FOCUS
High School
Economics

2nd Edition

WRITING TEAM

Michael Watts, Chair

Sarapage McCorkle

Bonnie Meszaros

Mark C. Schug

NCEE

National Council on Economic Education

AUTHORS

Michael Watts
Professor of Economics
Director, Center for Economic Education
Purdue University

Sarapage McCorkle
Director, Center for Entrepreneurship and Economic Education
University of Missouri-St. Louis

Bonnie T. Meszaros
Associate Director, Center for Economic Education and Entrepreneurship
University of Delaware

Mark C. Schug
Professor of Education
Director, Center for Economic Education
University of Wisconsin-Milwaukee

Suzanne Becker
Copy Editor

ISBN 1-56183-614-1   5 4 3 2

CONTENTS

FOREWORD

This is the latest edition of a key publication for what the research tells us – not surprisingly – is the single most important course in developing K-12 economic literacy: the high school economics course. Although we don't believe that a one-semester course in any subject is sufficient to develop student literacy in any field – let alone one as important, challenging, and open to daily use and misuse as economics – we don't believe economic literacy in the schools is likely to occur or endure without this capstone course.

Unfortunately, in many cases teachers are thrown into teaching high school economics with little or no formal training in economics, or in teaching this course. Even if they did have one or more college courses in economics, too little of the content and method of standard college economics courses is easily transferred or adapted for use with high school students.

This volume, and others that are listed in the Introduction to the volume – many of them also published by the National Council on Economic Education (NCEE) – can help students and teachers in the high school economics course. The help comes not only by focusing on key content (which is obviously important), but also by providing active teaching strategies that make the class more memorable, and more fun for both students and teachers. Many of these lessons also deal with current issues that students know are important, using current data.

The NCEE has always believed that providing solid, academic training in economics to teachers, and accurate and lively instructional materials for those teachers to use, are key elements of any program that seeks to make economic literacy a widespread and routine outcome in our nation's schools. This volume is a fine example of that approach with materials, and will undoubtedly be used extensively in teacher training programs in this country, and for that matter around the world. We are extremely proud of the fact that the previous edition of this volume was translated into Russian and Ukrainian.

The NCEE thanks the authors, Michael Watts, Professor of Economics and Director of the Center for Economic Education at Purdue University, who took the lead role on this project; Sarapage McCorkle, Director of the Center for Entrepreneurship and Economic Education at the University of Missouri-St. Louis; Bonnie Meszaros, Associate Director of the Center for Economic Education and Entrepreneurship at the University of Delaware; and Mark Schug, Director of the Center for Economic Education at the University of Wisconsin-Milwaukee.

Robert F. Duvall, Ph.D.
President and CEO
National Council on Economic Education

ACKNOWLEDGMENTS

The writing team for this edition thank Robert F. Smith and Robert Highsmith, members of the writing team for the first edition who have since left for greener pastures in retirement and new career directions, respectively. Some of their words, and more of their ideas, still appear in this edition. That may also be said of an earlier incarnation of the volume, affectionately known to economic educators as the "Silver Bullet" in the NCEE's Master Curriculum Guide series. The writing team for that volume was: John S. Morton, Chair; Stephen G. Buckles; Steven L. Miller; David M. Nelson; and Edward C. Prehn.

We also thank the following teachers, who field tested draft versions of the two new lessons in this edition, on very short notice and for very little financial reward:

Thomas J. Fugate, Homestead High School, Mequon, WI
James Stillman, Cedarburg High School, Cedarburg, WI

Our special thanks go to Julie Huffer and Alexander Skiba at Purdue University, and to Suzanne Becker, the Assistant Editor of the *Journal of Economic Education* at Indiana University. Julie was her usual invaluable self in all kinds of logistical and formatting issues, while Alex prepared many of the graphics included in the lessons, provided current data in many lessons, and identified many of the Internet/webpage references that are a new feature in this edition. Suzanne Becker improved all of the lessons with her invariably careful, compulsively consistent, and most of all insightful editing. She also contributed her good eye for page design and layout.

At the National Council on Economic Education (NCEE), Claire Melican joined the staff just in time to review and proofread lessons, and to oversee many administrative issues concerning this project. Heather Curtin secured reprint permissions for several graphs that were reprinted from commercially published textbooks, as noted in the sources for those graphs.

Finally, we thank the NCEE for undertaking this revision in the belief that marginal revenues would exceed marginal costs. We feel absolutely certain they are right, but then we weren't risking our money on the project, so that was easier for us to say than it was for them.

INTRODUCTION

This volume is one of several key resources published by the National Council on Economic Education (NCEE) for teachers of the high school course on economics. There are some worksheets in the volume to be used directly by students, but there are more simulations, role plays, and other types of active-learning strategies. Each lesson includes detailed, step-by-step instructions on conducting the activities, together with short reviews of the content to be covered, or longer content reviews on material that is less likely to be familiar to teachers, or less likely to appear in high school economics textbooks (such as the lessons on public choice and aggregate supply and aggregate demand). We also provide and use "real world" data on a wide range of issues and topics, and include references to print and Internet sources that teachers can use to update those data.

Other NCEE volumes that are also designed for use in high school economics courses cover more specialized topics, or generally use different instructional approaches. For example, *Capstone: The Nation's High School Economics Courses*, uses student worksheets and a "mystery" approach to teaching economic reasoning; *Advanced Placement Economics* provides hundreds of lessons with student worksheets and teacher reference material for use in the AP courses; *Focus: International Economics* provides 20 lessons on international trade and finance; and *Focus: Economic Systems* provides 12 lessons dealing with basic economic concepts and institutions – especially the economic role of government as viewed from a comparative systems approach, with extensive information on the transition economies of the former Soviet Union. The NCEE also publishes *The Test of Economic Literacy*, a nationally normed assessment instrument with two forms of 40 multiple-choice questions, appropriate for use as pre- and posttests in most secondary economics classes. Finally, the NCEE now offers a Webpage with teaching lessons designed for use in a wide range of courses and grade levels, at *http://www.nationalcouncil.org*.

What's New in This Edition?

The earliest version of this publication, widely and affectionately known as the "Silver Bullet," but officially as the *Master Curriculum Guide for High School Economics Courses*, was a pathbreaking document in many ways. It soon became popular with high school economics teachers and teacher trainers. In fact, it was so popular that most of its lessons were "recycled" in later documents published by the NCEE. As a result, the first edition of this volume that was published in the NCEE *Focus* series eliminated many lessons that had become available in *Focus: International Economics, Advanced Placement Economics,* and the *Capstone* volumes. In this edition, a similar fate befell one more lesson, which featured content and activities that have now been presented in greater detail and length in the recent NCEE volume, *Learning from the Market*, which is designed to be used with The Stock Market Game™. That provided enough page space to add two entirely new lessons: one dealing with saving, investing, financial intermediaries, and Adam Smith's "invisible hand" (Lesson 17), and the other with economic growth and development (Lesson 21). This does not mean that the lessons dropped over the past two editions were less important than the lessons that have been added. But because the material that has been dropped is still available in other NCEE publications, it seemed better (at least to us) not to use scarce pages reprinting identical or very similar lessons in more than one publication.

This is the first edition of this publication that ties lessons to the *Voluntary National Content Standards in Economics*, published by the NCEE in 1997. It is also the first to provide addresses for many Webpages that will allow teachers to easily update many of the tables or graphs provided, or to access other teaching resources over the Internet.

The previous edition added an Assessment section to each lesson. This edition sees the further addition of a Closure section, both as a reminder to summarize the key content of the lessons with students, and to make it easier for teachers to do that.

Almost every lesson contains at least one new activity, and many of the activities that remain have been revised. For example, the classroom market game (Lesson 3) now features a different product (oil, not wood), simplified calculations and student record sheets, and this most popular of all economic education simulations is now revisited in Lessons 4 and 14, to illustrate the effects of changes in supply and demand, and of moving from a competitive to an imperfectly competitive market. Of course, to make room for the new material, some of the old activities were cut back or entirely eliminated. Finally, wherever possible, data and figures that were carried over from the previous edition were updated. We hope, and believe, that these changes will make a good product even better.

Using These Lessons in the High School Economics Course

There are more important things to teach in a high school economics course than there is time to teach it, which of course is just one more example of the fundamental economic problem of scarcity. There are also many different ways to teach a good economics course, many different teacher methods and strategies you might use, and literally thousands of "real-world" examples and policy issues you might highlight. *The* one best way for everyone to teach the high school economics course probably doesn't exist; but there may well be *a* best way for *you* to teach economics to *your* students, given your particular background, interests, and skills, and those of your students.

We recommend that you start planning the course by thinking about yourself and your students, and making a list of the topics you want to be sure to cover as the course unfolds. For example, your list might include such things as career choices and the decision about whether or not to go on for a college degree; the public policy debates over health care reform and free trade agreements, price floors for agricultural products, and price ceilings on credit card interest rates and apartment rents in large cities; unemployment rates for skilled and unskilled workers; inflation rates; or the standard of living in the United States and other countries in different decades of this century.

Once you have chosen the mix of examples and issues you believe to be most important and interesting for you and your students, look at any curriculum guidelines your state or district has set for your course, and at the NCEE's voluntary content standards, and perhaps last of all at the basic textbook you will be using. Decide when and how you will feature the examples and issues you have chosen to teach the basic economic understandings identified in those publications. Finally, look for the specific activities that help you teach these concepts and introduce the issues and examples you have chosen to cover, such as (but certainly not limited to) the lessons in this publication.

Using basic economic concepts and the broader understandings identified in the NCEE national standards, and helping your students understand them with the activities included in this volume and others, will lead your classes to *analyze* the examples and issues you have chosen to study, not just talk and argue about them with little hope of reaching any conclusion or of learning anything from the discussion. Keep in mind that these pervasive, versatile, and enduring concepts and understandings – not the sometimes transitory issues and problems to which they are applied – are what distinguish economic analysis from history, sociology, mathematics, and other social, natural, and physical sciences. Put differently, taken together and used effectively, these concepts and understandings represent what John Maynard Keynes called "the economic way of thinking." But beware the trap of teaching concepts or even standards as dry, sterile theory, at least to any but the most capable and

From *Focus: High School Economics*, © National Council on Economic Education, New York, NY

theoretically oriented students. The excitement of economics for most people comes in applications – either to very familiar daily events involved in personal and family "making, getting, and spending," or to social issues at the local, state, or international levels.

In preparing this edition of this volume of lessons and activities, that is the approach we have also tried to follow, at least as a general rule. There will still be days when, even in very applied courses, it is essential to deliver a good, solid lecture on a key economic theory or model that students aren't likely to understand without that kind of instruction, or to use drill-and-practice worksheets and other, more regimented ways of learning to drive home those conceptual understandings. Indeed, some activities here are designed to help with those kinds of lectures, or assume that such a lecture is presented before an activity is conducted. But we have tried to make that approach the exception, not our rule. Accordingly, most of the lessons in this volume include direct applications to things or events students have already experienced themselves first hand, or at least read about in the popular press, or heard about on radio or television news programs.

Of course, no single manual can provide all of the activities, examples, and facts and figures you will want to use in a semester-long course. Other materials published by the NCEE or commercial publishers, including textbooks, are crucial in helping to cover more material, using other instructional methods. And as every experienced classroom teacher knows, it is also crucial to talk with your colleagues about the topics, activities, and tricks of the trade that they find most effective and innovative, and to share your own good ideas with them. Because once you stop looking for new ideas and new materials, and talking with other teachers about what works and what doesn't, your effectiveness will begin to diminish.

Finally, we strongly endorse the idea of using "real world" examples and, more specifically, real data to emphasize the relevance of economics, and the availability of data on the overall economy, or particular sectors and markets in the economy. The best way to start doing that is by using articles from the financial press (*The Wall Street Journal, The Economist,* and similar periodicals) and information from the three basic government publications and related websites listed below.

Key Data Sources on the U.S. Economy

Economic Report of the President – published each February by the President's Council of Economic Advisors, featuring articles on current economic issues and a long statistical appendix with data on the U.S. economy and many key sectors of the economy. Contact the U.S. Government Printing Office or go to *http://w3.access.gpo.gov/eop/.*

Economic Indicators – a monthly publication of the Joint Economic Committee of the U.S. Congress, with the most recent statistics on the key macroeconomic data series that are collected and published by federal agencies. Contact the U.S. Government Printing Office or go to *http://www.gpo.gov/congress/eibrowse/broecind .html.*

The Federal Reserve Bulletin – published monthly by the Federal Reserve System, with key data on money, banking, and credit in the U.S. economy. Many of the 12 regional Federal Reserve banks publish a wide range of economic education print and video materials for use in precollege classes, and some have regular newsletters or electronic networks for teachers. Contact the Federal Reserve System or the branch banks, or go to *http://www.federalreserve.gov/pubs/bulletin.*

LESSON ONE
CHOICE, OPPORTUNITY COSTS, AND DECISIONS

INTRODUCTION

Scarcity, choice, and cost are sometimes referred to as a basic trilogy of economics, because of the strong interrelationships between these fundamental concepts. Resources are limited, compared to wants; therefore, individuals and families face the problem of scarcity in deciding how to allocate their incomes and their time. All societies must also make choices about how to use their scarce resources. And every economic choice involves an opportunity cost – the foregone opportunity to make a different choice and use resources in a different way.

CONCEPTS

Scarcity
Opportunity costs
Tradeoffs

CONTENT STANDARD

Productive resources are limited. Therefore, people cannot have all the goods and services they want; as a result, they must choose some things and give up others.

BENCHMARKS

Scarcity is the condition of not being able to have all of the goods and services one wants. It exists because human wants for goods and services exceed the quantity of goods and services that can be produced using all available resources.

Like individuals, governments and societies experience scarcity because human wants exceed what can be made from all available resources.

The opportunity cost of a choice is the value of the best alternative given up.

Choices involve trading off the expected value of one opportunity against the expected value of its best alternative.

The choices people make have both present and future consequences.

The evaluation of choices and opportunity costs is subjective; such evaluations differ across individuals and societies.

OBJECTIVES

♦ Students define the opportunity cost of a decision as the value of the best alternative given up.

♦ Students analyze tradeoffs involved in making decisions.

♦ Students analyze the consequences of a choice and determine when those consequences occur.

LESSON DESCRIPTION

This lesson provides examples of individual and group decision-making involving specific considerations of opportunity costs and tradeoffs. Students make choices concerning the last school dance for seniors and a class project. They plan a monthly budget and then adjust that budget because of unexpected expenses.

TIME REQUIRED

Two class periods. Day one – procedures 1-6; day two – procedures 7-10 and Assessment.

MATERIALS

- Activity 1: Planning a Dance, one copy for each student
- Activity 2: Budget Tradeoffs, one copy for each student
- Activity 3: Assessment, one copy for each student

- Visual 1: Dance Choices
- Visual 2: Unexpected Expenses

PROCEDURES

1. Ask students how many of them never seem to have enough time to do all the things they want to do. Tell them to imagine that for some reason they find themselves with an hour of free time this evening that they did not expect to have. Ask students what they might like to do with this hour of free time. List their ideas on the board. (Expect some rather standard suggestions such as watch TV, read, sleep, talk on the telephone, study, surf the Internet, etc.)

2. After a sizable list is developed, ask students why they cannot do all of the things listed on the board. (Limited time and numerous alternative uses for this time.) Explain that this problem is called scarcity. **Scarcity** is the condition of not being able to have all of the goods and services one wants. Scarcity exits because there are never enough available resources to produce all the goods and services people want. Point out that individuals, families, governments, and societies experience scarcity.

3. Ask each student to write down the four or five activities they would most like to do with one hour of free time. Then ask each student to indicate the one thing they would do by placing a star next to their first choice. Also have them circle their second choice.

4. Draw a T-chart on the board. Label the first column *choice* and the other *cost*. Ask three or four students for their first and second choices. Write each first choice in the choice column. Place each second choice in the cost column.

5. Ask students: "Why did I place your second choice under the column labeled cost?" (In order to get the first choice, I gave up the second choice. In choosing the first option, I lost the opportunity to do the second alternative.) Stress that there is a *real* or

opportunity cost in making this decision, even though money is not involved. Rename the second column "Opportunity Cost." Point out that the cost of the alternative selected was the *one* most valuable alternative that was not selected, because it was never possible to do more than one of the choices in the limited time available. Therefore, not all of the alternatives are considered the opportunity cost, only the next-best alternative that was given up when the choice of what to do was made. Note that different people make different choices and have different opportunity costs.

6. Distribute a copy of Activity 1 to each student. Divide the class into groups of four or five students each. Review the instructions. Ask each group to reach a decision about how the funds should be used and be prepared to explain their decision. Defining the senior class project in a way that will make the decision more difficult will make this problem more interesting and realistic. For example, if the class project is defined as raising money to buy a motorized wheel chair for a disabled classmate, the project is likely to generate more support.

7. Have groups present their decisions. Record choices on Visual 1. Discuss:

A. Tell students that a **tradeoff** involves giving up some of one thing to get more of another. What tradeoffs did each group have to make? (*Answers will vary.*)

B. What was the opportunity cost of each group's decision? (*the group's second choice in each category*)

C. How did group preferences influence decisions? (*Different preferences resulted in different choices, tradeoffs, and decisions on how to use the funds.*)

D. In what ways is this problem similar to the "economizing behavior" faced by your family, and in what ways is it different? (*The problem is similar to family decisions in that difficult choices must be made, and tradeoffs are necessary because of varying opinions of family members. But this problem is unlike family decision making in some critical ways. This is one of the few decisions students will make together, as a group. A family has to make continuous spending decisions concerning food, shelter, clothing, and transportation, as well as entertainment. Also, many family decisions must be considered with respect to their long-run effects as well as immediate impacts.*)

8. Distribute one copy of Activity 2 to each student. Explain to students that their monthly income is $2100 and the proposed budget is merely a suggestion. In the column labeled Month 1, students should establish their own budgets. The amounts for taxes, housing, a car payment and insurance cannot be changed (because as Benjamin Franklin said, death and taxes are inevitable and it would take time to sell a car or move). Point out that the two blank lines are for items students might want to add that aren't in the proposed budget.

9. Ask students to share changes they made if any. Have students state the tradeoffs they made and the opportunity costs of their decisions.

10. Display Visual 2. Inform students they have had some unexpected expenses and must adjust their budget for month 2. Discuss:

A. Tell students that a tradeoff involves giving up some of one thing to get more of another. What tradeoffs did you have to make? (*Answers will vary.*)

B. What was the opportunity cost of your decision? (*whatever was given up to pay the dental bill and repair the washing machine*)

C. In what way did the decisions that you made in your month 1 budget affect your decisions in month 2? Remind students that choices have both present and future consequences.

CLOSURE

Review the key points of the lesson.

1. What is opportunity cost? (*Opportunity cost is the value of the best alternative given up when a choice is made.*)

2. State the choice and identify the opportunity cost of a decision you have made. (*Answers will vary.*)

3. What are the present and potential future consequences of this choice? (*Answers will vary.*)

4. Define tradeoffs. (*A tradeoff means giving up some of one thing to get more of something else.*)

5. Describe a decision you have made and identify a tradeoff you made.

ASSESSMENT

Distribute a copy of Activity 3 to each student. Instruct students to review the areas of the budget scheduled for possible cuts and write a recommendation for the mayor. Tell them to be sure to include in the recommendation the areas of the budget that should be cut, a description of the tradeoffs involved, identification of the opportunity cost, and a summary of the likely future consequences of the recommendation.

Activity 1
Planning a Dance

Your class has been engaged in various fund-raising projects during the past several years, and you now have a total of $9,635 to spend on a big bash – your last school dance. You may not spend more than this amount on the dance, but you do not have to spend all of it on the dance. Any remaining money can be used for a class project, designed to help your school or community.

You have decided that there are three categories of expenditures for the dance: 1) hiring a band or disc jockey, 2) renting a place to hold the dance, and 3) providing refreshments and decorations. A committee has provided the following information:

Music for Dance
Cost
  Disc Jockey
    $1000   Pig Sty—cheap but good
    2000   Good Vibrations—excellent music selections and sound system
  Live Bands
    $2500   Pumkin Chunkin—good progressive country
    4000   Angelic Sinners—good hard rock
    5000   Our Rage—a popular group featuring rap music
    6500   Funky Fugues—nationally known touring group, classic rock and roll

Places Available for Dance
Cost
    $200   School Gym
    600   American Legion Hall
    1500   Holiday Inn
    2000   The Hilton Hotel
    3000   The Knob Hill Country Club

Refreshments and Decorations for Dance
Cost
    $800   School Service Club prepares sandwiches, chips, etc. and limited decorations
    1200   Catered – pizza, wings, sandwich platter and decorations
    3000   Catered – pizza, chicken fingers, salad bar, taco bar, pasta bar and neat decorations
    5000   Package deal – before-dance meal at a restaurant; good snacks and decorations at dance

Your task now is to decide, with the other members of your group, which band or disc jockey to hire, where to hold the dance, what type of refreshments and decorations to provide and how much money to spend on a class project. Your group must select one item from each expenditure category.

From *Focus: High School Economics*, © National Council on Economic Education, New York, NY

Activity 2
Budget Tradeoffs

You are a graduate of a technical community college and have a job as a surgical technician. Your salary for the current year is $2100 per month. Below is a possible budget for you. It is only a proposed budget and you can make changes, but you cannot change the taxes, housing, car payment, and car insurance amount for next month. You may add other budget categories in the spaces provided, if you wish.

Plan your budget for month 1 using the proposed budget as a guide. Your total for the month cannot be more than $2100.

MONTHLY BUDGET

Budget Category	Proposed	Month 1	Month 2
All taxes	$ 420	$ 420	$ 420
Housing (includes utilities, cable TV, local phone)	625	625	625
Food – groceries	250		
Food – eating out	100		
Clothing	85		
Car payment	200	200	200
Car – operation (gas, oil)	65		
Car – insurance	50	50	50
Car – repairs	30		
Medical insurance (deductibles and co-payments)	25		
Entertainment - movies, hanging out, snacks, beverages, etc.	75		
Newspapers, books, magazines	20		
Gifts (birthdays, Mother's Day, etc.)	25		
Savings (for stereo)	100		
Miscellaneous (haircuts, toiletries, laundry, etc.)	30		
TOTAL	$ 2100	$ 2100	$ 2100

1. Did you make any changes in your actual budget for month 1? Explain.

2. What tradeoffs did you make?

Activity 3
Assessment

The recently elected mayor has inherited a budget deficit. He has asked you as budget director to cut $500,000 from the city's budget. The areas targeted for budget cuts and their current appropriations are below.

Department	Current	Final Budget
Parks and Recreation		
Opening and maintaining six citywide swimming pools	$240,000	
Youth Programs		
Summer work program	200,000	
High school grade incentive program	200,000	
After school athletic program	100,000	
After school tutorial program	100,000	
Public Safety		
Safety patrols		
Downtown business district	50,000	
Five adjacent neighborhoods	75,000	
Police and fire		
Three additional police officers	150,000	
Fire education program	40,000	
TOTAL	**$1,155,000**	**$655,000**

Your task is to prepare a recommendation for the mayor. Your recommendation should

- State which areas of the budget should be cut
- Describe the tradeoffs involved
- Identify the opportunity cost of your recommendation
- Summarize the likely future consequences of your recommendation

From *Focus: High School Economics*, © National Council on Economic Education, New York, NY

Visual 1
Dance Choices

Group	Band/DJ	Place	Food	Project

Visual 2
Unexpected Expenses

Month 2

You have an unexpected dental bill of $400. Your dental insurance covers 80%. You owe the dentist $80.

Your washing machine needs repairs. It will cost $60.

LESSON TWO
BROAD SOCIAL GOALS OF AN ECONOMIC SYSTEM

INTRODUCTION

All economic systems strive to achieve a set of broad social goals, including economic efficiency, equity, freedom, growth, security, and stability. How these goals are prioritized, and how successful an economy is at attaining these goals, influences the quality of life for its citizens. Recent events such as the breakup of the former Soviet Union; the aging of the population in the United States, Japan, and most nations in Western Eurpoe; remarkable advances in technology; and public policy discussions relating to social security, health care, job training, and international trade have focused attention on the broad social goals, and especially on how different countries and types of economic systems tend to value some goals over others.

American citizens and policymakers must decide how best to achieve these goals, working within the framework of a market economy. Achieving these goals is often difficult to do, because although the goals complement each other in some cases, in many cases there are serious tradeoffs to face. When that happens, policies or programs designed to achieve one goal often interfere with achieving another goal or goals. Resolving these conflicts when people have different opinions about the relative importance of each of these goals, and even different interpretations of what the goals mean, is a perennial challenge in every country, and in every economic system.

CONCEPTS

Broad social goals (economic efficiency, equity, freedom, growth, security, stability)

Tradeoffs
Market economy
Command economy

CONTENT STANDARDS

Productive resources are limited. Therefore, people cannot have all the goods and services they want; as a result, they must choose some things and give up others.

Different methods can be used to allocate goods and services. People, acting individually or collectively through government, must choose which methods to use to allocate different kinds of goods and services.

BENCHMARKS

The evaluation of choices and opportunity cost is subjective; such evaluations differ across individuals and societies.

National economies vary in the extent to which they rely on government directives (central planning) and signals from private markets to allocate scarce goods, services, and productive resources.

There are essential differences between a market economy, in which allocations result from individuals making decisions as buyers and sellers, and a command economy, in which resources are allocated according to a central authority.

OBJECTIVES

♦ Students define the six broad social goals of an economic system.

♦ Students discuss and evaluate the relative importance of the six goals in different economic systems.

♦ Students evaluate various public policy actions with respect to their impact on the American economy and the achievement of the six broad social goals.

LESSON DESCRIPTION

Students read diaries of two students, one living in a country with a command economy and one in a country with a market economy. Based on these readings, students identify the broad social goals that are viewed as most important in each of the two countries. They learn about the characteristics of command and market economies, and identify tradeoffs each type of economic system makes among the competing goals. Finally, students choose a current social issue and develop a public policy to deal with that issue, identifying the goals they are attempting to achieve and goals that may be less well achieved because of the policy they develop.

TIME REQUIRED

One class period

MATERIALS

- Six pieces of 8 ½" × 11" paper, each labeled with one of the six broad social goals – economic efficiency, economic equity, economic freedom, economic growth, economic stability, and economic security
- Tape
- 40 sticky dots in two different colors
- Activity 1: Broad Social Goals, one per student and a visual
- Activity 2: Student Diary A, one copy for half the students and a visual
- Activity 3: Student Diary B, one copy for half the students and a visual
- Activity 4: Broad Social Goals in Command and Market Economies, one per student
- Activity 5: Creating Public Policies, one per student

PROCEDURES

1. Explain to students that all nations, regardless of the type of economic system they may have, face the same basic economic problem of deciding how to use scarce resources to satisfy the wants of their citizens. Point out that this problem is universal and that no system can provide all the goods and services that its citizens desire. The public policies a nation adopts to deal with issues related to this basic economic problem reflect the importance a nation places on different broad social goals, including economic efficiency, equity, freedom, growth, security, and stability. People do not always agree about which of these goals are most important, especially people living in different types of economic systems.

2. Display a visual of Activity 1 and distribute a copy to each student. Review the definitions of each goal and make the following points.

A. Economic efficiency means an economy is using its limited resources to produce the most goods and services possible to satisfy people's wants, and is also producing the kinds of goods and services that people want most. To achieve economic efficiency decisions about the use of resources to produce additional goods and services must be made by analyzing the costs incurred and benefits received. When the additional benefits exceed the additional costs, it is efficient to use resources to produce more of a good or service.

B. Economic equity involves fairness. The manner in which this goal is implemented depends on people's beliefs about what is right and wrong. Public policies that deal with equity are usually programs dealing with the redistribution of income or wealth. For example, how much should income from one group be taxed to provide more income or goods and services for other groups? Other examples of government programs that deal with equity issues include income assistance to low income families, Medicare, food stamps, subsidized housing, job training programs, and unemployment compensation.

C. Economic freedom entails the freedom to choose what to buy and sell, where to work and live, open new businesses or close old ones, etc. Total economic freedom is never possible, however, because some individual freedoms must be restricted to benefit the general welfare of society. For example, consumers are not free to purchase illegal drugs, nor are producers free to produce and sell them. Taxes also restrict economic freedom, because paying taxes, as required by law, limits individuals' ability to decide how to spend some portion of their income.

D. Economic growth is a sustained increase in the goods and services an economy produces. For an economy's standard of living to increase, real gross domestic product (GDP) per capita must increase. To do this an economy with a stable or growing population must increase the number of goods and services produced each year. That is possible if the economy is investing in capital goods and the education and training of its workers, and experiencing some level of technological progress. Economic growth is closely related to a nation's long-term ability to use resources to achieve other goals, such as economic stability, security, efficiency, and equity.

E. Economic security focuses on the desire of consumers and producers to be protected against economic risks over which they may have little or no control. These risks include loss of jobs, inability to work due to illness or old age, business and bank failures, or other kinds of unexpected social or economic disasters, including wars, earthquakes, droughts, and epidemics. Individuals attempt to provide economic security for themselves and their families by saving and purchasing different kinds of insurance. Government programs such as Social Security, food stamps, aid to families with dependent children, unemployment compensation, subsidized housing, and farm price supports are designed to reduce risks for different groups of people. Even national defense programs are a kind of insurance against economic, political, and military risks.

F. Economic stability implies three basic things: steady economic growth with no sudden swings in output and consumption levels; employment stability with no dramatic swings in employment levels or the rate of unemployment, and price stability. Price stability is achieved when the general level of prices for goods and services is neither rising nor falling rapidly. Unexpected changes in the price level hurt some groups of people and help others. For example, inflation is an increase in the average level of prices that hurts those on fixed incomes, and those who have loaned money at a fixed interest rate. It helps those who have borrowed money at a fixed interest rate. Price stability improves economic security by allowing both consumers and businesses to do more and better long-term planning. When an economy experiences high unemployment valuable resources are wasted and overall levels of production, income, and spending decrease. But if workers live in a country that allows workers the freedom to change jobs, some level of unemployment is considered normal and acceptable. In fact, this kind of economy will have some unemployment even when it is said to be at the level of full employment, because even then some workers are temporarily unemployed as they change jobs.

3. Divide the students into groups of two or three. Give half of the groups copies of Activity 2 and half copies of Activity 3. Tell students that each handout is a page from a diary of a high school student. Instruct the groups to read the diary entries and determine which economic goals are apparently given highest priority in the society in which the student who wrote the diary lives.

4. As students read the diary pages, post a sign for each of the six broad social goals in the front of the room. Distribute four sticky dots to each group. Make sure groups reading Activity 2 receive sticky dots that are a different color from those given to the groups reading Activity 3.

5. Allow time for group discussion, then instruct a representative from each group to place sticky dots on the two to four goals that are given highest priority in the country described by the diary entry in Activity 2 or 3. (*Students with Activity 2 will most likely put dots on the goals of stability, security, and equity. Students with Activity 3 will most likely put dots on the goals of freedom, efficiency, growth, and equity.*) Students may not select all of these goals initially. In procedures 6 and 7, discuss only the goals that the students marked with dots.

6. Display a visual of Activity 2 and ask students to identify portions of the diary that support the goals they selected. (*Security – job, apartment, retirement benefits, and health care provided by government; equity – everyone has job and is paid similar wages; stability – low prices, no unemployment.*) Students may not choose all of these goals or may choose others. Again, at this time only discuss the goals students have marked with dots.

7. Repeat procedure 6, but this time using a visual of Activity 3. (*Freedom – start a business, choice of careers and level of education, choose to spend or save money, buy or sell property; stability – low unemployment*

and little inflation; growth – economy growing at 3 percent a year; incentives to work hard and invest in capital resources and training.)

8. It is quite likely that students from both groups will put dots on the equity goal. If not, ask students if it is possible that some people from both economic systems would believe that their system was more fair than the other kind of economic system. Ask students to identify differences in how the two students who wrote the diary entries felt about equity. (*The student in Activity 2 focused more on the equality or equity of outcomes; the student in Activity 3 focused more on the equality or equity of opportunity.*)

9. Distribute a copy of Activity 4 to each student. Allow time for students to read the characteristics of command and market economies. Discuss with students how supporters of market and command (central planning) economic systems may value and rank the six broad social goals.

10. Ask students in which type of economy the students who wrote the diary entries lived. (*Activity 2 command, Activity 3 market*)

11. Direct students to reconsider the goals they originally marked with the sticky dots and ask if there are any changes they want to make. They may want to move or add sticky dots based on the information in Activity 4.

12. Point out that public policies and programs instituted by governments are designed to help achieve one or more of the broad social goals. However, some policies may help societies meet some goals while reducing their ability to meet others. Individuals and societies must often make **tradeoffs** when trying to achieve more than one goal, by giving up something that promotes one goal to get more of something that promotes another goal. But not everyone agrees on the extent and type of tradeoffs that should be made among goals. That makes developing policies

and programs challenging and often controversial.

13. Ask students to identify tradeoffs among goals that were made in the countries in which each of the students who wrote the diary entries in Activities 2 and 3 lived. (*Command: gives up freedom for security, equity of outcome, and stability; gives up economic efficiency and economic growth for stability and security . Market: gives up some security and equality of outcomes for more freedom; may give up some stability for growth and efficiency.*)

14. Discuss with the students several examples of how, in a market system, specific government policies help to achieve one or more broad social goals while restricting others. The following examples could be used:

A. Requiring motorcycle riders to wear helmets reduces their freedom, but may help to achieve the goal of economic efficiency (by reducing medical costs) and economic equity (taxpayers and consumers with auto and health insurance don't have to pay so much to cover costs for motorcycle riders who suffer serious head injuries).

B. Taxes tend to restrict economic freedom by reducing people's ability to decide how to spend a portion of their incomes, but tax revenues may be used to support activities that promote the achievement of many goals. For example, some people argue that by requiring and providing a minimum level of education for all citizens, government expenditures and taxes help to achieve all of the broad social goals.

C. New welfare rules limit the length of time individuals can receive welfare payments. Welfare payments and food stamps are methods for redistributing income from those who earn more to those who earn less. Limiting the length

of time these payments may be received is an equity issue as well as an issue of economic security and efficiency. These payments provide some level of security for those who are unable to provide for themselves. It is also an issue of economic freedom for the taxpayers whose tax dollars fund the welfare payments.

D. Banning the import of all red meat from Europe because of fears of Mad Cow Disease. Security is increased but consumers' economic freedom is restricted because they have fewer alternatives to choose from, and the price of red meat will rise. Producers' freedom is restricted because those wanting to sell imported beef will have less to sell. Efficiency is also affected – more U.S. resources will go into the production of red meat, which means those resources cannot be used to produce other things.

CLOSURE

Review the key points of the lesson using the following questions.

1. What are the six broad social goals? (*economic efficiency, equity, freedom, growth, security, and stability*)

2. Define each of the goals? (See Activity 1 for definitions.)

3. Describe how the broad social goals are valued in a command economy and in a market economy. (See Activity 4.)

4. Explain why achieving one goal might interfere with the achievement of another goal, and give an example. (Answers will vary.)

ASSESSMENT

Divide students into groups and distribute a copy of Activity 5 to each student.

Instruct the groups to select one of the issues and complete the following assignments:

1. Create a public policy that addresses the problem.

2. State what goal or goals the public policy is attempting to support, and explain how implementing the policy might interfere with the achievement of another goal or goals.

3. State in which type of economic system this policy is more likely to be implemented and explain why.

Have groups share their public policies. Ask the class to identify the goal or goals each group is attempting to achieve and the effects the policy might have on other goals.

Activity 1
Broad Social Goals

Economic Efficiency refers to how well scarce productive resources are allocated to produce the goods and services people want and how well inputs are used in the production process to keep production costs as low as possible.

Economic Equity means what is "fair." Economic actions and policies have to be evaluated in terms of what people think is right or wrong. Equity issues often arise in questions dealing with the distribution of income and wealth. Some people judge equity based on providing equal opportunity. Others judge based on equality of outcomes.

Economic Freedom refers to such things as the freedom for consumers to decide how to spend or save their incomes, the freedom of workers to change jobs and join unions, and the freedom of individuals to establish new businesses or close old ones.

Economic Growth refers to increasing the production of goods and services over time. Economic growth is measured by changes in the level of real gross domestic product (GDP). A target annual growth rate of 3 to 4 percent in real GDP is generally considered to be reasonable and sustainable.

Economic Security refers to protecting consumers, producers, and resource owners from risks that exist in society. Each society must decide from which uncertainties individuals can and should be protected, and whether individuals, employers, or the government should provide or pay for this protection.

Economic Stability refers to maintaining stable prices and full employment and keeping economic growth reasonably smooth and steady. Price stability means avoiding inflation or deflation. Full employment occurs when an economy's scarce resources, especially labor, are fully utilized.

Activity 2
Student Diary A

Monday, 2/1—Dad was really discouraged today. The plant where he works is old and poorly maintained. His suggestions for improvements are discouraged and ignored. I heard him telling Mom that he's tired of doing work that he hates and of getting paid the same as other men at the plant who often don't show up for work or do little once they arrive. He says they have no incentive to work. They get paid even if their work is poor. Mom reminded him we have much to be thankful for. The government provides us with an apartment, guaranteed retirement benefits, free health care, and job security.

Mom tries to lift Dad's spirits. I'm not so sure he isn't right about many things. Prices for consumer goods are kept low but we have so few choices, and sometimes the stores run out of even the few things they usually have to sell. It can take hours standing in line just to get a loaf of bread or a piece of meat. Last week I stood in line for 50 minutes to buy meat for dinner and then couldn't get what Mom wanted. I took what they had, even though I knew Mom would be disappointed. I want new shoes but there are so few choices and they are not well made. My friend has a pair of blue jeans. I'd love a pair! But I'd have to buy them illegally, like he did.

Monday, 2/8—I passed the entrance exam for the university, to study engineering. I don't want to be an engineer. My teachers tell me I should go to the school, because there are always jobs for engineers in the government factories. I really want to be a writer.

Tuesday, 2/9—It snowed today and our apartment was cold. The government is always promising things will be better next year. I doubt it. The government cares more about supplies for the military, the space program, and Olympic sports than it does for its citizens.

Thurs., 2/11—I took Grandma to the doctor. She has many problems, but fortunately health care is free. We waited all afternoon before she got to see the doctor. She needs an operation. The doctor says there's a long waiting list, maybe as long as a year.

Friday 2/12—Mom and Dad were arguing again. Dad said what good is a guaranteed job when you don't like the work and you are not free to change jobs or start your own business. Mom points out that it's the same for everyone. Do as you're told and be happy with what you have. We don't have much but at least the government will take care of us.

Activity 3
Student Diary B

Monday, 2/3—I hate babysitting my younger brothers. Mom says it's just until Dad gets his new consulting firm off the ground. Then we can afford extended daycare. Why did his old employer need to downsize? The paper says the economy is doing well. 3% growth and inflation is under control, whatever that means. Did they really need to cut my Dad's job and make my life miserable? Starting a business is risky. He's never around. Mom isn't either these days. She's opening a second restaurant. They took out a second mortgage on the house to help pay for the restaurant renovations. It's a huge risk but something she's been wanting to do. Dad encourages her. Says consumer spending is up and she'll have people filling her new restaurant in no time at all. But what about me? Don't they realize I have things to do?

Tuesday 2/4—I couldn't go out with my friends. Mom and Dad are working late and I had to watch my brothers. I complained. It's not fair! They said to be patient. I didn't say too much. They're upset with me. My brother told them I haven't been wearing my seatbelt. I hate wearing it when I drive. I got a lecture. I already know the pros and cons. We've been debating the issue in school. The state legislature passed a law making it mandatory. What right do they have to dictate wearing seat belts? It's bad enough that my parents are on my case.

Wednesday, 2/5—I reminded my parents I work after school on Thursday and Friday and can't help out at home. Then they wanted to know how much of my paycheck I have been saving. Well, not much since I had to pay for my car insurance, buy new clothes, movie tickets, CDs, and pay for gas. That started it. I got another lecture on the importance of saving for college. As if I don't know how much college costs. They're so concerned about college and getting a good job. My best friend went to college and then couldn't get a job in her field. Maybe I'll work for a year before college, or just go part time. I bet that won't go over well.

Thursday, 2/6—I got a raise! My boss complimented me on my "work ethic." I didn't even know I had one. He fired his other after-school employee because she was always late and made too many mistakes. I was surprised he did it, because finding workers is tough with the unemployment rate so low. He asked me if I wanted to increase my hours. He's willing to send me for training on the new computer he bought. Wow! I could really use the money, but there goes what little free time I have now.

Activity 4
Broad Social Goals in Command and Market Economies

Broad Social Goals	In Command Economies	In Market Economies
Economic Efficiency	Resource allocation established by central planners. State-owned businesses are often inefficient but rarely allowed to fail.	Most allocation decisions made by consumers and producers in markets. Extensive specialization and international trade increase productivity and competition.
Economic Equity	Wages often set by government to provide greater equality of income. Opportunities for moving or changing jobs are limited, so jobs may not make use of individuals' skills and abilities.	Equality of opportunity, people are free to make own decisions on how to use their resources and capabilities but no guarantee of success. Income depends on the value of labor and other resources an individual has to sell.
Economic Freedom	Government ownership of most capital and land resources, many decisions made by central planners.	Private ownership of all kinds of resources is allowed, and individual freedom and control of resources is highly valued.
Economic Growth	Growth targets set by central planners who assign output quotas for different firms. Weak incentives to reduce waste. Plant facilities and equipment maintenance often a problem.	Incentives for individuals and businesses to produce more and avoid waste encourage efficient use of resources. Specialization, investment in capital and workers' education and training, and trade encourage higher levels of output.
Economic Security	Pensions, jobs, income, housing, and health care provided or guaranteed by the government.	Generally, individuals are responsible for their own health care, retirement benefits, housing, and income. But there are some government programs to reduce risks and provide increased economic security such as assistance for low-income families, unemployment compensation, social security, and government job training programs.
Economic Stability	No unemployment, prices usually set below market price to ensure that goods are sold, which controls official measures of inflation.	Some unemployment is tolerated, income depends on the resources an individual has to sell, the federal government uses monetary and fiscal policies to reduce unemployment and inflation and encourage economic growth.

From *Focus: High School Economics*, © National Council on Economic Education, New York, NY

Activity 5
Creating Public Policies

Public Policy Issues

- **All citizens are entitled to adequate health care.**

- **Smoking should be banned from all public places.**

- **Textile manufacturers are asking for a tariff on imported clothing.**

Working with your group, select one of the above issues and complete the following assignment:

- Create a public policy (a law, regulation, or government program) to address the issue.

- State which broad social goal or goals* the public policy is attempting to achieve, but also explain how implementing the policy might interfere with achieving another goal or goals.

- State in which type of economic system (market or command/central planning) this policy is more likely to be implemented and explain why.

* Economic freedom, efficiency, security, stability, equity, and growth – or add other goals if they are especially important for the policy you develop.

LESSON THREE
A CLASSROOM MARKET FOR CRUDE OIL

INTRODUCTION

Every day in communities all around the nation, decisions are made on what goods and services will be produced, how many will be produced and purchased, and at what prices. How are these decisions made? In a market economy there is no central planning committee to answer these basic economic questions. Instead, prices are established through the interaction of buyers and sellers in the marketplace. Those prices allocate goods and services to the uses that individual buyers value most, in terms of what they are willing and able to pay for different products. At the same time, any producer can decide to supply these goods and services. Producers will be successful and earn profits as long as they can make a product that consumers are willing to buy at an average cost that is not higher than the market price.

Despite the importance of markets in the U.S. economy and other market systems, most people who live in these countries know relatively little about how they operate. Understanding more about how markets work can help students make better choices today as consumers and perhaps as workers and savers. In the future, it can help them make better decisions as investors and perhaps even as producers and entrepreneurs. Participating in the simulation described in this lesson should also help students see that market allocations of goods and services are extremely decentralized; even though decisions are made by individual buyers and sellers, in fact the overall process is automatic and impersonal.

CONCEPTS

Supply
Demand
Market clearing price
Surplus
Shortage

CONTENT STANDARD

Markets exist when buyers and sellers interact. This interaction determines market prices and thereby allocates scarce goods and services.

BENCHMARKS

Market prices are determined through the buying and selling decisions made by buyers and sellers.

The market clearing or equilibrium price for a good or service is the one price at which quantity supplied equals quantity demanded.

If a price is above the market clearing price, it will fall, causing sellers to produce less and buyers to purchase more; if it is below the market clearing price, it will rise, causing sellers to produce more and buyers to buy less.

OBJECTIVES

♦ Students explain how the interaction of buyers and sellers in the marketplace determines a market clearing price.

♦ Students define market clearing price as the one price at which quantity supplied equals quantity demanded.

♦ Students explain how changes in the price of a good or service affect the quantities that are demanded and supplied.

LESSON DESCRIPTION

Students participate in a simulation to experience how a competitive market works. Although most markets for goods and services are not as competitive as the market in this activity, by playing "A Market in Oil" students gain a better understanding of how the interaction of buyers and sellers determines prices in any market.

TIME REQUIRED
One class period.

MATERIALS
- Thirty-two Buy Cards (4 copies of Activity 1) and 32 Sell Cards (4 copies of Activity 2). Use different colors for the buy and sell cards. Make cards in the following amounts:

$ per barrel	24	26	28	30	32	34	36	38	40	42	44
# Buy Cards	--	4	4	4	4	4	3	3	2	2	2
# Sell Cards	2	2	2	3	3	4	4	4	4	4	--

- Activity 3: Score Sheet for "A Market in Crude Oil," one per student
- Activity 4: Supply and Demand Schedules, one per student
- Activity 5: Crude Oil Supply and Demand (graph sheet), one per student
- Activity 6: A Market Survey, one per student
- One colored armband (construction paper, crepe paper, or yarn) for each seller
- NOTE: This activity requires a class of at least 20 students to be effective. Up to 50 students can participate if your room is large enough.
- Visual 1: Sample Buy/Sell Cards
- Visual 2: Class Tally Sheet
- Visual 3: Graphing Supply, Demand, and Market Clearing Price

PROCEDURES
1. Tell students they are going to participate in a simulation in which half the students will be buyers of barrels of crude oil and half will be sellers. In the real market, exchanges are made for millions of barrels, but to keep calculations simple, students will deal with one barrel at a time.

2. Display Visual 1. Explain that each buyer will receive a buy card. Read the Buy Card, pointing out that cards have various prices. Explain that students must try to buy a barrel of crude oil at the lowest possible price. They should not buy for more than the price on their card, although this is sometimes necessary to make a transaction and get another buy card. Stress that buyers should not reveal the price on their cards at any time.

3. Repeat procedure 2 with a Sell Card. Tell sellers that each seller will receive one sell card at a time. Explain that students must try to sell their barrels of crude oil at the highest possible price. They should try not to sell for less than the price on their cards, although sometimes this is necessary in order to make a transaction and get another sell card. Stress that sellers should not reveal the price on their cards at any time.

4. Explain the following rules for the simulation:

A. Any buyer can talk with any seller.

B. The goal of both buyers and sellers is to make as much money as they can. The buyers do this by buying a barrel of oil for a lower price than the one shown on their cards. The sellers make money by selling for a higher price than the price shown on their cards.

C. All students are free to make as many transactions in a round as time permits.

D. All transaction prices must be made in whole dollar increments.

E. When a transaction is made, both the seller and the buyer report the agreed upon price to the recorder who will enter it on Visual 2. Display Visual 2. Remind students to watch the tally sheet so that they will know what prices are being paid for a barrel of oil.

F. After a transaction, students should turn in their cards and receive new ones, re-enter the marketplace, and resume making transactions. It is important that students receive a new card after every transaction. [NOTE: You may wish to assign two students to handle the distribution and collection of the buy and sell cards during the game, and another student to record each transaction on the Class Tally Sheet (Visual 2). Buy and sell cards should be kept in separate piles and shuffled between each of the three rounds.]

5. Hand out individual score sheets, Activity 3. Review procedures for completing the score sheet.

6. Clear a large area in the classroom and designate it as the marketplace.

7. Divide the class into two equal-sized groups. One group will be sellers, the other buyers. Distribute a colored armband to each seller. Explain that buyers will be buyers throughout the game and sellers will be sellers throughout the game.

8. Explain that you will conduct three rounds of trading lasting five minutes each. Announce when one minute remains in each round.

9. Use Visual 2 to record transactions.

10. Encourage students to make as many deals as they can in the time permitted. Remind students that it is permissible to take a loss in order to get a new transaction card.

11. During the time between trading rounds, direct students' attention to the record of all transactions on the Class Tally Sheet, Visual 2. Point out that it contains useful information for them. Do not elaborate.

12. At the end of the three rounds, allow students time to calculate their total net gain or net loss. Remind students that in the real market exchanges would be made for millions of

barrels, so their gains or losses would be in millions of dollars too.

13. Determine the buyer and seller who had the largest net gains.

14. Conduct post game discussion:

A. At what price was crude oil most frequently sold in each round? (Have students examine data on their score sheets and on the Class Tally Sheet.)

B. In which round did the greatest spread in prices occur? (Examine data.)

C. Why did the prices become more clustered in later rounds? (*Competition among buyers and sellers based on greater information is the most important cause. Markets tend to move toward an equilibrium price as buyers and sellers obtain information about the quantity of products available at different prices.*)

D. Did buyers or sellers determine the final market price for crude oil? (*Both buyers and sellers determined the market price by their interaction in the marketplace.*)

E. How did competition among sellers and buyers influence price? (*Because of competition within both groups, no single buyer or seller controlled the price. Note that buyers compete with other buyers, sellers with other sellers.*)

15. Distribute Activities 4 and 5. Inform students that the information on the buyer and seller cards can be converted to supply and demand schedules and used to construct a graph that illustrates the behavior of buyers and sellers. The focal point of the graph – the point at which the line for market supply and the line for market demand intersect – is called the

market clearing price or the equilibrium price of the product traded (in this case, crude oil).

16. Tell students to construct the graph by placing dots at the points that correspond to all combinations of prices and quantities shown in the supply schedule on Activity 4. Then do the same, but use small crosses instead of dots, for the demand schedule. Connect the dots to produce the supply schedule; connect the crosses to produce the demand schedule. Tell students to label each curve. Assist students who have difficulty. When they have finished, project Visual 3 and have students compare their graphs to it.

17. Tell the class the graph indicates that, given enough time, this competitive market would generate a market price of $34 per barrel of crude oil. At that price, 16 barrels of crude oil would be sold. Ask: How does this compare with the market clearing price in the class simulation? (*May vary. Typically, a price of about $34 will not prevail until students play several rounds of the game. But in later rounds, their transactions should converge toward the market price.*)

18. After students complete the graphing exercise, summarize the important points by asking:

A. What does the demand schedule show? (*The quantities of crude oil buyers are willing and able to purchase at all possible prices.*) Explain that this entire schedule is what economists call **demand**.

B. What does the supply schedule show? (*The quantities of crude oil sellers are willing to produce and sell at all possible prices.*) Explain that this entire schedule is what economists call **supply**.

C. When the only thing that changes is the price of a product, what relationship exists between the price of a good or service and the quantity people are willing to buy? (*As price rises the quantity demanded decreases, and vice versa.*)

D. When the only thing that changes is the price of a product, what relationship exists between the price of a good or service and the quantity producers are willing to sell? (*When price rises, the quantity supplied increases, and vice versa.*)

E. What happens in the market if the price is set higher than the market clearing price? (*Quantity supplied is greater than quantity demanded.*) Point out that this is called a **surplus**.

F. At what pries does a surplus occur? (*all prices above the market clearing price of $34*)

G. What happens in the market if the price is set lower than the market clearing price? (*Quantity demanded is greater than quantity supplied.*) Point out that this is called a **shortage**.

H. At what prices does a shortage occur? (*all prices below the market clearing price of $34*)

19. Tell students that they will learn more about shortages, surpluses, and imperfect competition in future lessons (Lessons 4 and 14).

CLOSURE

Use the questions below to review the key points of the lesson.

1. What is the market clearing price? (the price at which quantity demanded equals quantity supplied)

2. How is the market clearing price determined? *(by the interaction of buyers and sellers in the marketplace)*

3. When will a shortage occur? *(Shortages occur when price is below the market clearing price.)*

4. How does competition influence price? *(With competition, no one buyer or seller controls price. Competition among buyers pushes price up. Competition among sellers pushes price down.)*

ASSESSMENT

Distribute copies of Activity 6. Instruct students to complete the activity.

1. What is the market clearing price for bananas? *($.69 per pound)*

2. In the marketplace, how will this price be determined? Remember, the store managers don't have the survey information on expected purchases that the students collected. *(The market clearing price will be determined by both buyers and sellers through their interaction in the marketplace. The market in bananas will tend to move toward an equilibrium price as buyers and sellers obtain information about the quantity of bananas available at different prices.)*

3. What will happen if the store managers try to sell their bananas at $.89 per pound? *(There will be a surplus.)*

4. Describe an example of a surplus or a shortage that you have experienced in the marketplace, or that you have read about or heard about from someone else. *(Answers will vary.)*

Activity 1
Buy Cards

You are authorized to **BUY 1 barrel of crude oil**, paying as **little** as possible. If you pay more than $_____, you lose money.	You are authorized to **BUY 1 barrel of crude oil**, paying as **little** as possible. If you pay more than $_____, you lose money.
You are authorized to **BUY 1 barrel of crude oil**, paying as **little** as possible. If you pay more than $_____, you lose money.	You are authorized to **BUY 1 barrel of crude oil**, paying as **little** as possible. If you pay more than $_____, you lose money.
You are authorized to **BUY 1 barrel of crude oil**, paying as **little** as possible. If you pay more than $_____, you lose money.	You are authorized to **BUY 1 barrel of crude oil**, paying as **little** as possible. If you pay more than $_____, you lose money.
You are authorized to **BUY 1 barrel of crude oil**, paying as **little** as possible. If you pay more than $_____, you lose money.	You are authorized to **BUY 1 barrel of crude oil**, paying as **little** as possible. If you pay more than $_____, you lose money.

Activity 2
Sell Cards

You are authorized to **SELL 1 barrel of crude oil** for as **much** as possible. If you accept less than $_____, you lose money.	You are authorized to **SELL 1 barrel of crude oil** for as **much** as possible. If you accept less than $_____, you lose money.
You are authorized to **SELL 1 barrel of crude oil** for as **much** as possible. If you accept less than $_____, you lose money.	You are authorized to **SELL 1 barrel of crude oil** for as **much** as possible. If you accept less than $_____, you lose money.
You are authorized to **SELL 1 barrel of crude oil** for as **much** as possible. If you accept less than $_____, you lose money.	You are authorized to **SELL 1 barrel of crude oil** for as **much** as possible. If you accept less than $_____, you lose money.
You are authorized to **SELL 1 barrel of crude oil** for as **much** as possible. If you accept less than $_____, you lose money.	You are authorized to **SELL 1 barrel of crude oil** for as **much** as possible. If you accept less than $_____, you lose money.

Activity 3
Score Sheet for "A Market in Crude Oil"

Name_____   **Circle one: Buyer Seller**

Keep track of your progress during the game on this score sheet. Each time you receive a card, record the price on the card in column A. After you have made a sale or a purchase, write that amount in column B. Repeat this procedure as often as possible until you have completed all three rounds of the game. At the end of the game determine your gain (column C) or loss (column D) on each transaction. Determine total number of sales, total gains, total losses, and total net gain or loss. Sellers make a gain when they sell for more than the price on their Sell Cards. Buyers make a gain when they pay less than the price on their Buy Cards. Losses are made in just the opposite direction.

Transaction Number	Price on Card (A)	Transaction Price (B)	Gain (C)	Loss (D)
1				
2				
3				
4				
5				
6				
7				
8				
9				
10				
11				
12				
13				
14				
15				
16				
17				
18				
19				
20				
21				
22				
23				
24				
25				
26				
27				
28				

Total Number of Transactions_____   Total Gains_____ Total Losses_____
Total Net Gain or Loss (circle one) _____

Activity 4
Supply and Demand Schedules

SUPPLY: In the following table, the supply schedule in the third column equals the cumulative number of barrels of crude oil available for sale at the price indicated. The cumulative total is found by adding up in the second column all the barrels that will be produced and sold at a given price *and* at all lower prices. (Obviously, any producer willing to sell a barrel at a price of $28 will still be willing to sell that barrel at a higher price.)

Price	Number of Sellers Willing to Sell 1 Barrel of Crude Oil at the Price Indicated or at a Higher Price	Total Quantity Supplied
$24	2 sellers	2
26	2 sellers	4
28	2 sellers	6
30	3 sellers	9
32	3 sellers	12
34	4 sellers	16
36	4 sellers	20
38	4 sellers	24
40	4 sellers	28
42	4 sellers	32

DEMAND: In the following table, the demand schedule in the third column equals the cumulative number of barrels of crude oil buyers would be willing and able to buy at the price indicated. The cumulative total is found by adding up in the second column the barrels that will be purchased at a given price *and* at all higher prices. (Obviously, any buyer willing to purchase a barrel at a price of $38 will still be willing to buy that barrel at a lower price.)

Price	Number of Buyers Willing to Buy 1 Barrel of Crude Oil at the Price Indicated or at a Lower Price	Total Quantity Demanded
$44	2 buyers	2
42	2 buyers	4
40	2 buyers	6
38	3 buyers	9
36	3 buyers	12
34	4 buyers	16
32	4 sellers	20
30	4 sellers	24
28	4 sellers	28
26	4 sellers	32

From *Focus: High School Economics*, © National Council on Economic Education, New York, NY

Activity 5
Crude Oil Supply and Demand

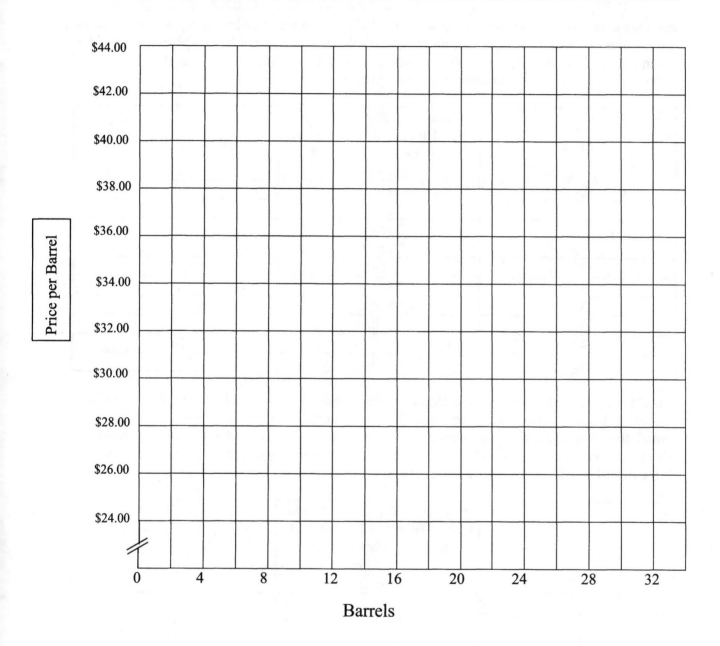

Activity 6
A Market Survey

Students in an economics class interviewed store managers of local grocery stores. They asked the managers to estimate how many pounds of bananas they would likely try to sell at their store next month, at each of five different prices selected by the class.

This is the average response for all of the stores, based on what the students learned from the managers.

Price per pound	$.89	$.79	$.69	$.59	$.49
Quantity sold	1000	900	800	700	600

The students also asked 100 adult shoppers at these grocery stores to estimate how many pounds of bananas each of them would buy next month at each of the prices selected by the class. Then they multiplied the average response from these 100 shoppers by the typical number of shoppers who will use the stores next month, based on what the store managers told them about their usual number of customers. This is what the students learned about average purchases of bananas that could be expected next month, based on the information provided by the consumers and store managers.

Price per pound	$.89	$.79	$.69	$.59	$49
Quantity bought	600	700	800	900	1000

Based on this information, answer the following questions:

1. What is the market clearing price for bananas?

2. In the marketplace, how will this price be determined? Remember, the store managers don't have the survey information on expected purchases that the students collected.

3. What will happen if the store managers try to sell their bananas at $.89 per pound?

4. Describe an example of a surplus or a shortage that you have experienced in the marketplace, or that you have read about or heard about from someone else.

Visual 1
Sample Buy/Sell Cards

You are authorized to **BUY 1 barrel of crude oil**, paying as **little** as possible. If you pay more than $_____, you lose money.

You are authorized to **SELL 1 barrel of crude oil** for as **much** as possible. If you accept less than $_____, you lose money.

Visual 2
Class Tally Sheet

Price per Barrel	Round 1	Round 2	Round 3	Total of Rounds 2 & 3
$24				
25				
26				
27				
28				
29				
30				
31				
32				
33				
34				
35				
36				
37				
38				
39				
40				
41				
42				
43				
44				

Visual 3
Graphing Supply, Demand, and Market Clearing Price

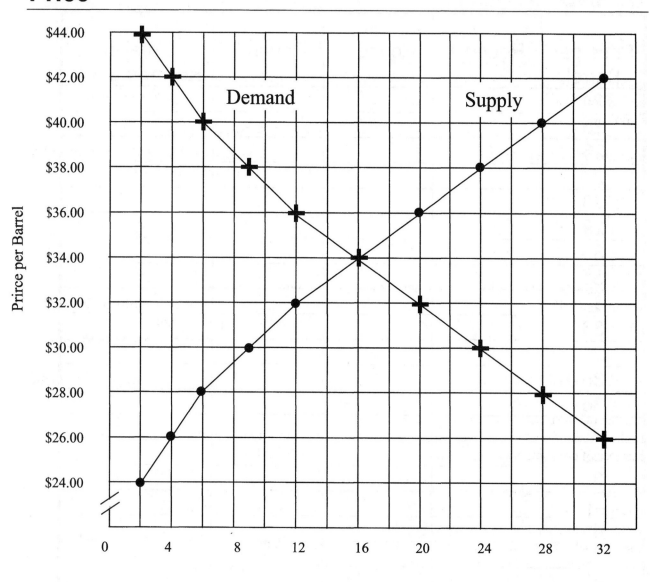

Barrels

LESSON FOUR
THE MARKET NEVER STANDS STILL

INTRODUCTION

Prices of goods and services fluctuate as conditions that influence the behavior of buyers and sellers change. This lesson examines the major reasons for such changes in supply and demand, and the resulting effects of these changes on market prices.

CONCEPTS

Determinants of demand shifts
Determinants of supply shifts

CONTENT STANDARD

Prices send signals and provide incentives to buyers and sellers. When supply or demand changes, market prices adjust, affecting incentives.

BENCHMARKS

Demand for a product changes when there is a change in consumers' incomes or preferences, or in the prices of related goods or services, or in the number of consumers in a market.

Supply of a product changes when there are changes in the prices of the productive resources used to make the good or service, the technology used to make the good or service, the profit opportunities available to producers by selling other goods and services, or the number of sellers in the market.

Changes in supply and demand cause relative prices to change; in turn, buyers and sellers adjust their purchase and sales decisions.

OBJECTIVE

♦ Students explain how demand and supply shift in response to changes in factors affecting consumers and producers, respectively. Then they predict the effects of changes in demand and supply on market prices and quantities traded.

LESSON DESCRIPTION

Students complete several worksheets to study the factors (determinants) that affect the position of supply and demand curves in order to understand why market prices and output levels fluctuate. After learning these determinants, students predict the effects of changes in the determinants on market prices and quantities.

TIME REQUIRED

Two class periods. Day one – procedures 1-9. Day two – procedures 10-15 and Assessment.

MATERIALS

- Activity 1: Reasons for Changes in Demand, one per student
- Activity 2: Reasons for Changes in Supply, one per student
- Activity 3: Reasons for Shifts in Demand Curves, one per student
- Activity 4: Reasons for Shifts in Supply Curves, one per student
- Activity 5: Changes in Supply and Demand Change Market Price and Quantity, one per student
- Activity 6: Market Game Test, one per student
- Visual 1: Determinants of Demand
- Visual 2: Shifts in Demand and Supply
- Visual 3: Determinants of Supply

PROCEDURES

1. Explain to the class that markets never stand still. Prices in a market economy change often, reflecting shifts in supply and demand. The purpose of this lesson is to examine more specifically how people's choices regarding buying and selling result in shifts in demand and supply.

2. Display Visual 1. Use the **determinants of demand** (consumer income, consumer tastes and preferences, prices of substitute goods, prices of complementary goods, consumers'

expectations about the future price of the product, and the number of consumers in the market) to explain a shift in demand.

3. Distribute Activity 1 to the class. Read the directions for Part I, and have students complete the tasks described. Have students explain their responses to see if there is a consensus, or confusion. Read the directions for Part II and direct students to complete it. Carefully discuss and correct students' responses by referring to the following answers.

Part I:
   A. *No change in demand, only in quantity demanded*
   B. *Increase*
   C. *Decrease*
   D. *Decrease*
   E. *Decrease*
   F. *Increase*
   G. *Decrease*
   H. *Increase*

Part II:
   Not listed, no change in demand – A
   Change in consumer tastes – D, F
   Change in income – E
   Change in the number of consumers – B
   Change in price of substitute good – C
   Change in price of complementary good – G
   Change in consumers' price expectations – H

4. Display Visual 2. Explain that using diagrams that show changes in demand and their effects on prices can reduce the confusion of the sort likely encountered in Activity 1. Use the top half of Visual 2 to explain that an increase in demand for a product means a larger quantity is demanded at every price. This is represented by the shift from curve D_1 to curve D_2. Conversely, a shift from D_2 to D_1 represents a smaller quantity demanded at every price, or a decrease in demand.

5. Emphasize that an increase in the demand for doughnuts means that more doughnuts are demanded at every price.

Provide students with practice in interpreting the graph. Ask:

A. What quantity of doughnuts is demanded at point A? (*20*) At point B? (*40*)

B. What quantity is demanded at point C? (*40*) At point D? (*60*)

C. What quantity is demanded at point E? (*50*) At Point F? (*70*)

D. What conclusion can be drawn from these data? (*On demand curve D_2, 20 more doughnuts are demanded at every price than on demand curve D_1.*)

6. Ask students to predict how one should draw a curve that illustrates a decrease in demand from D_1, and explain why. Draw such a curve, and label it D_0. (*Curve D_0 should be to the left of D_1.*)

7. Ask students whether a movement from point A to point C on curve D_1 shows an increase in the demand for doughnuts? (*No. It shows an increase in the quantity demanded, caused by a decrease in price from $2.00 to $1.00. It does not show that more doughnuts were demanded at all prices – e.g., at $2.00 the quantity demanded does not change.*) Stress that a movement along a demand curve is called a change in the quantity demanded; a shift in the position of the entire curve is called a change in demand.

8. Display Visual 3. Use the **determinants of supply** (the cost of productive resources, technology, change in producers' profit opportunities producing other products, changes in producers' expectations about the future price of the product, and the number of sellers in the market) to explain a shift in supply.

9. Distribute copies of Activity 2. Read the directions for Part I, and have students complete the tasks described. Have students explain their responses to see if there is a consensus, or confusion. Read the directions for Part II, and

direct students to complete it. Carefully discuss and correct students' responses by referring to the following answers.

Part I:
A.   *Increase*
B.   *Increase*
C.   *Decrease*
D.   *Increase*
E.   *Decrease*
F.   *No change in supply, only in quantity supplied.*
G.   *Decrease*

Part II:
Not listed, no change in supply – F
Costs of factors of production – A, C
Technology – B
Number of sellers – D, E
Profit opportunities from producing other products – G

10. Distribute Activity 3 to the class. Read the instructions and have students complete the activity sheet, using Part II of Activity 1 as a reference. Discuss the following answers.

A.   *No change, 3*
B.   *Increase, 4*
C.   *Decrease, 3*
D.   *Decrease, 2*
E.   *Decrease, 1*
F.   *Increase, 2*
G.   *Decrease, 1*
H.   *Increase, 2*

11. Display Visual 2 again. Using the bottom half, point out to students that a movement from curve S_1 to curve S_2 is an increase in supply, because the quantity supplied increases for every price. A shift from curve S_2 to S_1 indicates a decrease in quantity supplied at every price, so this is a decrease in supply.

12. Emphasize that an increase in the supply of doughnuts means that more doughnuts are supplied at every price. Ask:

A.   What quantity of doughnuts is supplied at point A? (*60*) At point B? (*70*)

B.   What quantity is supplied at point C? (*40*) At point D? (*50*)

C.   What quantity is supplied at point E? (*30*) At point F? (*40*)

D.   What conclusions can be drawn from these data? (*On supply schedule S_2, 10 more doughnuts are supplied at every price compared with schedule S_1.*)

13. Ask students to predict how one should draw a curve that illustrates a decrease in supply from S_1. Draw such a curve, and label it S_0. (*Curve S_0 should be to the left of S_1.*)

14. Ask students whether a movement from point D to point B shows an increase in the supply of doughnuts. (*No. It only shows an increase in the quantity supplied, caused by the increase in price from \$1.00 to \$2.00. At the price of \$1.00, more doughnuts are not supplied.*) Stress that a movement along a supply curve is only a change in the quantity supplied; a shift of the entire curve is called a change in supply. This verbal distinction is crucial to understanding one another in discussing economic topics, because the two phrases clearly refer to very different things.

15. Distribute Activity 4 to the class. Read the instructions and have students complete the activity sheet, using Part II of Activity 2 as a reference. Discuss the answers to Activity 4.

A.   *Increase, 4*
B.   *Increase, 5*
C.   *Decrease, 4*
D.   *Increase, 5*
E.   *Decrease, 4*
F.   *No change, 4*
G.   *Decrease, 3*

CLOSURE

Conclude the lesson by reviewing some of the key points. Ask:

1. What are the determinants of demand? (*Consumer income, consumer tastes, the prices of substitute goods, the prices of complementary goods, consumers' expectations about the future price of the good, and the number of consumers in the market*)

2. What are the determinants of supply? (*The cost of productive resources, technology, producers' profit opportunities producing other products, producers' expectations about the future price of the good, and the number of sellers in the market*)

3. What is the difference between a change in quantity demanded and a shift in demand? (*A movement along a demand curve is called a change in quantity demanded; a shift in the position of the entire curve is called a change in demand.*)

4. What is the difference between a change in quantity supplied and a shift in supply? (*A movement along a supply curve is called a change in quantity supplied; a shift in the position of the entire curve is called a change in supply.*)

5. Distribute a copy of Activity 5 to each student. After students have completed Activity 5, discuss their answers in class to reinforce understanding.

A. *E_1, equilibrium price = 1.50, equilibrium quantity = 40 million gallons*
B. *Quantity demanded equals quantity supplied, and that is only true at this price*
C. *E_2, equilibrium price = 1.75, equilibrium quantity = 55 million gallons*
D. *E_3, equilibrium price = 2.00, equilibrium quantity = 40 million gallons*

Questions C and D Demand Schedule

If the price of gasoline is:	Consumers would be willing to buy:
$1.25	85 M gallons
1.50	70 M
1.75	55 M
2.00	40 M
2.25	35 M
2.50	31 M

Question D Supply Schedule

If the Price of Gasoline is:	Producers would be willing to sell:
$1.25	-5 M gallons (i.e., will sell none)
1.50	10 M
1.75	25 M
2.00	40 M
2.25	55 M
2.50	60 M

ASSESSMENT

1. Encourage students to visit a business selling a product in which they are interested. Ask the owner or manager to identify the last time prices for the product changed. Also ask him or her to list as many reasons as possible why the price changed. In class, review the determinants of changes in demand and supply. Help students put the reasons for the price change that were suggested by the owner/manager into categories that list the appropriate determinants of supply or demand. Put students into cooperative learning groups, and draw graphs that reflect the reasons for changes in price identified during their interviews – i.e., show the shifts in supply and/or demand.

2. Conduct one or more rounds of the Classroom Market in Crude Oil (see Lesson 3) to simulate a decrease in supply. Use the number of *sell* cards available at each price shown in the following table. Give each student a score sheet (Activity 3 from Lesson 3). If you have used that activity very recently, simply remind students of

the activity and tell them you are going to play the game again, but with something changed. In the original version, or in the first rounds played now if you did not use the Classroom Market for Crude Oil in earlier classes, equilibrium price is $34 – with both quantity supplied and quantity demanded 16 (million) barrels. In the classroom market, prices should converge toward this level as more and more trades take place and students discover the equilibrium price. Continue by replacing the original deck of seller cards with a new deck as shown in the following table. (You will now have one seller card from Visual 1 in Lesson 3 with a price of $28, one seller card with a price of $30, etc.) **Don't** tell students at this time that the supply deck has changed, or that the demand deck has not changed. Shuffle both decks, and distribute a new card to buyers and sellers, as explained in Lesson 3. Have students start a new record of trades on their score sheet, clearly separated from information from any earlier rounds. Warn students again that things have changed, and that prices from the earlier rounds may no longer hold. Play the simulation again for about 10 minutes, as explained in Lesson 3. Have students record their transaction prices and gains or losses on their score sheets, and report their scores during the trading so that you can prepare the class tally sheet (Visual 2 in Lesson 3). When trading is completed and students have calculated their individual gains and losses, display the class tally sheet and ask students to discuss how and why prices changed as they did. (*Prices should increase because of the decrease in supply*.) To show the decrease in supply, draw the old and new supply curves on Activity 5 of Lesson 3, either shown on an overhead transparency or on individual copies of the activity distributed to students. Take the numbers for the original supply curve from the top chart in Activity 4 of Lesson 3, and the numbers for the new supply curve from the chart below. Putting this schedule together with the demand curve – which did not change – from the bottom chart on Activity 4 in Lesson 3, shows that the new equilibrium price is $38.

Change in Supply (Assessment Item 2)

Price	Number of sellers willing to sell 1 barrel of crude oil at the price indicated or at a higher price	Total quantity supplied at this price
$28	1 seller	1
30	1 seller	2
32	1 seller	3
34	2 sellers	5
36	2 sellers	7
38	2 sellers	9
40	4 sellers	13
42	5 sellers	18
44	7 sellers	25
46	7 sellers	32

3. Conduct one more round of the Classroom Market for Crude Oil to simulate an increase in demand. Once again, collect the old buyer and seller decks from the students, and warn them that something else is going to change. Do **not** tell them that this time the supply curve will remain unchanged (at the lower level established by using the new supply deck in the previous procedure), but demand will increase (perhaps because of an increase in income, a change in tastes and preferences, or other reasons explored in this lesson). Replace the original deck of buyer cards with the new deck shown in the following table. (Make two buyer cards from Visual 1 in Lesson 3 with a price of $50, three buyer cards with a price of $48, etc.) Shuffle both decks and distribute a new card to buyers and sellers. Have students start a new record of trades on their score sheet, clearly separated from information from any earlier rounds. Warn students again that things have changed, and that prices from the earlier round(s) may no longer hold. Play the simulation again for about 10 minutes. Have students record their transaction prices and gains or losses on their score sheets. Also have them report their trades during the activity, so that you can prepare the class tally sheet (Visual 2 in Lesson 3). When trading is

completed, display the class tally sheet and ask students to discuss how and why prices changed as they did. (*Prices should increase again, to even higher levels, this time because of the increase in demand.*) To show the increase in demand, draw the old and new supply and demand curves on Activity 5 of Lesson 3, either shown on an overhead transparency or on individual copies of the activity distributed to students. Take the numbers for the original demand curve from the bottom chart in Activity 4 of Lesson 3, and the numbers for the new demand curve from the chart below. Putting this schedule together with the new supply curve developed in the previous procedure – which did not change here – shows that the new equilibrium price is $42.

Change in Demand (Assessment Item 3)

Price	Number of buyers willing to buy 1 barrel of crude oil at the price indicated or at a lower price	Total quantity demanded
$50	2 buyers	2
48	3 buyers	5
46	4 buyers	9
44	4 buyers	13
42	5 buyers	18
40	6 buyers	24
38	8 buyers	32

4. Distribute a copy of Activity 6 to each student, to assess students' understanding of the key ideas in this lesson.

A. *The schedule showing how much of a product producers are willing and able to sell at all possible prices.*

B. *The schedule showing how much of a product consumers are willing and able to buy at all possible prices.*

C. *Law of supply: Producers are willing to sell more of a product at higher prices and less at lower prices.*

Law of demand: Consumers are willing to buy more of a product at lower prices and less at higher prices.

D. 1. *Greater*
   2. *Less*
   3. *Decrease*
   4. *Remain unchanged*

Activity 1
Reasons for Changes in Demand

Part I

Read the following eight newspaper headlines. In each case decide if the event will cause a change in the current market demand for beef. If so, decide if it is an increase or a decrease, and write the correct answer. For example, if you think headline 1 means there will be a decrease in demand, write "decrease" in the first blank. For headline 2, if you think demand will increase, write "increase." If the event causes no change in demand, write "no change."

A.   PRICE OF BEEF RISES
        Demand _____

B.   MILLIONS OF IMMIGRANTS SWELL U.S. POPULATION
        Demand _____

C.   PORK PRICES DROP
        Demand _____

D.   SURGEON GENERAL WARNS THAT EATING BEEF CAN BE HAZARDOUS TO HEALTH
        Demand _____

E.   TAKE-HOME PAY FOR AMERICANS DROPS 3RD MONTH IN ROW
        Demand _____

F.   NATIONWIDE FAD: THE JAPAPEÑO BURGER
        Demand _____

G.   HIGHER PRICE FOR CHARCOAL THREATENS MEMORIAL DAY COOKOUTS
        Demand _____

H.   BEEF PRICES EXPECTED TO SKYROCKET NEXT MONTH
        Demand _____

Activity 1 (continued)

Part II

   Put each change in demand from Part I into one of the following categories, based on the reason for the change. Write the letter of the headline(s) next to the appropriate reason for the change in demand. Some categories may have more than one headline letter, and any event that did not change demand should *not* be listed with any of the determinants.

_____   A change in consumer tastes
_____   A change in consumer incomes
_____   A change in the number of consumers in the market
_____   A change in the price of a substitute good
_____   A change in the price of a complementary good
_____   A change in consumers' price expectations

Activity 2
Reasons for Changes in Supply

Part I

Read the following seven newspaper headlines. In each case, decide if the event will cause any change in the current market supply of new cars sold in the United States. If so, decide if it is an increase or a decrease, and write the correct answer. For example, if you think headline 1 means there will be a decrease in supply, write "decrease" in the first blank. For headline 2, if you think supply will increase, write "increase." If the event causes no change, write "no change."

A.   AUTO WORKERS AGREE TO WAGE AND FRINGE CUTS
Supply _____

B.   NEW TECHNOLOGY INCREASES EFFICIENCY IN DETROIT FACTORIES
Supply _____

C.   STEEL PRICES RISE 10%
Supply _____

D.   QUOTAS ELIMINATED: FOREIGN CAR IMPORTS RISE
Supply _____

E.   LARGE AUTO PRODUCER GOES BANKRUPT, CLOSES FACTORIES
Supply _____

F.   BUYERS REJECT NEW CAR MODELS: SELLERS LOWER PRICES
Supply _____

G.   SHORTAGES ABOUND IN CONSUMER ELECTRONICS – CONSUMERS CAN'T BUY ENOUGH NEW GADGETS
Supply _____

Activity 2 (continued)

Part II

Put each change in supply from Part I into one of the following categories, based on the reason for the change. Write the letter of the headline next to the appropriate reason for the change in supply. Some categories may have more than one headline letter, and any event that did not change supply should *not* be listed with any of the determinants.

_____ A change in the cost of factors of production
_____ A change in technology
_____ A change in the number of sellers in the market
_____ A change in profit opportunities from producing other products

From *Focus: High School Economics*, © National Council on Economic Education, New York, NY

Activity 3
Reasons for Shifts in Demand Curves

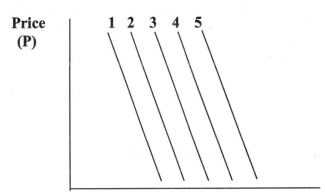

Read the following eight newspaper headings. In each case decide if the event will cause a change in the current demand for beef. If so, determine whether it is an increase or a decrease, and write the correct answer. Begin at curve 3. If you think headline A means there will be a decrease in demand, write "decrease" in the first blank and "2" in the second blank; move to curve 2 to do headline B. Or, if you think headline A means demand will increase, write "increase" and "4" in the blank for headline A; move to curve 4 to do headline B.

Move only one curve at a time. Do not skip two curves, say from 1 to 3, even if you think the headline means there will be a large change in demand. Do not go beyond the five curves. If you are at 1 and the next headline implies a decrease in demand, you goofed somewhere. There is one headline which implies that the demand for beef does *not* change.

A.   PRICE OF BEEF RISES
       Demand _____ Curve _____

B.   MILLIONS OF IMMIGRANTS SWELL U.S. POPULATION
       Demand _____ Curve _____

C.   PORK PRICES DROP
       Demand _____ Curve _____

D.   SURGEON GENERAL WARNS THAT EATING BEEF CAN BE HAZARDOUS TO
       HEALTH
       Demand _____ Curve _____

Activity 3 (continued)

E.   TAKE-HOME PAY FOR AMERICANS DROPS 3RD MONTH IN ROW
Demand _____ Curve _____

F.   NATIONWIDE FAD: THE JALAPEÑO BURGER
Demand _____ Curve _____

G.   HIGHER PRICE OF CHARCOAL THREATENS MEMORIAL DAY COOKOUTS
Demand _____ Curve _____

H.   BEEF PRICES EXPECTED TO SKYROCKET NEXT MONTH
Demand _____ Curve _____

Activity 4
Reasons for Shifts in Supply Curves

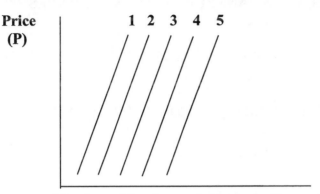

Number of foreign and domestically produced
cars in the U.S. (Q)

Read the following seven newspaper headlines. In each case, decide if the event will cause any change in the supply of cars. If so, determine whether it is an increase or a decrease, and write the correct answer. Begin at curve 3. If you think headline A means there will be a decrease in supply, write "decrease" in the first blank and "2" in the second blank; move to curve 2 to do headline B. Or, if you think headline A means supply will increase, write "increase" and "4" in the blank for headline A; move to curve 4 to do headline B.

Move only one curve at a time. Do not skip two curves, say from 1 to 3, even if you think the headline means there will be a large change in supply. Do not go beyond the five curves. If you are at 1 and the next headline implies a decrease in supply, you goofed somewhere. There is one headline which implies that the supply of cars does *not* change.

A. AUTO WORKERS AGREE TO WAGE AND FRINGE CUTS
    Supply _____ Curve _____

B. NEW TECHNOLOGY INCREASES EFFICIENCY IN DETROIT FACTORIES
    Supply _____ Curve _____

C. STEEL PRICES RISE 10%
    Supply _____ Curve _____

D. QUOTAS ELIMINATED: FOREIGN CAR IMPORTS RISE
    Supply _____ Curve _____

Activity 4 (continued)

E. LARGE AUTO PRODUCER GOES BANKRUPT, CLOSES FACTORIES
    Supply _____ Curve _____

F. BUYERS REJECT NEW CAR MODELS: SELLERS LOWER PRICES
    Supply _____ Curve _____

G. SHORTAGES ABOUND IN ELECTRONICS: CONSUMERS CAN'T BUY ENOUGH
    NEW GADGETS
    Supply _____ Curve _____

Activity 5
Changes in Supply and Demand Change Market Price and Quantity

Economists studied the gasoline market to find out how many millions (M) of gallons consumers would be willing to buy each day and how many gallons sellers would be willing to sell each day at various prices. This research showed that:

If the price of a gallon of gasoline was	Consumers would be willing to buy	Producers would be willing to sell
$1.25	55 M	25 M
1.50	40 M	40 M
1.75	25 M	55 M
2.00	10 M	70 M
2.25	5 M	85 M
2.50	1 M	90 M

A.   According to the table, the market clearing (or equilibrium) price for gasoline is _____ and at this price the number of gallons of gasoline bought and sold is _____. Label the equilibrium price E_1.

B.   How do you know this is the market clearing price?_____

_____

C.   Assume that sports utility vehicles gain new popularity by meeting improved safety standards for tires and operating designs. Because consumers buy so many sports utility vehicles, they want to buy 30 million more gallons of gasoline per day at every price. For example, at $1.25 per gallon people now want to buy 85 million gallons rather than 55 million. Complete a new table below showing the amount that people would like to buy at each price. What is the new market-clearing price? _____ How many gallons will be bought and sold at this price? _____ Label the new equilibrium price E_2.

If the price of a gallon of gasoline was	Consumers would be willing to buy	Producers would be willing to sell
$1.25	___ M	25 M
1.50	___ M	40 M
1.75	___ M	55 M
2.00	___ M	70 M
2.25	___ M	85 M
2.50	___ M	90 M

Activity 5 (continued)

D.   Now assume that two oil producing countries get into a war and destroy each other's oil wells. Because of this, sellers are willing to sell 30 million fewer gallons of gasoline per day at every price. For example, at $1.50 per gallon sellers are willing to sell only 10 million gallons rather than 40 million gallons. Write another table showing the new amount that people would like to sell at each price. What is the new market-clearing (or equilibrium) price, assuming the demand schedule from question C is used again? _____ How many gallons will be bought and sold at this price? _____ Label this new equilibrium price E_3.

If the price of a gallon of gasoline was	Consumers would be willing to buy	Producers would be willing to sell
$1.25	85 M	___ M
1.50	70 M	___ M
1.75	55 M	___ M
2.00	40 M	___ M
2.25	35 M	___ M
2.50	31 M	___ M

Activity 6
Market Game Test

A.   What does the term supply mean? _____
_____
_____

B.   What does the term demand mean? _____
_____
_____

C.   Explain the laws of supply and demand, i.e., (1) the relationship between quantity supplied and price and (2) the relationship between quantity demanded and price.
_____
_____
_____

D.   Use the following terms to complete the sentences below. You will not have to use all of the terms.

> Increase   Remain Unchanged   Less
> Decrease   Greater

1.   If everything else remains the same, the amount of wheat available for sale at a price of $4.90 per bushel will usually be _____ than the amount available for sale at a price of $3.90 per bushel.

2.   However, the amount of wheat demanded would be _____ at $4.90 than at $3.90 per bushel.

3.   All other things being equal, if the demand for wheat falls, then the market price for wheat will _____.

4.   If the supply of wheat for sale doubles and the demand for wheat doubles, the price of wheat will probably _____.

Visual 1
Determinants of Demand

- **Change in Consumer Income**: When there is an increase in income, demand for most goods increases. If there is a decrease in income, demand for most goods decreases. The exceptions to this rule are called inferior goods, because people buy less of them as their income rises.

- **Change in Consumer Tastes**: If consumers like a product more based on advertising or experience in using the good, demand increases. If consumers like a good less over time, demand decreases.

- **Change in the Price of a Substitute Good**: If the price of a substitute good increases, this will increase demand for the original good. If the price of Coca Cola increases, for example, the demand for Pepsi Cola will increase. If the price of a substitute good decreases, this will result in a decrease in demand for the original good. If the price of Coca Cola decreases, the demand for Pepsi Cola will decrease.

- **Change in the Price of a Complementary Good**: If the price of a complementary good increases, this will decrease demand for the original good. If the price of camera film sharply rises, for example, the demand for cameras will decrease. If the price of a complementary good decreases, this will result in a increase in demand for the original good. If the price of CD players decreases, the demand for CD's will increase.

- **Change in Consumers' Price Expectations**: Consumers' expectations about the future price of a good influence demand. If consumers expect the price to increase, they try to buy more now, before the price rises.

- **Change in Number of Consumers in the Market**: If there is an increase in the number of consumers, this will result in an increase in demand. If there is a decrease in the number of consumers, this will result in a decrease in demand.

 From *Focus: High School Economics,* © National Council on Economic Education, New York, NY

Visual 2
Shifts in Demand and Supply

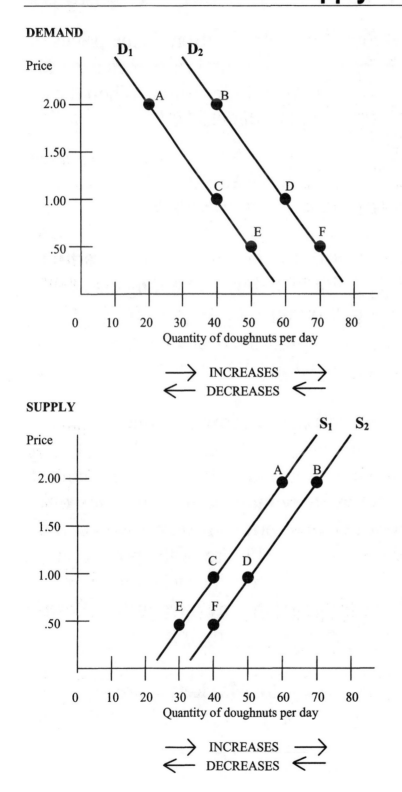

DEMAND

Price

D₁ D₂

SUPPLY

Price

S₁ S₂

→ INCREASES →
← DECREASES ←

Visual 3
Determinants of Supply

- **Change in the Cost of Factors of Production**: If the prices of natural resources, labor resources, or capital resources used to produce a product increase, supply will decrease. When these costs of production decrease, supply increases.

- **Change in Technology**: New technology often reduces producers' costs, leading to an increase in supply.

- **Change in Profit Opportunities Producing Other Products**: If producers expect to make more selling something else the supply of what they currently produce decreases. If profit opportunities producing other things decrease, more sellers will begin producing this product, increasing supply.

- **Change in Producers' Price Expectations**: Producers' expectations about the future price of the product they sell influence current supply. If sellers expect the price for their good to increase in the future, they may reduce what they offer to sell today, to wait for the higher price. If sellers expect the price to decrease, they may try to sell more of the product now, before the price falls. For example, consider wheat farmers deciding whether to store or sell grain they have just harvested, or people who are thinking about selling their houses.

- **Change in Number of Sellers in the Market**: More sellers in a market will usually increase supply. Fewer sellers will likely decrease supply.

 From *Focus: High School Economics*, © National Council on Economic Education, New York, NY

LESSON FIVE
MARKETS INTERACT

INTRODUCTION

Supply and demand analysis is most often used to show the impact of market changes on equilibrium price and quantity for a particular good or service. But it can also be used to show how changes in one market lead to changes in many other markets. Doing that is an important step towards building an understanding of how a *system* of markets works. It can also demonstrate the inherent difficulty of trying to use laws, regulations, or other public policies to raise or lower price and quantity outcomes in just one market. Often, such policies set off a long chain of events, including unintended consequences that were not at all what policy makers wanted to see happen.

CONCEPTS

Equilibrium price and quantity
Supply and demand
Interdependence

CONTENT STANDARD

Prices send signals and provide incentives to buyers and sellers. When supply or demand changes, market prices adjust, affecting incentives.

BENCHMARK

Markets are interrelated; changes in the price of one good or service can lead to changes in prices of many other goods and services.

OBJECTIVES

♦ Students analyze how changes in determinants of supply or demand affect market prices and quantities exchanged.

♦ Students analyze how changes in one market may affect other markets.

LESSON DESCRIPTION

Using supply and demand analysis and building flow charts, students investigate how markets interact.

TIME REQUIRED

One class period.

MATERIALS

- Activity 1: Markets Interact, one per student, cut apart
- Activity 2: Markets Interact – The Sequel, one per student
- Nine 8½" × 11" sheets of paper
- Yarn and tape

PROCEDURES

1. Review how changes in demand or supply bring about changes in **equilibrium price and quantity** exchanged. (See Lesson 4.)

2. Explain that a change in one market tends to affect related markets. For example, if the cost of producing beef increases, the supply of beef will decrease, which will increase the price of beef and reduce the quantity exchanged. When the price of beef increases, the market for pork will be affected. The demand for pork will increase because of an increase in the price of a substitute good. As a result, the price of pork will increase and the quantity of pork exchanged will increase.

3. Divide the class into nine groups. Distribute a sheet of paper and a card from Activity 1 to each group. Explain that each group will analyze and present to the class changes in the market listed on its card. Instruct each group to write the name of its market at the top of the sheet of paper and draw a supply and demand diagram.

4. Explain that the "News Event" on each card describes something that has happened that affects their market. Instruct each group to: (a) determine whether supply or demand has been affected, (b) describe how and why it has

changed, (c) draw the change on its diagram, and (d) indicate how equilibrium price and quantity have changed. When finished, each group should tape its card to the sheet of paper.

5. As groups complete their diagrams, circulate among the groups to make sure their diagrams are correct. Note: It is especially important to check if group #1 has shown an increase in demand. That group may be tempted to show a decrease in supply, but the supply of sugar produced *in the U.S.* has not changed.

Market Changes for Activity 1: Key to symbols: ↑ (increase); ↓ (decrease); = (no change); ? (indeterminate)

Market

#	S	D	P	Q	Reason for Change
1	=	↑	↑	↑	*(increase in the number of consumers)*
2	↓	=	↑	↓	*(increase in the price of an input causes higher production costs)*
3	=	↑	↑	↑	*(increase in price of a substitute)*
4	=	↓	↓	↓	*(initially, a decrease in the number of consumers reduces demand; in time, supply will also decrease due to a decrease in the number of producers)*
5	=	↓	↓	↓	*(decrease in number of buyers [i.e., employers])*
6	↑	=	↓	↑	*(increase in number of producers, reflecting better profit opportunities in this "crop")*
7	↑	=	↓	↑	*(increase in number of producers [workers], reflecting better wage opportunities in the U.S.)*
8	↓	=	↑	↓	*(increase in profits from producing other products)*
9	=	↑	↑	=/↑	*(increase in number of buyers [farmers] resulting from increased demand and profits for U.S. agricultural production; some students may argue that the amount of farmland in the U.S. is fixed, but there will probably be a small increase in the amount of land available for farming as rents increase)*

6. Explain that while, so far, each group has considered only one market, the main point of the activity is to show **interdependence** (how these markets interact). A change in one market can affect another market, which in turn affects yet another market. Instruct a spokesperson from each group to read its card and describe its supply and demand analysis.

7. After all of the groups have explained their analysis of their individual markets, announce that the class will create a flow chart, using the diagrams each group drew to show how the markets are linked together. Discuss:

A. Which market/news event initiated the market changes? (*Market 1*.) Tape the diagram to the wall.

B. Which market changes occurred directly because of the increase in the price of sugar? (*Markets 2, 3, 4, 8, and 9*.) Tape diagrams 2, 3, 4, and 8 around the four sides of the market 1 diagram, and tape a piece of yarn from market 1 to each of the other four markets. See the sample flow chart below. Tape a piece of yarn from market 1 to market 9 now, or after discussing market 3.

C. Were any market changes caused by the change in market 2? (*No.*) Market 3? (*Yes, markets 8 and 9.*) Market 4? (*Yes, markets 5 and 6.*) Tape yarn from market 4 to markets 5 and 6, and between markets 3 and 8 and 3 and 9.

D. Were any market changes caused by changes in markets 5 and 6? (*None because of changes in market 6, but the change in market 7 was caused by the change in market 5.*) Tape yarn between markets 5 and 7.

E. Were any market changes caused by the change in market 7? (*No.*)

Sample Flow Chart

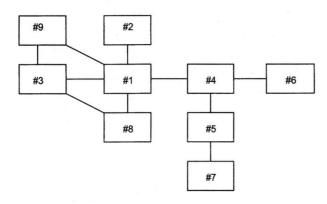

8. Explain that the U.S. government really has used sugar quotas to support sugar prices and the incomes of sugar growers. In fact, the market changes described in this lesson are discussed in a series of *Wall Street Journal* articles: 9/26/86 (pp. 1, 20); 10/9/86 (p. 39); 12/16/86 (p. 14); and 6/26/90 (pp. 1, 11).

9. Instruct students to use the flow chart and supply and demand analysis to write a fictitious newspaper article about U.S. trade policy in the sugar market.

10. Distribute a copy of Activity 2 to each student. Have students draw a flow chart

similar to the classroom flow chart, using the oil market example. Each box should contain a supply-and-demand graph, analyzing how the event affected the market.

Market Changes for Activity 2:

Market #	S	D	P	Q	Reason for Change
1	↓	=	↑	↓	(*In effect, collusion by the OPEC cartel reduces competition and the number of independent sellers in this market. Like most cartels, OPEC has been through periods of relatively effective, and relatively ineffective, collusion. The assumption here is that conditions currently favor more effective collusion.*)
2	↓	=	↑	↓	(*increase in the price of an input causes higher production costs*)
3	↓	=	↑	↓	(*increase in the price of an input causes higher production costs*)
4	↓	↑	↑	?	(*increase in the price of an input causes higher production costs; bad weather increases demand; price will definitely increase, but the quantity exchanged may go up or down*)
5	=	↑	↑	↑	(*increase in the price of a substitute good*)
6	↓	=	↑	↓	(*increase in the price of an input causes higher production costs*)

7 ↓ = ↑ ↓ *(increase in the price of an input causes higher production costs)*

8 = ↓ ↓ ↓ *(decrease in the number of consumers [i.e., employers])*

9 ↓ = ↑ ↓ *(increase in the price of an input causes higher production costs)*

CLOSURE

Discuss the following:

1. If demand or supply changes in a given market, what will be the effects in that market? (*The price and quantity exchanged in that market will change.*)

2. When economists say that "markets interact," what do they mean? (*Price and output changes in one market affect other markets, changing prices and quantities exchanged in those markets, too.*)

3. If natural gas prices increase, how will that affect the supply of electric power and the equilibrium price and quantity exchanged? (*The cost of producing electricity will rise for power-generating plants that use natural gas as a source of energy. That will cause supply to decrease, the price of electricity to increase, and the quantity purchased to decrease.*)

4. If natural gas prices increase, what will happen to the demand for home and business insulation and the equilibrium price and quantity exchanged? (*More consumers will insulate their homes and businesses to reduce their gas bills, thereby increasing the demand for insulation. Equilibrium price and quantity for insulation will also increase.*)

ASSESSMENT

1. Instruct groups to add new market events and analyses to the flow charts developed in Activities 1 and 2 to demonstrate further possible market interactions. The events may be related to any of the cards from these activities.

2. Have students find and turn in a newspaper article that shows how a change in one market has affected other markets. Based on the article, students should develop a simple flow chart, similar to those developed in Activities 1 and 2.

From *Focus: High School Economics,* © National Council on Economic Education, New York, NY

Activity 1
Markets Interact

Market: sugar produced in the United States   #1 **News Event:** The U.S. government reduces the amount of sugar that U.S. companies may import. As a result, U.S. sugar consumers, such as candy companies, buy more sugar from U.S. sugar producers.
Market: candy   #2 **News Event:** Because of a federal policy designed to protect U.S. sugar producers, the price of sugar increases.
Market: corn   #3 **News Event:** Because of a federal policy supporting sugar prices, soft-drink bottlers use more high-fructose corn syrup as a substitute for sugar.
Market: sugar market in Caribbean countries   #4 **News Event:** Because of legal quotas on sugar imported to the United States, sales of sugar to the United States decrease, and sugar producers in Caribbean countries reduce sugar production.
Market: unskilled labor market in Caribbean countries   #5 **News Event:** Because of decreased sugar exports to the United States, sugar plantations lay off workers, and some sugar mills close.
Market: marijuana in Caribbean countries   #6 **News Event:** Because of reduced demand for sugar grown in the Caribbean, some sugar growers begin to grow marijuana to earn more income.
Market: unskilled labor market in the United States   #7 **News Event:** Because of lower sugar production in their countries, some Caribbean sugar plantation and sugar mill workers begin to immigrate illegally to the U.S. to find work.
Market: soybeans produced in the United States   #8 **News Event:** As higher sugar prices lead more U.S. farmers to grow sugar cane, sugar beets, and corn (for corn sweetener), the production of wheat and soybeans decreases.
Market: U.S. farm land   #9 **News Event:** Higher crop prices and profits drive up rents on U.S. farm land.

Activity 2
Markets Interact – The Sequel

Market: world oil market	#1
News Event: OPEC (Organization of the Petroleum Exporting Countries) announces a significant reduction in the amount of oil that will be produced by each member.	
Market: diesel fuel	#2
News Event: The price of crude oil doubles.	
Market: trucking services	#3
News Event: Prices for diesel fuel increase dramatically.	
Market: home heating oil	#4
News Event: Crude oil prices rise substantially, and extremely cold weather hits northeastern states where heating oil is a major fuel for home furnaces.	
Market: wood	#5
News Event: Because of high fuel-oil prices, people use wood-burning fireplaces more, and sales of wood-burning fireplaces increase.	
Market: frozen vegetables	#6
News Event: Trucking firms charge higher prices to deliver products to factories, warehouses, grocery stores, and other retailers.	
Market: airline travel	#7
News Event: Jet fuel prices rise rapidly.	
Market: airline workers	#8
News Event: Airlines cut back on flight schedules as high ticket prices result in fewer people flying.	
Market: Barrels of chemicals used by water treatment plants	#9
News Event: High oil prices lead to higher diesel and gasoline prices, which increase shipping and transportation costs.	

LESSON SIX
PRICE CONTROLS – TOO HIGH OR TOO LOW

INTRODUCTION

Sometimes governments interfere with market forces by establishing minimum prices or maximum prices for specific goods and services. Examples of such legal price controls include minimum prices for milk and grain products to help agricultural producers; minimum wage laws in labor markets; and maximum prices for apartment rents, for gasoline in the 1970s, and for many products during World Wars I and II. Economists generally oppose these price controls, except perhaps during wartime conditions, or in markets characterized by very limited competition (see Lesson 14). Nevertheless, the policies continue to be an important part of some key markets in the U.S. economy.

CONCEPTS

Markets and prices
Supply and demand
Price ceiling
Price floor
Shortages and surpluses
Rationing

CONTENT STANDARDS

Markets exist when buyers and sellers interact. This interaction determines market prices and thereby allocates scarce goods and services.

Prices send signals and provide incentives to buyers and sellers. When supply or demand changes, market prices adjust, affecting incentives.

BENCHMARKS

Government-enforced price ceilings set below the market clearing price and government-enforced price floors set above the market clearing price distort price signals and incentives to producers and consumers. The price ceilings cause persistent shortages, while the price floors cause persistent surpluses.

OBJECTIVES

♦ Students define price ceilings and price floors.

♦ Students analyze the effects of price controls on competitive markets.

♦ Students describe the outcomes of price controls in terms of surpluses and shortages.

♦ Students evaluate the arguments for and against price controls.

LESSON DESCRIPTION

Students use supply-and-demand graphs to illustrate the effects of legal price controls in competitive markets.

TIME REQUIRED

One class period.

MATERIALS

- Activity 1: Price Floors and Ceilings, one per student
- Activity 2: Apartments to Rent, but How Many at What Price?, one per student
- Activity 3: The Market for Milk, one per student
- Visual 1: Price Ceilings
- Visual 2: Price Floors

PROCEDURES

1. After covering basic material on how market prices are set by the forces of supply and demand (see Lessons 3-5), begin a discussion of price controls by asking questions about a price that some students might think is "unfair." Examples of products with high prices might be CDs and DVDs, gasoline, tickets for movies or sporting events or rock concerts, houses, rents on apartments, and utilities (especially

electricity and natural gas). Students with part-time jobs may think that the minimum wage is too low, and in farming communities students may argue that prices for food crops and products are too low.

2. When the class has developed a list of prices that some students feel are too high or too low, ask: "Should the government do something about these prices that some of you think are unfair?"

3. Review the idea that most prices in the United States are set by market forces (i.e., supply and demand), not by government laws or regulations. (Of course, sales or excise taxes on most goods and services affect the final prices that consumers pay and producers receive for these products. But those taxes are usually set as some percentage of the market prices, which are determined by supply and demand.) The main reason for letting markets set prices, rather than government agencies, is to have prices reflect the preferences and circumstances of individual buyers and sellers, with decisions made in a very decentralized manner. In competitive markets, buyers compete with other buyers, and sellers compete with other sellers. The market price is determined through this process, and everyone who is willing and able to buy at the market price gets the product, while everyone who is willing and able to sell at that price can sell it. In this way the allocation decisions are made to determine which consumers will buy and use the product, and which producers will use productive resources to make and sell the product.

4. Point out that despite the efficiency and ease of letting prices for most goods and services be determined in the marketplace, even in the United States and other market economies there are some cases where either producers or consumers are able to convince government officials that market prices for some products are too high or too low. That may lead the government to set a legal maximum or minimum price.

5. Project Visuals 1 and 2 and introduce the terms **price ceiling** and **price floor**. Students often find it strange that price floors are above the market clearing price, and price ceilings are below the market clearing price – after all, ceilings are up and floors are down. But explain that a legally enforced price ceiling sets the maximum price that can be charged for a good or service. Therefore, price ceilings are adopted in cases where some consumers feel that prices for products are too high. Legally enforced price floors set a minimum price for some product, and are adopted when some producers feel that prices for some products are too low. Those who argue for price ceilings or floors will only be successful when they enjoy widespread public and political support (as with price controls on gasoline adopted in the early 1970s), or when they can form effective special-interest groups (see Lesson 13). But in some cases they are successful, which leads to many predictable kinds of problems that will be shown in the rest of the lesson.

6. Review the list of products students developed in procedure 1, for which they felt prices were too high or too low. Now, as an individual assignment or working in small groups (3-5 students), they will consider what would happen if the government set legal price ceilings to lower the prices that some students felt were too high, or legal price floors to raise the prices that some students felt were too low.

7. Distribute a copy of Activity 1 to each student, and ask the students to answer the questions. When they have done that individually or in small groups, lead a class discussion that covers the following points:

A. What is the market clearing price in the graph below? (*The market clearing price is $50 because this is the only price at which quantity supplied is equal to quantity demanded.*)

B. What quantity is demanded and what quantity is supplied at the market clearing price? (*The equilibrium level of quantity demanded and quantity supplied is 120 units.*)

C. What quantity is demanded and what quantity is supplied if the government passes a law setting a maximum price of $30? (*At a price of $30, quantity demanded is about 160 units and quantity supplied is about 60 units. Explain that this difference, the amount by which quantity demanded exceeds quantity supplied at a price below the market clearing price, is called a **shortage**.*)

D. What quantity would be demanded and what quantity would be supplied if the government passes a law setting a minimum price of $80? (*At a price of $80, the quantity supplied is about 220 and the quantity demanded is about 60. Explain that this difference, the amount by which quantity supplied exceeds quantity demanded at a price above the marketing clearing price, is called a **surplus**.*)

8. Ask students to identify examples of actual price ceilings and floors, and provide some additional examples. (*The minimum wage and agricultural price supports are examples of price floors; rent controls, "usury" laws setting maximum interest rates on credit card loans, and price controls on gasoline in the 1970s are examples of price ceilings.*)

9. Distribute a copy of Activity 2 to each student. Have students answer the questions, either in small groups or as an individual assignment.

Correct answers:

A. Everybody wants a place to live, so how can it be true that more apartments will be demanded at a lower price than at higher prices? (*At higher rents, more people will choose the following kinds of options: a) live with their parents, b) share an apartment, or c) buy a house rather than rent. At lower rents, more people will want to rent their own apartment – if they can find one.*)

B. On any given day, there are only a certain number of apartments in the city, so why isn't the supply curve of apartments a vertical line? In other words, can it really be true that there will be more apartments for rent at high prices than at low prices? (*More people and companies will be willing to rent rooms and apartments at higher prices than at lower prices. The rent controls will lead some people to stop renting rooms or apartments, and over time will slow or stop the construction of new apartments.*)

C. How many total apartments are available at the rent control price? (*40,000*)

D. How many apartments do people want to rent at the rent control price? (*70,000*)

E. What is the problem facing the city and the people who want to rent apartments? (*There is a shortage of apartments because quantity demanded is greater than quantity supplied at the current ceiling price. This creates an incentive for people who can't find an apartment to offer bribes or other favors when an apartment is available. Maintenance and other services at the apartments will probably be cut back because the apartment owners are receiving lower rents, and because they have no trouble finding people to rent any vacant apartments.*)

Comments concerning the mayor and city council's options may include:

Some students may consider letting rents increase to the market clearing price the fairest and most efficient thing to do. Others may see landlords as greedy, at the expense of renters, because many apartments have already been built, and would be rented even at the rent-control price. Try to bring out both the short-run and long-run effects of letting rents remain fixed or increase, both to prospective renters and apartment owners. Then ask students if the same arguments apply to prices of individually owned homes? In other words, should the price people receive when they sell their homes be limited with a price ceiling?

The first-come, first-served method may be considered unfair to those who are just moving into town, and therefore unable to search for an apartment as easily as someone who already lives in Ourtown. It also favors groups that include at least one adult who does not have an 8-to-5 job, and therefore has more time to spend searching for an apartment.

A random drawing might be considered fair in the sense that everyone who wants an apartment has an equal chance to rent one. But long-time residents and those who have been waiting a long time to get an apartment may think it is very unfair to give people who have just started looking the same chance they have.

10. Distribute a copy of Activity 3, Part I, to each student. After reviewing the explanation of how price controls were used in the dairy industry, ask students to answer the questions on their Activity sheet.

Correct Answers:

A. Is there a shortage or a surplus in the market? Explain. (*A surplus, because the quantity supplied exceeds the quantity demanded at a price floor of $1.40, which is higher than the market clearing price.*)

B. If there were no government price controls in the market, this graph suggests that the price of milk (the market-clearing price) paid to farmers would be approximately _____ per gallon. (*$1.00*)

C. Who would benefit and who would be hurt if price controls in the milk market were eliminated? (*Clearly the incomes of dairy farmers would decline considerably. Many small or high-cost dairy farmers would probably have to shift into other agricultural products or leave farming entirely. Consumers of milk and other dairy products would benefit from lower prices. The reduced costs of purchasing surplus products and administering the price-support program would reduce government expenditures and benefit taxpayers.*)

Explain that Part I of the activity indicates why most economists tend to be critical of price support programs. Public policy debates do include discussions, and different interpretations of, these *economic* effects of price support programs. However, *political* concerns often dominate the debates and the policies. Tell students you will use Part II of Activity 3 to discuss these aspects of price support programs.

11. Distribute a copy of Activity 3, Part II, to each student. Ask students to read the statements of each speaker and to answer the question at the bottom of the page. Discuss Part II, noting the following points: These statements indicate a typically messy mix of economic and political issues. There is not a

definite answer to the question of what would happen to the price of milk, but most economists believe that Miss Doright's comments are more accurate. Senator Foxfire's statement that milk prices might be even higher without price controls overlooks the effects of competition. Unless there are substantial barriers to entering the industry, competition can be expected to prevent monopolistic price levels – and there would probably still be a large number of milk producers without the price controls.

12. Note that the effects of price-support programs often hurt many people (in this case, milk consumers and taxpayers) a very small amount, and help a few people (in this case, milk producers) a great deal. Therefore, the comments of Senator Foxfire are often politically very persuasive. Special interest groups are willing to devote a lot of effort and money to their lobbying efforts because, for them, the stakes are high – they have a lot to gain or lose. Consumers and taxpayers who would gain from the lower milk prices aren't so clearly focused because, for them, the stakes are not so high – they have very little to gain or lose individually, even though in total they would often gain more than the special interest group would lose if the price controls were dropped. See Lesson 13 for more discussion and activities on special interest effects.

CLOSURE

1. What are legal price floors and ceilings? *(To have any effect on prices a price floor establishes a minimum legal price that is higher than the market clearing price and a price ceiling establishes a maximum legal price that is lower than the market clearing price.)*

2. Do price floors and ceilings have any effects other than raising and lowering prices? *(Yes. Legal price floors above the market clearing price lead to persistent surpluses.*

Legal price ceilings below the market clearing price lead to persistent shortages.)

3. Who favors, and who opposes, price floors and price ceilings? *(Price floors are usually supported by producers who receive higher prices for their products – especially if the government also agrees to purchase the surplus production. Consumers are generally hurt by price floors. Price ceilings, on the other hand, benefit consumers – or at least those consumers who are able to purchase the product subject to the price ceiling. Other consumers would actually be willing and able to pay more for the product. Producers are generally hurt by price ceilings.)*

ASSESSMENT

1. Tell students they must solve the following hypothetical problem:

The greatest rock group of all time – think of a group even better than any group you have ever heard of – is going to get together for one final tour of three concerts. The first two concerts will be one night each in New York, Chicago, or Los Angeles (choose the two cities that are farthest from your area), and the third will be in your hometown. This group has been around for a while, and they have many fans in their 30s and 40s as well as younger fans. For acoustical reasons, the concert cannot be held in a stadium. It will be held in a portable auditorium, with exactly 10,000 seats. The demand for tickets to this final concert in your town can be shown as a downsloping line on the following graph. (Draw this on the chalkboard or an overhead transparency, and draw a vertical supply curve at 10,000 seats. Do *NOT* put numbers on the vertical axis.)

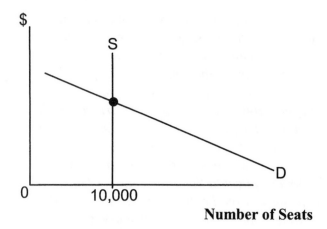

Number of Seats

The students' first problem is to estimate what the market clearing price would be for this concert. Assume that there are no especially good seats or bad seats, so any ticket is as good as another. At what price do students believe the quantity demanded will be exactly 10,000?

(Allow class discussion of this problem – if students say that the market price would be $50 or $60, they probably don't understand the assumptions – tickets for some concerts performed by existing groups already cost this much or more. If students say that the box office price will be $50, but scalpers will probably charge $100, they don't understand the concept of a market clearing price. One way to describe a market clearing price is as the lowest price at which no scalping is possible. In other words, anyone who wants to buy a ticket at that price can do so. Some classes may agree on a price as low as $100 or so, and some classes may think it would be as high as $1,000 – "The used ticket stub may be worth $100." "How many thousands of people from other cities will want tickets?" "These tickets would be worth more than ringside seats at a championship boxing match.")

After a few minutes, determine a reasonable price and announce: "All right, let's say that the market clearing price is $ _____ . But hold it! We have just received a telegram from the group. They say they want to make this final concert in our town a special thank you to their fans. They will forego any profits from this concert, and will even pay all necessary expenses. But they want to be absolutely sure that no ticket will be sold for more than $5. How will we do this?"

(Some students may suggest schemes such as selling a candy bar for $500 with a "free" concert ticket enclosed, but the band's statement is intended to rule out such approaches. Discussion is likely to center on two alternatives: first-come first-served, and some type of random drawings. In both cases, the number of tickets that can be purchased by one person is critical. Selling one ticket per person would greatly reduce the scalping problem, but attending concerts alone isn't much fun. Two tickets per person is probably a good compromise. Four tickets per person would allow a lot of scalping. The issue of reselling tickets, or scalping, is likely to generate considerable discussion. It might be suggested that reselling tickets should be made impossible by printing each purchaser's photo on the tickets and requiring a matching photo ID to enter the concert. Some students may argue that there is nothing wrong with scalping because it benefits both the buyer and the seller or it wouldn't take place. Those fortunate enough to get tickets, however they are distributed, shouldn't be prohibited from benefiting from the tickets either by using them or selling them.

A first-come, first-served policy should raise questions about riots and sanitation problems at sales points for tickets, but is likely to have the support of a lot of students who may say "Somebody willing to lie in sleeping bags in the mud for three weeks deserves the tickets." Other students may argue that "rich" people may hire others to wait in line for them. These students may think that a random drawing would be more fair – people who want tickets could send in a check for $10 with Social Security numbers used to make sure that there is only one check per person. Then, 5000 applications could be selected. Each of those people would get two tickets; everyone else gets their check back, less a handling fee.

Both alternatives have some unfair and inefficient results. The basic lesson about price controls is that when we don't let the market do its job, we face serious problems in trying to distribute goods and services in a fair and efficient way. Note that the make-up of the audience that attends the concert – younger vs. older, higher income vs. lower income, local residents vs. people from other cities – will depend on the specific rules imposed.)

Activity 1
Price Floors and Ceilings

1.   What is the market clearing price in the graph below?

2.   What quantity is demanded and what quantity is supplied at the market clearing price?

Quantity demanded _____
Quantity supplied _____

3.   What quantity is demanded and what quantity is supplied if the government passes a law setting a maximum price of $30?

Quantity demanded _____
Quantity supplied _____

4.   What quantity would be demanded and what quantity would be supplied if the government passes a law setting a minimum price of $80?

Quantity demanded _____
Quantity supplied _____

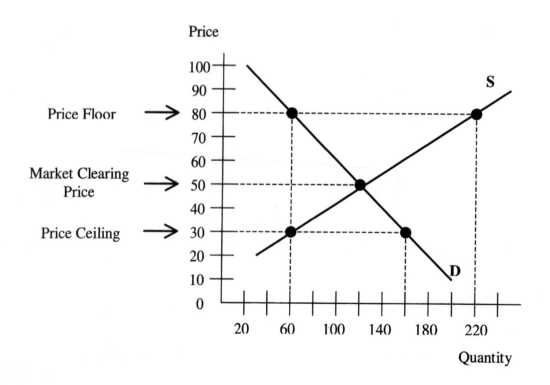

From *Focus: High School Economics*, © National Council on Economic Education, New York, NY

Activity 2
Apartments to Rent, but How Many at What Price?

Ourtown is a Midwest city with about two million residents, which grew rapidly over the past 10 years. That growth caused rents on apartments in the city to rise rapidly, and four years ago a new mayor and several new city councilors were narrowly elected after promising to set rent controls to help low-income families and the homeless. The rent on a basic apartment with a kitchen, living room, dining area, and two bedrooms, with no more than 1,000 square feet, was set at $500 a month. The debate over these rent controls is still heated, and the mayor and city council are now debating several options to deal with the problem. An economist at Ourtown University presented the following graph at the last meeting of the city council, which she feels shows the current market for these kinds of apartments in Ourtown.

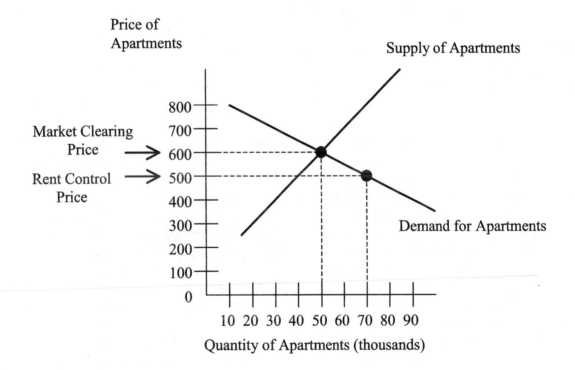

Activity 2
(Continued)

Discussion Questions:

A. Everybody wants a place to live, so how can it be true that more apartments will be demanded at a lower price than at higher prices?

B. On any given day, there are only a certain number of apartments in the city, so why isn't the supply curve of apartments a vertical line? In other words, can it really be true that there will be more apartments for rent at high prices than at low prices?

C. How many total apartments are available at the rent control price?

D. How many apartments do people want to rent at the rent control price?

E. What is the problem facing the city and the people who want to rent apartments?

The mayor and city council have been considering three options:

• Let apartment rents rise to the market price.

• Continue the rent controls, and let people find and rent apartments on a first-come, first-served basis. Anyone convicted of collecting or paying more than the rent control price will be subject to fines and imprisonment.

• Conduct random drawings each month to fill all vacant apartments.

Are any of these options fair? Who benefits and who loses under each option? Are there any other options that might work better? What do you think the mayor and city council should do?

Activity 3
The Market for Milk

MARKETS FOR MILK: Part I

Through the early 1990s, using a system of geographic "marketing orders," quotas, and price controls, the federal government establishes a minimum price paid to dairy farmers for milk. In 1992, the effect of that system was to set the price at about $1.40 per gallon. That year, U.S. dairy farmers produced and sold about 17.2 billion gallons of milk. About 6.5 billion gallons were sold to consumers at an average price of about $1.40 per gallon. The remaining 10.7 billion gallons were sold to manufacturers and used in the production of butter, cheese, and dried milk. Consumers purchased enough of these manufactured dairy products (butter, cheese, etc.) to account for about 10.9 billion gallons of milk. The federal government's Commodity Credit Corporation purchased the remaining products, or the equivalent of about 1.4 billion gallons of milk. The graph below presents this information using basic supply and demand curves for milk.

According to the information in this graph:
A. Is there a shortage or a surplus in the market? Explain.
B. If there were no government price controls in the market, this graph suggests that the price of milk (the market-clearing price) paid to farmers would be approximately _____ per gallon.
C. Who would benefit and who would be hurt if price controls in the milk market were eliminated?

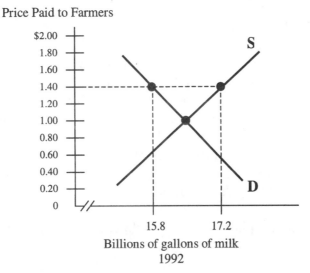

Price Paid to Farmers

Billions of gallons of milk
1992

Government payments to the U.S. farm sector fell sharply in 1995 and 1996, and were lower than they had been since 1983. The Federal Agriculture Improvement and Reform Act of 1996 further limited and restructured agricultural subsidies, and phased out price supports in the dairy industry. As a result, prices were allowed to fluctuate more, with the government providing emergency payments to farmers when prices and profits fell sharply. By 2001, a major public policy debate had resurfaced about how extensive the emergency payments should be, and whether some form of price supports should be reestablished.

Source: Publications of the US Department of Agriculture National Agricultural Statistics Service at *www.usda.gov/nass/pubs/agr00/acro00.htm*

Activity 3
(Continued)

MARKETS FOR MILK: Part II

Imagine that you are a member of the U.S. House of Representatives. You must decide whether to vote yes or no on a bill that would eliminate the price-support program for milk. In committee hearings on the bill, you hear testimony from people who favor eliminating the program and from people who favor retaining it.

For example, you hear Diane Doright, who works at University Public Policy Institute, say:

> This program is costly to consumers and taxpayers, and is an unnecessary and inefficient form of government interference in the economy. We estimate that, if the price support were ended, the price that people pay for milk would decrease by about 60 cents a gallon. Prices of other dairy products, such as butter and cheese, would also decrease. And one of the worst effects of this program is that it keeps small, inefficient farms in operation. We shouldn't fear the forces of market competition.

You also hear Senator William Foxfire, from a Midwestern state with many dairy farmers and cheese factories, say:

> People who want to eliminate this program just don't understand dairy farming. It is a very risky and unstable business. Feed costs may suddenly increase because of floods or droughts. Price supports bring some stability into this situation by making it possible for farmers to be sure of a certain price so they can ride out the rough times. And the so-called savings to consumers and taxpayers are an illusion. What would happen is that large, monopolistic dairy farms would take over the small family farms, and the price of milk might go even higher than it is now! As the displaced farmers moved into cities, taxpayers would be saddled with high costs of training and public assistance. Our small family farms represent the best American values of family, hard work, honesty, and thrift. We should not enact legislation that weakens these values.

Evaluate these statements and explain why you would vote for or against the bill.

Visual 1
Price Ceilings

PRICE CEILINGS

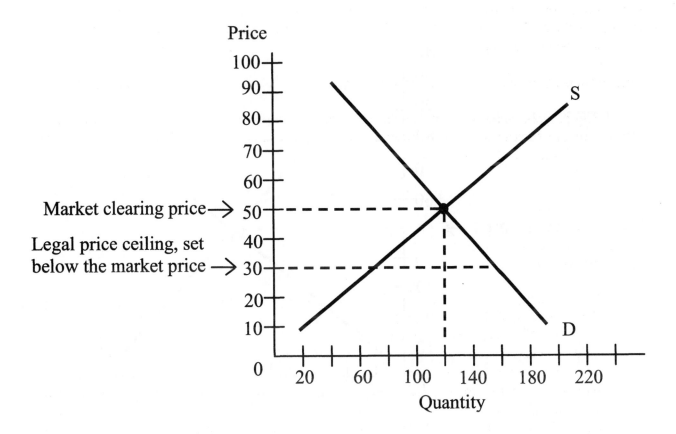

Visual 2
Price Floors

PRICE FLOORS

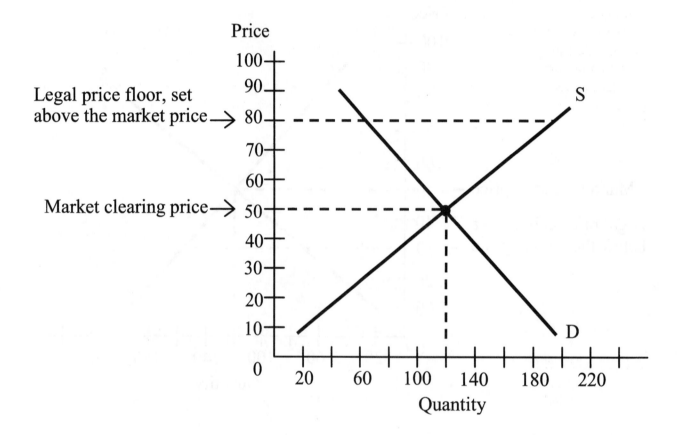

Legal price floor, set
above the market price →

Market clearing price →

LESSON SEVEN
PRICE CHANGES
MATTER

INTRODUCTION

The law of demand states that as the price of a product increases, the quantity demanded decreases. Conversely, as price decreases, the quantity demanded increases. But that still leaves an important question: will consumers purchase a great deal more or less when the price decreases or increases, respectively, or only a little more or a little less? Price elasticity of demand is a measure of consumers' responsiveness to price changes. Understanding price elasticity of demand helps students see more fully how businesses make pricing decisions, and what governments must consider as they make decisions about taxing a particular product.

CONCEPTS

Demand
Price elasticity of demand

CONTENT STATEMENTS*

Economists describe the demand schedules for various goods and services as inelastic if the quantity responses to a change in price are relatively small compared to the change in price. If the quantity responses are relatively large, demand is described as elastic.

Demand for products that have few close substitutes and that make up a small part of the consumer's budget tends to be inelastic. Demand for products with many close substitutes and those that represent a large part of consumers' total budgets tends to be elastic.

* Taken from *A Framework for Teaching Basic Economic Concepts with Scope and Sequence Guidelines, K-12.* Phillip Saunders and June Gilliard, eds. New York: National Council on Economic Education, 1995.

Demand is typically more elastic in the long run than in the short run.

OBJECTIVES

♦ Students define price elasticity of demand.

♦ Students distinguish between elastic and inelastic demand.

♦ Students describe the factors that tend to make demand elastic or inelastic.

♦ Students determine if demand is elastic or inelastic by using the total revenue test.

♦ Students use price elasticity of demand to analyze several kinds of economic problems.

LESSON DESCRIPTION

In this lesson, students examine the characteristics of products to determine price elasticity of demand, calculate changes in total revenue to determine elasticity, and analyze the impact of elasticity on public policy and business issues.

TIME REQUIRED

Three class periods. Day one – procedures 1 and 2. Day two – procedures 3-6. Day three – procedure 7 and Assessment.

MATERIALS

- Activity 1: What is Price Elasticity of Demand?, one per student
- Activity 2: Price Elasticity and the Total Revenue Test, one per student
- Activity 3: Applying Elasticity to the Real World, one per student
- Visual 1: Comparing Price Elasticities

PROCEDURES

1. Distribute a copy of Activity 1 to each student and tell students to read Part I. Discuss:

A. What does the law of demand state? *(Price and quantity demanded are inversely related.)*

B. What is price elasticity of demand? *(A measure of consumers' price responsiveness. It compares how much quantity demanded changes relative to a change in price.)*

C. What is elastic demand? *(A situation in which quantity demanded changes relatively more than price changes.)*

D. What is inelastic demand? *(A situation in which quantity demanded changes relatively less than price changes.)*

E. What factors tend to affect the price elasticity of demand for a product? *(Whether the product has many or few substitutes, whether the product takes a large or small portion of consumers' budgets, and how long consumers have to react to price changes.)*

2. Tell students to complete Part II of Activity 1. When students are finished, discuss the answers.

A. Salt – *Inelastic. It has few substitutes and takes a small portion of consumers' budgets.*

B. New cars – *Elastic. Used cars are a widely available substitute, and a new car takes a large portion of consumers' budgets.*

C. Pork chops – *Elastic. There are many substitutes.*

D. European vacation – *Elastic. There are many other places for a vacation, and travel to Europe is a large expenditure item for most consumers.*

E. Insulin – *Inelastic. Few substitutes.*

F. Insulin at one of four drug stores in a shopping mall – *More elastic. Competition provides substitute goods*

G. Gasoline purchased one day after a 20 percent price increase – *Inelastic. Consumers have not had enough time to adjust their purchases to higher gasoline prices.*

H. Gasoline purchase one year after a 20 percent price increase – *More elastic than in G, but perhaps still somewhat inelastic. Many consumers will switch to more fuel-efficient cars or find other alternatives, such as carpooling, public transportation, and more frequent tune-ups of their cars.*

3. Distribute a copy of Activity 2 to each student. Tell students to read Part I. Discuss:

• What is total revenue? *(Price times quantity demanded.)*

• What is the price effect on total revenue when price increases? *(To increase total revenue, because each unit is sold for more.)*

• What is the quantity effect on total revenue when price increases? *(To decrease total revenue, because fewer units will be sold at a higher price.)*

• What happens to total revenue when price increases? *(It may go up or down, depending on whether the price or quantity effect is larger. If the price effect is greater than the quantity effect, total revenue will increase. If the price effect is less than the quantity effect, total revenue will decrease.)*

• What is the price effect on total revenue when price decreases? *(To decrease* total revenue, because each unit is sold for less.)

- What is the quantity effect on total revenue when price decreases? *(To increase total revenue, because more units will be sold at a lower price.)*

- What happens to total revenue when price decreases? *(It may go up or down, depending on whether the price or quantity effect is larger. If the price effect is greater than the quantity effect, total revenue will decrease. If the price effect is less than the quantity effect, total revenue will increase.)*

- How would you describe elastic demand in terms of the price and quantity effects? *(With elastic demand, the price effect is smaller than the quantity effect, so price and total revenue move in opposite directions.)*

- How would you describe inelastic demand in terms of the price and quantity effects? *(With inelastic demand, the price effect is larger than the quantity effect, so price and total revenue move in the same direction.)*

- What would happen to total revenue if the price effect and quantity effect were the same? *(Total revenue would stay the same. This is called unitary elastic demand.)*

4. Instruct students to complete Part II of Activity 2. When finished, discuss the answers to the problems

A. *Completed on the activity.*

B. *1. $10 x 100 = $1,000; 2. $9 x 110 = $990; 3. P↓TR↓ inelastic*

C. *1. $6 x 60 = $360; 2. $9 x 50 = $450; 3. P↑TR↑ inelastic*

D. *1. $6.50 x 100 = $650; 2. $6 x 200 = $1,200; 3. P↓TR↑ elastic*

E. *1. $4 x 300 = $1,200; 2. $3.75 x 400 = $1,500; 3. P↓TR↑ elastic*

F. *The quantity effect is greater than the price effect.*

G. *The quantity effect is smaller than the price effect.*

(Procedures 5 and 6 are designed for use in strong classes making extensive use of graphical analysis.)

5. Display Visual 1 to provide an alternative explanation of how elasticity of demand and total revenue are related. Explain that the top graph shows the demand for product A. At a price of $2, 10,000 units would be demanded and total revenue would be $20,000. If the price rose to $4, the quantity demanded would decrease to 6,000 units and the total revenue would be $24,000. Price and total revenue both increased so demand is inelastic in this price range. Explain that the ▨ area shows the price effect on total revenue and the ▧ area shows the quantity effect on total revenue. The price effect is larger than the quantity effect, so the price change has a stronger influence on total revenue.

6. Explain that the bottom graph shows the demand for product B. Like product A, 10,000 units will be demanded at a price of $2. If the price rose to $4, however, the quantity demanded would decrease to 4,000 units and total revenue would be $16,000. In this case, price and total revenue moved in opposite directions, so demand is elastic in this price range. The diagram shows that the quantity effect is larger than the price effect.

7. Distribute a copy of Activity 3 to each student, and tell them to follow the instructions. When students are finished, discuss the answers to the handout. (This presents a good opportunity to make the point that incorrect assumptions about elasticity of demand can lead to poor policy choices.)

A. *I. M. Politico is wrong. He assumes that demand for these products is elastic, but it is not. He therefore falsely concludes that raising taxes on cigarettes and liquor will curb their consumption a great deal. Taxes on these commodities curb their consumption very little.*

B. *B. A. Green's assumption about price elasticity is wrong. People will reduce their consumption of gasoline but by a relatively small amount. It takes time to develop alternatives to gasoline use. In 2000, gasoline prices almost doubled in some parts of the United States, but consumption was not cut in half. It takes time for consumers to adjust their driving habits.*

C. *Vic Acqua's assumption is wrong. Demand for water is inelastic, but raising its price will curb consumption slightly, as people cut back on uses that are less important to them; e.g., watering lawns and washing cars, sidewalks, and driveways.*

D. *Sky King's assumption is wrong. She assumes that both business travelers and vacationers have an elastic demand for air travel. The fact is that business travelers' demand tends to be much less elastic because they often cannot postpone or give up their air travel, or schedule it as far in advance, or stay over weekend periods as easily as vacationers. Vacationers can more easily postpone their air travel, use other means of transportation, or change* *their destination to avoid air travel, or to require less of it.*

CLOSURE

1. What does the price elasticity of demand measure? *(It measures consumers' price responsiveness.)*

2. What does price elasticity of demand compare? *(It compares the relative size of changes in price and quantity demanded.)*

3. What is elastic demand? *(A situation in which quantity demanded changes relatively more than price changes.)*

4. What is inelastic demand? *(A situation in which quantity demanded changes relatively less than price changes.)*

5. Describe how the price and quantity effects work in opposite directions in their impact on total revenue. *(Because of the law of demand, the price effect will increase [decrease] total revenue with a price increase [decrease], but the quantity effect will decrease [increase] total revenue as consumers buy less [more] at the higher [lower] price.)*

6. If the price of a product increases and total revenue increases, is price elasticity of demand elastic or inelastic? *(inelastic)*

7. If the price of a product decreases and total revenue increases, is price elasticity of demand elastic or inelastic? *(elastic)*

8. Which factors affect consumers' price elasticity of demand? *(number of substitutes, portion of consumers' budgets, time)*

ASSESSMENT

Tell students to assume that your school receives 30 percent of its supplies budget from selling soft drinks. The school board is considering raising the price of soft drinks 20¢ to earn more revenue to buy computer software. Have each student conduct a market survey of 3 to 5 people in the high school to determine how many cans of soft drinks people buy per week at the current price and how many they would buy each week at the higher price. From this data, have them determine whether demand is elastic or inelastic in this price range, and write a recommendation for the school board based on their research.

Activity 1
What is Price Elasticity of Demand?

Part I: Overview

According to the law of **demand**, quantity demanded decreases when price increases. When price decreases, quantity demanded increases. However, it is not enough to know in what direction quantity demanded changes in response to price changes. It is also important to know *how much* the quantity demanded changes. A business may decide not to increase the price of its product if consumers will buy *much less* of it at the higher price. But a business will certainly increase the price of its product if consumers will buy only a *little less* of it at the higher price.

The measure of how much quantity demanded changes relative to price changes is called **price elasticity of demand**. If the quantity demanded changes more than price, in percentage terms, demand is elastic. Elastic demand means the quantity demanded is very responsive to changes in price. If the quantity demanded changes relatively little, the good or service has an inelastic demand.

Several factors determine whether the demand for a product is elastic or inelastic in some price range.

- Products that have many substitutes tend to have an elastic demand because it is easy to buy a substitute when its price rises. A product that has few substitutes tends to have an inelastic demand, because buyers don't have as many alternatives from which to choose.

- Goods and services that take a large portion of a consumer's budget tend to have an elastic demand because the price change has a bigger impact on the consumer's overall spending. Goods and services that represent a small portion of a consumer's budget tend to have an inelastic demand, because the impact of price changes for these products has a much smaller effect on the consumer's overall spending.

- The more time consumers have to adjust to price changes, the more they will increase purchases in response to price decreases, and decrease purchases in response to price increases. Therefore, long-run demand tends to be more elastic than short-run demand.

Activity 1
(Continued)

Part II: Elastic or Inelastic?

Instructions: Determine whether the demand for the following items is price elastic or inelastic. Write your answer on the line after the item. Then write the reasons for your answer.

A. Salt_____ Why? _____

_____

B. New cars_____ Why? _____

_____

C. Pork chops_____ Why? _____

_____

D. European vacation_____ Why? _____

_____

E. Insulin_____ Why? _____

_____

F. Insulin at one of four drug   Why? _____
    stores in a shopping mall
                                             _____
    _____

G. Gasoline purchased one day   Why? _____
    after a 20 percent price increase
                                             _____
    _____

H. Gasoline purchased one year   Why? _____
    after a 20 percent price increase
                                             _____
    _____

Activity 2
Price Elasticity and the Total Revenue Test

Part I: Overview

One way to determine price elasticity of demand is to examine what happens to total revenue when the price for a product changes. **Total revenue** is price times quantity demanded:

price	×	quantity demanded	=	total revenue
$10	×	150 items	=	$1,500

When the price for a good or service changes, the change in total revenue depends on the *relative* size of the changes in price and quantity demanded. First there is a *price effect* – a change in the amount the seller receives for each unit sold. The price effect of a price increase is to raise total revenue. The price effect of a decrease in price is to lower total revenue. However, there is also a *quantity effect*. Higher prices result in a decrease in quantity demanded, which means revenues are collected on fewer units. Therefore, the quantity effect of a price increase is to lower total revenue. On the other hand, when price decreases, quantity demanded increases, so revenues are collected on more units. That means the quantity effect of a price decrease is to increase total revenue.

The price effect and quantity effect work in opposite directions, so total revenue may go up, down, or remain the same whenever price changes. If the price effect is greater than the quantity effect, demand will be inelastic. If the quantity effect is greater than the price effect, demand will be elastic. By comparing the directions of the price and total revenue changes, you can determine whether the price effect or quantity effect is larger, and from that determine whether demand is elastic or inelastic. If total revenue remains constant due to exactly offsetting changes in price and quantity, demand is said to be unitary elastic.

Price	Total Revenue	Elasticity of Demand
↑	↓	elastic
↓	↑	elastic
↑	↑	inelastic
↓	↓	inelastic
↑ or ↓	=	unitary elastic

Part II:

To make sure you understand these points, complete each problem below, and circle the correct arrows in part 3 of each question. Then write whether demand is elastic or inelastic in this range of prices. The first problem is completed for you.

A. *Price rises* from $5 to $6. Quantity demanded decreases from 15 to 10.
1. Old price × old quantity demanded = old total revenue
   __5__ _____15_____ _____75_____
2. New price × new quantity demanded = new total revenue
   __6__ _____10_____ _____60_____
3. P ↓⑦ TR Ⓙ↑ <u>elastic</u>

Activity 2
(Continued)

B.   *Price falls* from $10 to $9. Quantity demanded increases from 100 to 110.
  1.   Old price × old quantity demanded = old total revenue

  _____   _____   _____

  2.   New price × new quantity demanded = new total revenue

  _____   _____   _____

  3.   P↓ ↑ TR↓ ↑ _____

C.   Price rises from $6 to $9. Quantity demanded decreases from 60 to 50.
  1.   Old price × old quantity demanded = old total revenue

  _____   _____   _____

  2.   New price × new quantity demanded = new total revenue

  _____   _____   _____

  3.   P↓ ↑ TR↓ ↑ _____

D.   Price falls from $6.50 to $6.00. Quantity demanded increases from 100 to 200.
  1.   Old price × old quantity demanded = old total revenue

  _____   _____   _____

  2.   New price × new quantity demanded = new total revenue

  _____   _____   _____

  3.   P↓ ↑ TR↓ ↑ _____

E.   Price falls from $4.00 to $3.75. Quantity demanded increases from 300 to 400.
  1.   Old price × old quantity demanded = old total revenue

  _____   _____   _____

  2.   New price × new quantity demanded = new total revenue

  _____   _____   _____

  3.   P↓ ↑ TR↓ ↑ _____

F.   Why do price and total revenue go in opposite directions when the demand for the good is elastic? _____

_____

_____

G.   Why do price and total revenue go in the same direction when the demand for the product is inelastic? _____

_____

_____

Activity 3
Applying Elasticity to the Real World

Instructions: Each of the following stories contains an assumption about elasticity of demand. For each story:

1. State whether the assumption made about elasticity of demand is correct or incorrect.

2. Justify your answer.

A. I. M. Politico, a candidate for the state legislature, is proposing a large increase in the taxes on cigarettes and liquor. He says, "I'm not proposing these taxes to raise revenue, but to discourage reckless drinking and the filthy habit of smoking. If the prices of cigarettes and booze go up, most people will quit using them. After all, no one has to drink or smoke."

B. In 2000, members of the Organization of the Petroleum Exporting Countries (OPEC) restricted production of crude oil. That was one reason for sharp increases in the price of oil and gasoline. B. A. Green, an environmentalist, has acclaimed this move by OPEC. "This is a step in the right direction for the environment. People will cut their consumption of nonrenewable petroleum products dramatically, and the air will be markedly cleaner."

C. Councilman Vic Acqua opposed a price increase for water during a recent drought. He claimed that there is no substitute for water, and that therefore increasing the price of water charged by the city-owned water company will not cause the amount of water people use to decrease at all.

D. Sky King, world traveler, says if the airlines want to attract more passengers, they should lower fares for business travelers as well as for vacationers. She believes both groups will respond equally to a price decrease.

Visual 1
Comparing Price Elasticities

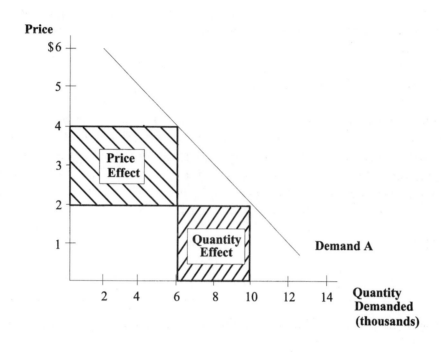

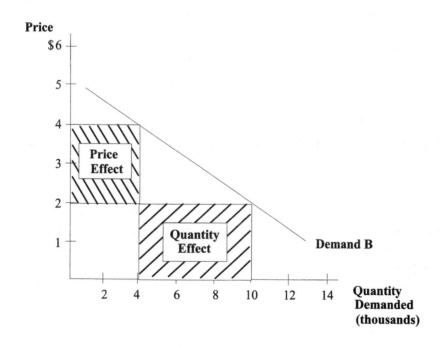

LESSON EIGHT
GETTING MORE OR USING LESS

INTRODUCTION

Although the problem of scarcity can never be eliminated, it can be moderated by finding ways to increase productivity. Productivity is the amount of goods and services produced (output) per unit of productive resources used (input).

Productivity can be increased by producing more goods and services with the same amount of resources, or by producing the same amount of goods and services with fewer resources. As productivity increases, production costs for each unit of a good or service decrease. That makes producers more competitive in the marketplace, and translates into higher wages for workers as productivity increases at the national level. In individual markets, however, productivity increases can sometimes reduce the number of workers employed.

Over time, both personal and national living standards are directly related to labor productivity. For a country to consume at high levels, it must have a highly productive labor force. Productivity can be increased by investing in capital goods such as factories, machines, and tools. Individual workers can also increase productivity and enhance their own earning power by investing in their human capital through education and training.

CONCEPTS

Productivity
Specialization and division of labor
Investment in capital goods
Investment in human capital

CONTENT STANDARD

Investment in factories, machinery, new technology, and the health, education, and training of people can raise future standards of living.

BENCHMARKS

Specialization and division of labor usually increase the productivity of workers.

Workers can improve their productivity by improving their human capital.

Workers can improve their productivity by using physical capital such as tools and machinery.

Standards of living increase as the productivity of labor improves.

Productivity is measured by dividing output (goods and services) by the number of inputs used to produce the output. A change in productivity is a change in output relative to input.

Economic growth is a sustained rise in a nation's production of goods and services. It results from investments in human and physical capital, research and development, technological change, and improved institutional arrangements and incentives.

Investments in physical and human capital can increase productivity, but such investments entail opportunity costs and economic risks.

OBJECTIVES

♦ Students define labor productivity as output per worker.

♦ Students explain how the division of labor and investment in human capital and capital goods improves productivity.

♦ Students explain why increased productivity is important to the economy and to individuals.

LESSON DESCRIPTION

Students observe or participate in a pizza production simulation to determine the effects on labor productivity of specialization, the division of labor, and investment in human capital and capital goods.

TIME REQUIRED

Two class periods. Day one – procedures 1-15. Day two – procedures 16-17 and Assessment.

MATERIALS

One set of the following four items for each team, 1-8 teams
- 50-60 pieces of 8 ½" × 11" paper
- 1 red ink and 1 black ink felt tip magic marker
- 1 pair of scissors (see procedure 1)
- 40-50 paper plates, 6" or 7" in diameter

- Activity 1: Productivity Data, one per student and a transparency
- Activity 2: News Headlines, one per student
- Visual 1: Output per Hour, Nonfarm Business Sector, 1972-2000

PROCEDURES

1. Select one team of four students to make "pizzas," or divide the entire class into teams of four, and use any remaining students as quality inspectors or helpers. Have one set of production materials, listed above, available for each team. Announce to the class that these students will produce pizzas in a simulated pizza production process.

2. Demonstrate how to make a pizza:

A. Trace the template (a small paper plate) on a piece of 8 ½" × 11" piece of paper.

B. Cut out the circle.

C. Draw 10 pepperoni pieces about ¾" to 1" diameter each on the circle using the red marker.

D. Draw 15 black olive slices ½" to ¾" diameter each on the circle, using the black marker.

3. To provide a workplace for each team, push four desks together to make a table. Place a large supply of paper, one black and one red marker, a pair of scissors, and the template (paper plate) on each table.

4. Announce that in Round 1 each worker on a team will produce entire pizzas working alone. They will share their team's materials and capital goods.

5. Inform students that you or helpers you choose will serve as quality control officers and inspect all finished pizzas. Any pizzas that do not meet production standards will be rejected and thrown away.

6. Give the factory workers three minutes to produce pizzas. Check the quality of the completed projects and reject those that do not pass inspection. Discard all rejects and all partially completed pizzas.

7. Display the transparency of Activity 1 and record the pizza factory data in lines 1-3 under Round 1. If you used more than one production team, either choose a representative team and use that team's data throughout the activity, or calculate the average production data for all teams and record that data throughout the activity. Distribute a copy of Activity 1 to each student. As a class, calculate the remaining lines for Round 1, using the designated team or average team data, as shown in the transparency of Activity 1 you have displayed to the class.

8. Ask the class to suggest another way the workers could organize the production process

to increase output. *(Students usually suggest dividing the labor and specializing.)*

9.   Round 2. Allow students to introduce **specialization and division of labor**. Point out that, as specialists, the students will each do just a part of the production process. Give students time to discuss breaking down the production of the pizza into a series of steps. Some students will probably ask for additional pens, scissors, or templates, but for the time being limit the teams to one pair of scissors, one black and one red marker, and one template.

10. Repeat procedures 6 and 7, recording the data on Activity 1 under Round 2.

11. If the factory workers do not experience an increase in productivity between Rounds 1 and 2, repeat Round 2. This is often necessary because the specialists require practice in their specific tasks (**investment in human capital**), the assembly line needs to be reorganized, or the specialists fail to cooperate.

12. Next round. Tell students that their factory has made an **investment in capital goods** and acquired a new piece of capital equipment, a machine that precuts the pizza. The rental for this machine is $2.50 per round. Record this on Activity 1 in row 8, and point out that because of this machine they will no longer use or pay for scissors.

13. Give students a supply of precut pizzas (paper plates) and allow them time to reorganize the assembly line.

14. Repeat procedures 6 and 7, and record the data on Activity 1 for the next round.

15. Using the information from Activity 1, discuss the following points:

A.   Explain that **productivity** is the ratio of the amount of output produced to the number of inputs used. How was the pizza factory's productivity ratio calculated on line 12? *(As labor productivity, measuring only the labor input.)* Point out in this case we are looking at labor productivity, which is output per worker. Note that the ratio rises as productivity rises, and also that if we looked at labor productivity for all goods and services, not just pizzas, as labor productivity increases, the goods and services available for people to consume, also known as average real income or the standard of living, would increase.

B.   Ask: "What happened to productivity between Round 1 and Round 2, and between Round 2 and Round 3? Why did this occur?" *(In most cases productivity should increase between Rounds 1 and 2 because of specialization and division of labor. However, sometimes this does not happen due to lack of skills, lack of cooperation among the assembly line workers, or inexperience. By Round 3, the pizza factory should see an increase in productivity as specialists have more practice, investment in human capital, and as the factory workers refine the assembly line process.)* Ask: "What happened to quality between Rounds 2 and 4?" *(Typically, fewer pizzas will be rejected and quality will improve.)*

C.   Ask: "What effect did investing in additional capital goods (the pizza cutting machine) have on productivity?" *(Productivity should increase.)*

D.   Ask: "What effect did increased productivity have on average costs – line 10 of Activity 1? Why is this important?" *(It lowered average cost. Lower average costs mean that the pizza factory can compete more effectively with other pizza factories, allowing it to stay in business and perhaps earn higher profits.)*

E. What effect will increased productivity in the pizza factory have on wages? (*More productive workers will receive higher wages and have greater job security, because they add more to the firm's revenue while lowering its per unit production costs. Less productive workers may be fired and have to search for jobs. It is possible that, for a particular product or factory, if productivity increases, the number of workers employed will decrease, if the firm can not sell additional output.*) Ask: "What will happen if labor productivity increases in the overall economy?" (*At this level, productivity increases translate into higher average wages, more consumption, and a higher material standard of living. Although there may be concerns about selling more units of some particular product made at one factory, there is not a concern about people wanting to buy more output of all goods and services.*)

F. What costs were incurred by attempts to increase productivity? (*Buying additional capital goods – the pizza cutting machine – increased total costs, but lowered per unit production costs if productivity increased.*)

G. What are the advantages and disadvantages of specialization and division of labor? (*Advantages: specialists become very skilled at doing one step of the production process, new equipment and machinery designed to help with the specialized production steps may be invented, product quality can improve, and productivity rises. Disadvantages: worker boredom, more problems if workers with highly specialized skills are ill or absent for other reasons, some workers may lose their jobs and have to look for a new employer.*)-

H. What other things could the pizza factory do to increase productivity? (*Provide practice time or training for the specialists [investment in human capital] or invest in the pizza cutter machine or other machinery, such as a machine that put olives and pepperoni on the pizzas at the same time, using only one worker rather than two.*)

I. What things should a company consider before investing in capital, such as the pizza cutter machine? (*It should weigh the cost of the paper cutter, the cost of training workers to use the pizza cutter, and the risk involved in borrowing money to pay for the paper cutter, against the expected benefits of higher productivity.*)

16. Why is it important to increase productivity? (*Increased productivity allows a country to produce more goods and services with its scarce resources. That allows a nation to improve the real standard of living of its people.*)

17. Display Visual 1. Use the following questions for discussion.

A. Did productivity grow in the United States between 1977 and 1982 and between 1988 and 1991? (*No.*)

B. Ask students to consider what kinds of effects this lack of productivity growth might have had on the U.S. economy? (*The price inflation for goods and services experienced between 1977 and 1982 was greater than it would otherwise have been, and the standard of living in the U.S. was essentially "flat" during these periods.*)

C. What happened to productivity from 1983 to 1988? (*An economic recovery began in December 1982. Productivity usually increases when the economy emerges from a recession, as was the case in early 1983. Businesses tend to have idle machinery and extra workers during a recession, so they can produce more output without adding machinery and labor when the recession ends.*)

D. What happened to productivity in the 1990s? (*Output per hour increased rapidly.* The percentage of unemployed workers who permanently lost their last jobs rather than being temporarily laid off reached an all-time high of over 45 percent in October 1992. This job loss was due in part to long-term adjustments U.S. businesses made to increase productivity and be more competitive in the global marketplace. The growth in productivity suggests that these policies were having that intended effect, at least to some degree. Other factors were also at work, including computers and other new technologies.)

CLOSURE

Discuss the following.

1. What is labor productivity? (*output per worker*)

2. How does specialization and division of labor and investment in human capital and capital goods affect productivity? (*Productivity increases.*)

3. What are advantages to a firm of increasing productivity? (*Higher output levels or lower input levels lead to lower per unit production costs; product quality typically improves.*)

4. Why is increasing productivity important to individuals and to the economy? (*Higher output levels allow for higher consumption and income levels – i.e., a higher standard of living.*)

ASSESSMENT

1. Distribute Activity 2 to the class. Instruct students to read the headlines and answer the questions.

2. Have groups share their answers. Suggested answers:

HEADLINE 1: **WHIRLPOOL FACTORY INCREASES PRODUCTIVITY**

A. What are some steps the Whirlpool factory might have taken to increase productivity?

B. How could this increase in productivity benefit the workers? (*The Whirlpool factory might have reorganized its production process, invested in new technology and capital, or invested in training its workers.*) In fact, the Whirlpool plant located in Benton Harbor, Michigan worked with its employees to teach them new ways to improve quality. Later, it raised the pay of its workers.

HEADLINE 2: **U.S. PRODUCTIVITY RISES RAPIDLY FOR 6TH CONSECUTIVE QUARTER**

A. How can rising productivity benefit workers? Producers? The nation? (*Increased productivity can result in higher wages for workers, allow U.S. businesses to remain competitive in international markets, and improve the nation's standard of living.*)

B. Could there be some disadvantages of increasing productivity, at least to some people? Explain. (*Yes. One disadvantage can be that some workers are laid off and have to find new jobs.*)

HEADLINE 3: **PRODUCTIVITY LAGS
FIRST THREE QUARTERS OF YEAR**

A. Why is lagging productivity a problem
for the nation, businesses, and individual
workers and consumers? (*Low
productivity growth over a long period
of time means that the standard of living
is rising slowly, and that firms are
probably becoming less competitive with
firms in other nations that are
experiencing faster productivity growth.*)

Activity 1
Productivity Data

	Sample	Round 1	Round 2	Round 3	Round 4	Round 5
1. Production method	Pizza-makers					
2. Number of pizzas produced	6					
3. Number of pizzas accepted	4					
4. Cost of materials ($.25 per pizza)	$1.50					
5. Number of workers	4					
6. Wages ($1.00 per worker)	$4.00					
7. $2.00 rent for factory (desks)	$2.00					
8. Investment in capital goods ($.25 per marker, $1.00 for scissors)	$1.50					
9. Total costs	$9.00					
10. Cost per pizza (average cost): Total cost (Line 9) ÷ accepted pizzas produced (Line 3)	$9.00/4 = $2.25					
11. Total time worked: 3 minutes × number of workers (Line 5)	12 min.					
12. Output per minute worked: number of pizzas (Line 3) ÷ total time worked (Line 11)	4/12 = 0.333					

Activity 2
News Headlines – Assessment

READ the headlines below and answer the questions.

HEADLINE 1: **WHIRLPOOL FACTORY INCREASES PRODUCTIVITY**

A. What are some steps the Whirlpool factory might have taken to increase productivity?

B. How could this increase in productivity benefit the workers?

HEADLINE 2: **U.S. PRODUCTIVITY RISES RAPIDLY FOR 6TH CONSECUTIVE QUARTER**

A. How can rising productivity benefit workers? Producers? The nation?

B. Could there be some disadvantages of increasing productivity, at least to some people? Explain.

HEADLINE 3: **PRODUCTIVITY LAGS FIRST THREE QUARTERS OF YEAR**

A. Why is lagging productivity a problem for the nation, businesses, and individual workers and consumers?

Visual 1
Output per Hour, Nonfarm Business Sector, 1972 - 2000

VISUAL 1
Output per Hour, Nonfarm Business Sector, 1972-2000
(1992=100)

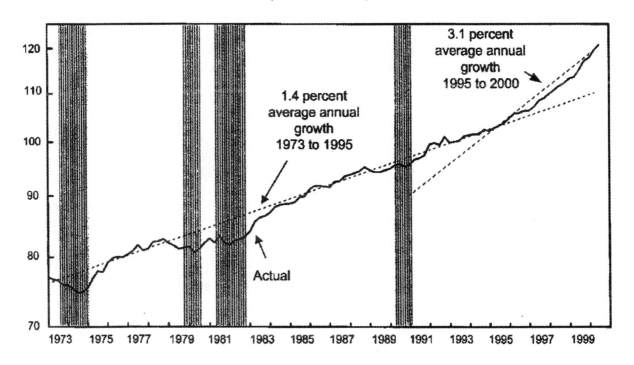

The vertical axis uses a scale that shows equal percentage changes in output per hour as equal distances.

Source: *Economic Report of the President*, January, 2001 (Washington, DC, US Government Printing Office, 2001) at *http://w3.access.gpo.gov/eop*

LESSON NINE
LEARN MORE, EARN MORE

INTRODUCTION

Human capital refers to the knowledge, skills, and experience that people bring to the workplace. With education and training, people increase their human capital and improve their productivity, which usually allows them to increase their income.

It is important for students to understand these connections now. The choices they make today to improve their human capital can have a direct effect on their future standard of living.

CONCEPTS

Human capital
Income
Standard of living

CONTENT STANDARD

Income for most people is determined by the market value of the productive resources they sell. What workers earn depends, primarily, on the market value of what they produce and how productive they are.

BENCHMARKS

More productive workers are likely to be of greater value to employers and earn higher wages than less productive workers.

People's income, in part, reflect choices they have made about education, training, skill development, and careers. People with few skills are more likely to be poor.

OBJECTIVES

♦ Students explain the relationship between investment in human capital (education and training) and income.

♦ Students describe how making choices to improve knowledge and skills directly affect a person's standard of living.

LESSON DESCRIPTION

Working in small groups, students analyze data and generalize about the relationship between the level of workers' education and their annual incomes. Students then randomly draw occupations and representative income levels, and establish a monthly budget to see in much greater detail the relationship between a person's education and standard of living.

TIME REQUIRED

Two class periods. Day one – procedures 1-7. Day two – procedures 8-11 and Assessment. Note: Day two will probably be presented several days after day one.

MATERIALS

- Activity 1: Occupation Slips, one copy cut into slips, put in a shoebox or envelope
- Activity 2: Monthly Wage Slips, one copy cut into slips, then sorted into shoeboxes or envelopes labeled A – D
- Activity 3: Standard of Living Worksheet, one per student
- Activity 4: Standard of Living Questions, one per student
- Activity 5: Monthly Wages by Occupation and Level of Education, one per student
- Five shoeboxes or large envelopes
- Visual 1: Education and Income, and Unemployment Rates by Years of Education
- Visual 2: Average Annual Expenditures and Expenditure Shares

PROCEDURES

1. Display Visual 1 and discuss:

A. Why do some individuals earn more money than others? (*The earning power of individuals with more education is, on average, greater than that of individuals with less education. People also have different physical and intellectual abilities, and some people work longer and harder than others.*)

B. What relationship exists between workers' level of education and unemployment rates? (*Workers with more education are less likely to be unemployed than workers with less education.*)

C. What relationship exists between the earning power of men and women? (*Women earn less money than men at all education levels.*)

D. What would explain this? (*Studies suggest some direct discrimination in terms of wages paid for identical work. However, other factors are also important. Women still tend to take different subjects in school than men, and to enter lower-paying occupations. Many middle-aged and older women workers entered the labor force later in life, or left the labor market for some years to raise children. Point out to students that somewhere between 1/3 and 1/2 of the earnings difference between men and women can be explained by these differences in human capital variables, especially work experience.*)

2. Make a copy of Activity 1. Cut apart the occupation slips and place all of them in the shoebox or envelope labeled Occupations. Each occupation slip is coded with a letter, A-D, which corresponds to one of the levels of education shoeboxes or envelopes described below.

3. Put one of the following labels on each shoebox: 1) Occupations; 2) College Graduate (A); 3) 1-3 Years Beyond High School (B); 4) High School Graduate (C); and 5) Less Than 4 Years of High School (D).

4. Make a copy of Activity 2 and cut apart the various income levels. Place these in the appropriate shoeboxes using the letter codes A-D. The wage ranges are taken from the 2000-2001 *Occupational Outlook Handbook*, U. S. Department of Labor, Bureau of Labor Statistics. The data is published annually and is available on the web at *http://stats.bls.gov/ocohome.htm*. In future years you might want to update the ranges.

5. Distribute copies of Activity 3 to the class.

6. One at a time have students draw an occupation slip. Then use the letter code on that slip to identify the appropriate education/earnings shoebox, and draw an earnings slip. Instruct students to announce their occupation and monthly earnings to the class and record the information on their Standard of Living Worksheet.

7. Allow several days for students to complete the Standard of Living Worksheet in Activity 3 outside of class. Encourage them to use the classified section of the local newspaper, grocery store flyers, restaurant menus, the internet, personal knowledge, and interviews to gather information to complete their budgets. They should turn in a paragraph explaining how they collected the information they used in setting these budget figures.

8. Once budgets are finished, divide students into small groups with at least one representative from each of the education/income levels. Distribute copies of Activity 4 and Activity 5 to the class. Instruct students to answer the questions.

9. Have groups share their findings. Possible answers to discussion questions are:

A. What type of choices did you have to make? How were your choices different from other members of your group? How were your choices similar to those made by other members of your group? (*Answers will vary. However, in general, students with higher incomes will have more choice in both the quality and quantity of goods and services they are able to purchase than individuals with lower incomes.*)

B. What surprised you most about your final monthly budget? (*Answers vary.*)

C. Write a brief description describing your standing of living using the budget you have developed. (*Answers vary.*)

D. How did your monthly wage compare with that of other occupations in your level of education? How did your monthly wage compare with the median monthly wage for your occupation? How did your monthly income compare with that of individuals who had a level of education different from yours? How did you explain these differences? (*Some students will have incomes different from the median or monthly wage for their occupations. Explain that median means the middle number in a series. Half of the workers earn more and half of them earn less than the median income. Some of the students will have higher incomes than other individuals with the same level of education and those who have a different level of education. Some will have lower incomes. Point out that different work habits and effort, levels of job responsibility, social "connections," etc., can explain these differences. Also, investment in human capital is risky. Some people with a great deal of education may not do as well as others with considerably less education. Ask students for reasons this might occur – for example, some people do not stay in the labor market very long, their training may be in an area that is not in demand, they are not very* productive, or they don't get along with others.*)

E. In general, what is the relationship between workers' earnings and their level of education? (*In general, individuals with more education have higher incomes than individuals with less education.*)

F. The standing of living can be defined as the material well-being of an individual, group or nation. What is the relationship between wage earnings and a family's standard of living? (*In general, individuals with higher income levels have a higher level of material well-being or **standard of living** than individuals with lower income levels.*)

10. Review with students that education will have a major impact on their potential earnings. With more **human capital** (education, training, and experience), they will have more career opportunities from which to choose, and the ability to earn more income.

11. Display Visual 2. Discuss:

A. As the level of income goes up, what happens to the actual amount consumers spend on items such as food, housing, utilities, entertainment, transportation, and health care? (*Increases*)

B. What happens to the percentage of personal income spent on these items? (*Goes down*) Why? (*The actual amount people spend goes up but it does not go up as much as their income.*)

C. What is the relationship between the amount and percentage of income spent on pensions and Social Security across all three groups? (*Both the dollar amount spent and percentage of income spent go up as income rises.*)

D. What is the relationship between income and average annual expenditures for the three groups? (*Consumers in the first two groups spend more than they earn.*) How can this happen? (*Credit.*)

E. Given this information, what could we conclude about the standard of living as incomes rise? (*In general, consumers with higher income levels have a higher level of material well-being than individuals with lower income levels.*)

F. How does this compare with the income and budget you just completed? (*Results should be similar.*)

G. This data does not give us any information on the level of education for members of the three groups. Based on what you have learned in this lesson, what would you predict the education level would be for individuals in these groups? (*In general, individuals in the higher income ranges have more education than those in the lower income ranges.*)

CLOSURE

Use the questions below to review the key points of the lesson.

1. What relationship exists between workers' level of education and unemployment? (*Workers with more education are less likely to be unemployed than workers with less education.*)

2. In general, what is the relationship between workers' earnings and level of education? (*Individuals with more education have higher incomes than individuals with less education.*)

3. What is the relationship between wage earnings and a family's standard of living? (*In general, individuals with higher income levels have a higher standard of living than individuals with lower income levels.*)

4. Why might individuals with the same level of education earn different incomes? (*Different work habits and effort, levels of job responsibility, years in the labor market, training in area that is not in demand, social connections, discrimination, inability to get along with other workers.*)

ASSESSMENT

1. Working in groups, have students prepare a presentation for a younger group of students explaining how these students can improve their human capital and how this investment in their human capital can affect career choices and future income and standard of living. Presentations should include visuals.

2. If possible, make arrangements for students to give their presentations to a group of younger students, preferably middle school students who will be making future course selection decisions for high school, or who may even be debating whether to stay in school or drop out.

Activity 1
Occupation Slips

(Occupation Shoebox – The letters in parentheses designate the shoebox from which students should draw their monthly wage slip.**)**

Industrial Production Engineer (A)	Hotel Manager (A)	Accountant (A)
Physical Therapist (A)	Dietitian (A)	Chemist (A)
Federal Government Mathematician (A)	Loan Officer (A)	Landscape Architect (A)
Registered Nurse (A)	Surveyor (B)	Licensed Practical Nurse (B)
Health Information Technician (B)	Optician (B)	Cardiology Technologist (B)
Surgical Technologist (B)	EKG Technologist (B)	Musical Instrument Repairer (B)

Activity 1
(Continued)

Jeweler (B)	Receptionist (C)	Home Appliance Repairer (C)
General Office Clerk (C)	Payroll Clerk (C)	EEG Technologist (C)
Corrections Officer (C)	Account Collector (C)	Adjustment Clerk (C)
Medical Secretary (C)	Bank Teller (C)	Maintenance Mechanic (D)
Grounds Keeper (D)	Concrete Worker (D)	Equipment Operator (D)
Nonsupervisory Worker (D)	Food Processor (D)	Textile Machine Operator (D)
Housekeeper (D)	Cook (D)	Nursing Aid (D)

Activity 2
Monthly Wage Slips

COLLEGE GRADUATE
(Shoebox A)

2200	2400
2600	2800
3000	3200
3400	3600
3800	4000
4200	4400
4600	4800
5000	5200

Activity 2
(Continued)

1-3 YEARS BEYOND HIGH SCHOOL
(Shoebox B)

1780	1800
1900	1900
2000	2000
2100	2100
2200	2200
2300	2400
2500	2600
3000	3000

From *Focus: High School Economics*, © National Council on Economic Education, New York, NY

Activity 2
(Continued)

HIGH SCHOOL GRADUATE
(Shoebox C)

1400	1500
1500	1600
1600	1700
1700	1800
1800	1900
1900	2000
2000	2100
2200	2200

Activity 2
(Continued)

LESS THAN FOUR YEARS OF HIGH SCHOOL
(Shoebox D)

800	900
1000	1100
1300	1300
1400	1400
1400	1400
1500	1500
1500	1600
1700	1800

From *Focus: High School Economics*, © National Council on Economic Education, New York, NY

Activity 3
Standard of Living Worksheet

Median Monthly Income_____

Education Level_____

Occupation_____

Directions: Use the classified section of your local newspaper, the yellow pages of a telephone book, grocery store flyers, restaurant menus, personal knowledge, the internet, and interviews to gather information to determine your monthly budget.

BUDGET ITEM	DOLLAR AMOUNT/MONTH
Rent	
Food	
Transportation (Bus, train, or car with fuel and insurance)	
Taxes (30% of monthly income)	
Clothing	
Insurance	
Entertainment/Recreation	
Savings	
Miscellaneous (Household supplies, toiletries, cosmetics, haircuts)	
TOTAL:	

From *Focus: High School Economics*, © National Council on Economic Education, New York, NY

Activity 4
Standard of Living Questions

Share your Monthly Budget with other members of the group. Use this information and a copy of Activity 5, **Monthly Wages by Occupation and Level of Education**, to answer the questions below.

A. 1. What type of choices did you have to make?

   2. How were your choices different from other members of your group?

   3. How were your choices similar to those made by other members of your group?

B. What surprised you most about your final monthly budget?

C. Write a brief description describing your standard of living using the budget you have developed.

D. 1. How did your monthly wage compare with that of other occupations in your level of education?

   2. How did your monthly wage compare with the median monthly wage for your occupation?

   3. How did your monthly income compare with that of individuals who had a level of education different from yours?

   4. How do you explain these differences?

E. In general, what is the relationship between workers' earnings and their level of education?

F. Standard of living can be defined as the material well-being of an individual, group or nation. What is the relationship between wage earnings and a family's standard of living?

From *Focus: High School Economics*, © National Council on Economic Education, New York, NY

Activity 5
Monthly Wages[1] by Occupation and Level of Education

Occupation	Monthly Median Wage	Occupation	Monthly Median Wage
College Graduate			
Industrial Production Engineer	4693	Hotel Manager	2225
Accountant	3155	Dietitian	2918
Physical Therapist	4717	Federal Government Mathematician	3108
Chemist	4175	Loan Officer	2945
Landscape Architect	3160	Registered Nurse	3391
1-3 Years Beyond High School (Including Graduates of Technical/Community Colleges)			
Surveyor	3137	Optician	1867
Health Information Technician	1716	Musical Instrument Repairer	1918
Jeweler	1985		
Surgical Technologist	2148	Cardiology Technologist	2980
EKG Technologist	2672	Licensed Practical Nurse	2245
High School Graduate			
Medical Secretary	1963	Home Appliance Repairer	2168
Bank Teller	1433	Receptionist	1552
General Office Clerk	1632	Adjustment Clerk	1837
Payroll Clerk	2030	Corrections Officer	1378
EEG Technologist	1947	Account Collector	1878
Less Than Four Years of High School*			
Cook	1520	Grounds Keeper	1318
Equipment Operator	1402	Nursing Aid	816
Maintenance Mechanic	1808	Concrete Worker	1664
Nonsupervisory Worker	1427	Food Processor	1592
Textile Machine Operator	1499	Housekeeper	824

[1] Median monthly earnings for all workers in the occupation.
*For these occupations median monthly earnings are based on 40-hour work weeks.

Source: ***Occupational Outlook Handbook***, Bureau of Labor Statistics, 2000-01.

Visual 1
Education and Income, 1998 (Age 18 or Older)

EDUCATION LEVEL	AVERAGE ANNUAL INCOME	
	Male	Female
Graduated college (Bachelor's degree)	$59,448	$31,928
Associate degree	$40,584	$24,485
1-3 years of college (no degree)	$34,396	$20,704
Graduated high school	$30,036	$17,031
9th to 12th grade, no diploma	$17,726	$10,827

Source: U.S. Department of Commerce, Bureau of the Census, *Current Population Reports,* 2000.

Unemployment Rates[1] By Years of Education: Persons Aged 25-64

YEAR	ALL WORKERS	Workers By Highest Level of Education:			
		LESS THAN 4 YEARS OF HIGH SCHOOL	HIGH SCHOOL GRADUATE	1-3 YEARS OF COLLEGE	4 OR MORE YEARS OF COLLEGE
1999	3.5	7.7	4.0	3.1	1.9
1998	4.0	8.5	4.8	3.6	1.8
1995	4.8	10.0	5.2	4.5	2.5
1992	6.7	13.5	7.7	5.9	2.9

[1] March unemployment rates. Source: U.S. Department of Commerce, Bureau of the Census, *Statistical Abstract of the United States*, 2000.

Visual 2
Average Annual Expenditures and Expenditure Shares

Income Range	$10,000 to 14,999		$30,000 to 39,999		$70,000 and over	
Consumer average income after taxes	$12,163		$34,353		$113,441	
Average annual expenditures	$19,722		$35,077		$76,812	
Item	Actual	% of Income	Actual	% of Income	Actual	% of Income
Food	$2917	23.9	$5060	14.7	$8725	7.7
Housing	7112	58.5	10862	31.6	23066	20.3
Personal care products & service	219	1.8	452	1.3	794	0.7
Utilities	1825	15.0	2297	6.7	4311	3.8
Housekeeping supplies	285	2.3	515	1.5	945	0.8
Apparel & services	893	7.3	1904	5.5	3625	3.2
Gasoline & motor oil	603	5.0	1124	3.3	1666	1.5
Vehicle purchases (net outlay)	1797	14.8	3239	9.4	6437	5.7
Health care	1162	9.6	1970	5.7	2670	2.4
Entertainment	643	5.3	1682	4.9	4121	3.6
Life & other personal insurance	119	1.0	342	1.0	970	0.9
Pensions & Social Security	187	1.5	2750	8.0	11202	9.9

Source: U.S. Department of Commerce, Bureau of the Census, *Current Population Reports*, 1999.

LESSON TEN
RICH MAN, POOR MAN . . .

INTRODUCTION

The issue of income distribution has been controversial throughout history. Decisions about the distribution of income are made by individuals and firms making exchanges in the markets for productive resources (inputs), and also through the political process. Public policies, such as taxation and transfer payments, are often targeted at particular income groups to redistribute income. Some of these policies redistribute income from the rich to the poor; but surprisingly, some policies increase the share of income going to middle and upper-income families, making the distribution of income less equal.

CONCEPTS

Income
Transfer payments
Personal distribution of income
Functional distribution of income
Proprietors' income
Corporate profits

CONTENT STANDARDS

Income for most people is determined by the market value of the productive resources they sell. What workers earn depends, primarily, on the market value of what they produce and how productive they are.

There is an economic role for government to play in a market economy whenever the benefits of a government policy outweigh its costs. Governments often provide for national defense, address environmental concerns, define and protect property rights, and attempt to make markets more competitive. Most government policies also redistribute income.

BENCHMARKS

To earn income, people sell productive resources. These include their labor, capital, natural resources, and entrepreneurial talents.

People's incomes, in part, reflect choices they have made about education, training, skill development, and careers. People with few skills are more likely to be poor.

Two methods for classifying how income is distributed in a nation – the personal distribution of income and the functional distribution – reflect, respectively, the distribution of income among different groups of households and the distribution of income among different businesses and occupations in the economy.

Governments often redistribute income directly when individuals or interest groups are not satisfied with the income distribution resulting from markets; governments also redistribute income indirectly as side-effects of other government actions that affect prices or output levels for various goods and services.

OBJECTIVES

♦ Students analyze the personal distribution of income.

♦ Students identify sources of income differences.

♦ Students classify resource payments (income) as wages, rent, interest, and profit.

♦ Students analyze the structure of the functional distribution of income over the past 70 years.

LESSON DESCRIPTION

Students participate in an income redistribution simulation and interpret statistics about the distribution of income.

TIME REQUIRED

Two class periods. Day one – procedures 1-16. Day two – procedures 17–19 and Assessment.

MATERIALS

- Activity 1: What's Your EQ (Economics Quotient)?, one per student
- Activity 2: What's My Income?, one per student
- Activity 3: Selected Percentage Shares of Income (1987 – 1998), one per student
- Visual 1: Answers to What's Your EQ?
- Visual 2: The Personal Distribution of Family Income: Percentage of National Money Income Received by Family Quintiles
- Visual 3: The Functional Distribution of Income (%)

PROCEDURES

1. Give a copy of Activity 1 to two students the day before teaching this lesson. Tell them to study for the exam but keep the information confidential. If they share the exam with any other student, they will receive a zero.

2. Distribute a copy of Activity 1 to each student. Announce that grades received will be included as a part of the semester grade. Allow 7-10 minutes for completion. Write the possible scores 20-0 on the board, in descending order.

3. Have students exchange exams for grading. Display Visual 1. Tell graders to report the scores and tally them next to each possible score on the board. Establish a distribution with + and – categories in which a few students receive As, a few receive Fs, and most fall in between. (For example: A+ (20), A (19), A– (18), B+ (17), B (15-16), B– (14), C+ (13), C (10-12), C– (9), D+ (8), D (6-7), D– (5), F (4 or below)).

4. Explain that you have received many complaints about unequal grades. Today you will try to do something about the usual grade distribution.

5. Explain that graders should put an "X" through the exam score because you will make some adjustments. Tell graders to add one point to the score if a student has an F. They should subtract one point if a student has a B+ or above. Inform students that you will explain your rationale later.

6. Tell graders to add one point to scores of students who are 16 years or older and subtract one point from students who are younger than 16. (Or pick an age that roughly divides the class into two equal-sized halves.)

7. Have graders subtract one point from the scores of students who are shorter than 5'4" and add one point to the scores of students who are taller than 5'4". Those who are exactly 5'4" keep the same point count.

8. Tell graders to calculate the new point score. Tally the new scores but do not change the letter grade ranges. Tell graders to return exams to test takers.

9. Explain that this exercise about grade distribution is designed to reflect several controversial issues concerning income distribution in our economy, and announce that student scores will *NOT* be a part of their semester grades. Point out that some students were "rich" in points on the test, some were "poor," and most were somewhere in the middle.

10. Display Visual 2 and explain that a quintile represents 20 percent of families. For example, the first quintile is the 20 percent of families receiving the lowest money income; the second quintile is the 20 percent of families receiving the next-lowest income; etc. Discuss:

A. In 1999, what percentage of national money income did the 20 percent of

From *Focus: High School Economics*, © National Council on Economic Education, New York, NY

families with the lowest income receive? *(4.3 percent)*

B. In 1999, what percentage of national money income did the 20 percent of families with the highest incomes receive? *(47.2 percent)*

C. If we define the middle class as the middle 60 percent (the 3 middle quintiles), what percentage of national money income did those families receive in 1999? *(9.9 + 15.6 + 23.0 = 48.5 percent)*

D. In this table, how have those percentages changed over time? *(The portion of total income received by the first (lowest income) quintile increased until 1967 and then decreased until 1993. The portion of total income received by the fifth (highest income) quintile decreased until 1967 and then increased. The portion received by the middle quintiles rose from 1947-1957, and then decreased.)*

Note: Students may be interested in the range of family income levels associated with the quintiles for 1999. Those divisions were:

1st quintile	$22,824 or less
2nd quintile	$22,825 to $39,599
3rd quintile	$39,600 to $59,399
4th quintile	$59,400 to $88,081
5th quintile	$88,082 or above

Source: U.S. Census Bureau, "Table F-1. Income Limits for Each Fifth and Top 5 Percent of Families (All Races): 1947 to 1999;" *<http://www.census.gov/hhes/income/histinc/f01.html>*

(Optional: Students could calculate quintiles for their grade distributions before and after adjustments.)

11. Remind students that Visual 2 shows the personal distribution of family income. Define **personal distribution of income** as income received after cash transfer payments and before taxes. This distribution, therefore, reflects some redistribution of income in our society because of cash transfer payments. Note that **transfer payments** can be cash or in-kind (noncash) benefits (such as food stamps, housing subsidies, or gifts between friends and family members). Define transfer payments as cash or in-kind benefits that are given to someone who does not have to provide any goods or services in exchange for these payments. Discuss:

A. Name some government cash transfer payments you have heard about. *(Social Security payments, Aid to Families with Dependent Children, unemployment compensation, worker's compensation)*

B. Although the figures in Visual 2 do not include in-kind transfers, name some government in-kind transfer payments you have heard about. *(food stamps, housing assistance, and free and reduced-price school lunches)*

C. Why do you think the federal government distributes monetary and non-monetary transfer payments? *(to redistribute income and assist low-income families)*

D. Which adjustments made on the class exams would parallel cash transfer payments? *(giving points to students with scores less than D- and to older students)*

12. Explain that students have seen that people's incomes differ and now they will examine why those differences occur. Discuss:

A. Why were some student scores higher than others? *(They may be smarter or better students in economics than others; therefore, they earned a higher score.*

Explain that differences in ability account for some income inequalities, but not all of them.)

B. Do you think people's level of education makes a difference in their income? *(Statistics from the U.S. Bureau of the Census show that, in general, income increases as the level of education increases. For example, in 1998, the median income of males who graduated from high school was $30,036. For those who attended high school but did not graduate, the median income was $17,726. For male college graduates, the median income was $59,448. See Visual 1 in Lesson 9.)*

C. Do people who perform unpleasant or dangerous jobs tend to earn more income? *(Yes, but only after adjusting for other differences such as education and physical skills. For example, coal miners and workers who put out oil fires tend to earn more because their jobs are dangerous.)*

D. Is all income earned from work? *(No, some people inherit wealth. Others earn interest or profits on savings and investments. Others receive transfer payments from the government, private agencies, or from friends and families.)* Explain that two students were given the test ahead of time. This "inherited wealth" allowed the students to get higher scores.

E. Are some rich or poor people just lucky or unlucky? *(Yes. A landowner might discover oil on his or her land. An investor might buy a certain stock just before it doubles in value. A student might study hard to become a civil engineer and graduate at a time when demand and salaries are very low. Some rock bands have big hits; others flop. A new actor may get a big break by*

starring in a movie that becomes very popular.)

F. Do any students live in a family with two income earners? One? *(Generally, more income earners in a family means more income.)*

G. Ask students to explain what you were trying to demonstrate when you instructed them to add a point for students who are taller than 5'4" and subtract for those who are shorter than 5'4". *(Discrimination accounts for some income differences.)* Ask students taller than 5'4" to raise their hands. Count how many males and females are in that group. Now count the males and females in the group shorter than 5'4". Gender discrimination is one type of discrimination that occurs in the workplace. Ask students for other examples. *(Race, age, and so on.)* Explain that differences because of discrimination are very difficult to calculate. In the past, men have been paid more than women, on average; but men were better educated, worked longer hours, and had more work experience. These performance-related differences have to be eliminated before determining how much of the wage difference is accounted for by current discrimination in paying different wages for identical work. However, the wage differences also led women to invest less in their own education and training, perpetuating the differences to some degree.

13. Remind students that transfer payments redistribute income. Explain that income taxes can also redistribute income from the rich to the poor. The U.S. federal income tax is a progressive tax system. It is designed for people with higher incomes to pay a larger percentage of their incomes as taxes than people with lower incomes. High-income people are

taxed more and the low-income taxpayers receive tax credits (e.g., the earned income tax credit) as well as government transfer payments.

14. Ask how higher-income families may legally reduce their tax burden. (*An important tax deduction for many families is the home mortgage interest deduction. That deduction helps high-income families more than low-income families. Poorer families tend to rent rather than buy homes; therefore, they do not receive the interest deduction. Higher-income families buy more expensive houses, have larger mortgage interest payments, and pay higher tax rates on income. Therefore, they tend to have larger tax deductions for interest payments on mortgages.*)

15. Point out that our overall system of transfer payments and taxes redistributes income from the rich to the poor. However, some tax or cash transfer policies favor low-income families and some policies favor high-income families. Studies have shown that the federal tax system tends to be progressive, but state and local tax systems are less progressive given their use of sales and property taxes. Also, social security taxes tend to be regressive. Many studies have concluded that, across income levels earned by the vast majority of taxpayers, the overall tax system in the United States is broadly proportional.

16. Have students compare the first and second grade distributions (prepared in procedures 3 and 8, respectively). Ask whether the second distribution is more or less equal. Then ask them to discuss whether they believe the new distribution is more or less fair, and why. Relate their discussion to the debate over various tax and assistance programs that redistribute family incomes.

17. Explain that income distribution can be described in other ways. Display Visual 3. Explain that the **functional distribution of income** classifies income received by individuals and businesses according to the type of productive resources sold in markets for productive resources.

18. Point out that there are four basic categories of income: wages, rent, interest, and profit. Explain that profits are included in both the corporate profits and proprietors' income columns. Define **proprietors' income** as income earned by individually or family-owned business firms (sole proprietorships). Note that some of this income represents wages for work the proprietors do in their own business; the rest is profit for risking assets in a business that might go bankrupt. **Corporate profits** include dividends, corporate income taxes, and retained earnings. Discuss:

A. How is the majority of income earned in the U.S.? *(wages and salaries – income earned working for an organization not owned by the worker)*

B. What is the smallest category of income earned? *(rental income)*

19. Give a copy of Activity 2 to each student. Explain that students should read the statement and determine what type of income is described.

A. Mary Jones received $365 this year on her certificate of deposit. (*I*)

B. William Walker received $3600 from tourists using his Florida condo. (*R*)

C. Terrence Harris received $675 in tips this year as a waiter. (*W*)

D. Florence Smith received a $250 dividend check from General Motors. (*P*)

E. Joel Lander sold potatoes for $40,000 this year and paid expenses (including the cost of his own time) of $30,000, thereby netting $10,000. (*P*)

F. Maria Gonzalez is a manger at a local grocery store, where she earns $27,000. (*W*)

G. Aunt Ethel received her Social Security check for $567 this month. (*TP*)

H. The Hulls received $5,000 this year leasing land to a farmer. (*R*)

I. Mr. Chang received a bonus of $2000 this year for being such a valuable salesperson. (*W*)

J. Tyrone Jackson earned $330 on his savings account. (*I*)

CLOSURE

1. Define the personal distribution of income. (*income received after cash transfer payments and before taxes*)

2. How do transfer payments affect the distribution of income. (*Cash or in-kind [noncash] benefits, such as food stamps, housing subsidies, or gifts between friends and family members, redistribute income from givers to recipients.*)

3. Why do governments make transfer payments to some people? (*Many families have relatively low incomes, and governments consider transfer payments as an appropriate action to redistribute income and help those in need. But some transfers reflect the political influence of special-interest groups.*)

4. Why do some people earn more income than others? (*Some people have knowledge, skills, or education that are highly valued in the workplace. Some people have jobs that are more difficult, unpleasant, or dangerous. Some people have inherited wealth and earn income from that wealth. Some people are lucky; others are discriminated against and earn lower incomes.*)

5. What does a progressive tax system have to do with income redistribution? (*It is designed so that people with higher incomes pay a larger percentage of their incomes as taxes than people with lower incomes.*)

6. How does the functional distribution of income classify income received by individuals and businesses? (*according to the type of productive resources sold in markets for productive resources*)

7. What are the four basic types of income reported in the functional distribution of income? (*wages, rent, interest, and profit*)

ASSESSMENT

1. Do you favor or oppose the following proposals for government policies? Explain your position in terms of the policy's effect on the distribution of income. (The effect of each policy, in terms of making the distribution of income more or less equal, is noted in parentheses.)

A. Employers contribute to pension plans for employees. The IRS does not count their contributions as income. (Less equal.)

B. Income earners may take a tax deduction for property taxes paid on the homes in which they live. (Less equal.)

C. Low income families may be eligible for an earned income tax credit that reduces their taxes. (More equal.)

D. Retired workers who earn less than $50,000 a year would not have to pay taxes on their Social Security benefits. (More equal.)

E. Tax credits are given to the disabled. (More equal.)

F. Income earners are allowed a tax credit for childcare expenses. (Unclear –

depends on whether more high income
or low-income families take the tax
credit, and how much the credit lowers
their taxes.)

2. Distribute a copy of Activity 3 to each
student. Instruct students to select one country
that has a relatively equal income distribution
and one country that is relatively unequal. Have
students study the two countries and write a
short paper on why the distributions are so
different in the two countries.

From *Focus: High School Economics*, © National Council on Economic Education, New York, NY   **119**

Activity 1
What's Your EQ (Economics Quotient)?

Write "true" or "false" in the spaces below. Do *NOT* write "T" or "F."

_____	1.	Money is one of the four basic types of productive resources.
_____	2.	When economists refer to "capital," they mean the amount of money necessary to start a business.
_____	3.	The law of demand states that price and quantity demanded are inversely related.
_____	4.	An increase in the costs of production will decrease supply.
_____	5.	A price floor above the equilibrium price will result in a shortage.
_____	6.	A pure market system with no government sector will not produce enough public goods.
_____	7.	If a business facing elastic demand for its product raises the price of the product, the business will receive more revenue.
_____	8.	An increase in the price of chickens will cause the supply curve for beef to shift to the right.
_____	9.	Voluntary exchange between two parties tends to make both parties better off.
_____	10.	The Social Security program is a social insurance and retirement program.
_____	11.	An increase in the rate of inflation will cause interest rates to fall.
_____	12.	U.S. currency is backed by the gold at Fort Knox and in government banks.
_____	13.	The amount of money in the U.S. is controlled by the Treasury Department.
_____	14.	If U.S. citizens would only "buy American," most of them would be better off economically.
_____	15.	New technology has been a major source of economic growth.
_____	16.	Highly paid athletes earn a large salary because they are worth it to their teams.
_____	17.	The value of money varies inversely with the price level.
_____	18.	When Congress lowers taxes, the level of total spending in the economy increases.
_____	19.	Whenever people make economic decisions, they incur an opportunity cost.
_____	20.	Any adult who does not have a job is counted as unemployed.

From *Focus: High School Economics*, © National Council on Economic Education, New York, NY

Activity 2
What's My Income?

Each statement below indicates a type of income. In the space provided, write "W" if the statement describes wages and salaries, "R" for rent, "I" for interest, "P" for profit, or "TP" for transfer payment.

_____ A.   Mary Jones received $365 this year on her certificate of deposit.

_____ B.   William Walker received $3600 from tourists using his Florida condo.

_____ C.   Terrence Harris received $675 in tips this year as a waiter.

_____ D.   Florence Smith received a $250 dividend check from General Motors.

_____ E.   Joel Lander sold potatoes for $40,000 this year and paid expenses (including the cost of his own time) of $30,000, thereby netting $10,000.

_____ F.   Maria Gonzalez is a manager at a local grocery store, where she earns $27,000.

_____ G.   Aunt Ethel received her Social Security check for $567 this month.

_____ H.   The Hulls received $5,000 this year leasing land to a farmer.

_____ I.   Mr. Chang received a bonus of $2000 this year for being such a valuable salesperson.

_____ J.   Tyrone Jackson earned $330 on his savings account.

Activity 3
Selected Percentage Shares of Income (1987-1998)

Country	1st Quintile	2nd Quintile	3rd Quintile	4th Quintile	5th Quintile
Algeria (1995)	7.0	11.6	16.1	22.7	42.6
Australia (1987)	5.9	12.0	17.2	23.6	41.3
Brazil (1996)	2.5	5.4	10.0	18.3	63.8
Bulgaria (1995)	8.5	13.8	18.0	22.7	37.0
Canada (1994)	7.5	12.9	17.3	23.0	39.3
Chile (1994)	3.5	6.6	10.9	18.0	61.0
China (1998)	5.9	10.2	15.1	22.2	46.6
Denmark (1992)	9.6	14.9	18.3	22.7	34.5
Dominican Rep. (1996)	4.3	8.3	13.1	20.6	53.7
France (1995)	7.2	12.6	17.2	22.8	40.2
Germany (1994)	8.2	13.2	17.4	22.7	38.5
Japan (1993)	10.6	14.2	17.5	22.0	35.7
Israel (1992)	6.9	11.4	16.3	22.9	42.5
Kenya (1994)	5.0	9.7	14.2	20.9	50.2
Malaysia (1995)	4.5	8.3	13.0	20.4	53.8
Mexico (1995)	3.6	7.2	11.8	19.2	58.2
Norway (1995)	9.7	14.3	18.0	22.2	35.8
Phillipines (1997)	5.4	8.8	13.2	20.3	52.3
Russia (1998)	4.4	8.6	13.2	20.1	53.7
Senegal (1995)	6.4	10.3	14.5	20.6	48.2
Switzerland (1992)	6.9	12.7	17.2	22.9	40.3
Ukraine (1996)	6.6	13.0	16.2	23.0	41.2
United Kingdom (1991)	6.6	11.5	16.2	22.7	43.0
United States (1997)	5.2	10.5	15.5	22.4	46.4
Zambia (1996)	4.2	8.2	12.7	20.1	54.8

Source: The World Bank, *World Development Report 2000/2001: Attacking Poverty.*

Visual 1
Answers to What's Your EQ?

False 1. Money is one of the four basic types of productive resources.

False 2. When economists refer to "capital," they mean the amount of money necessary to start a business.

True 3. The law of demand states that price and quantity demanded are inversely related.

True 4. An increase in the costs of production will decrease supply.

False 5. A price floor above the equilibrium price will result in a shortage.

True 6. A pure market system with no government sector will not produce enough public goods.

False 7. If a business facing elastic demand for its product raises the price of the product, the business will receive more revenue.

False 8. An increase in the price of chickens will cause the supply curve for beef to shift to the right.

True 9. Voluntary exchange between two parties tends to make both parties better off.

True 10. The Social Security program is a social insurance and retirement program.

False 11. An increase in the rate of inflation will cause interest rates to fall.

False 12. U.S. currency is backed by the gold at Fort Knox and in government banks.

False 13. The amount of money in the U.S. is controlled by the Treasury Department.

False 14. If U.S. citizens would only "buy American," most of them would be better off economically.

True 15. New technology has been a major source of economic growth.

True 16. Highly-paid athletes earn a large salary because they are worth it to their teams.

True 17. The value of money varies inversely with the price level.

True 18. When Congress lowers taxes, the level of total spending in the economy increases.

True 19. Whenever people make economic decisions, they incur an opportunity cost.

False 20. Any adult who does not have a job is counted as unemployed.

Visual 2
The Personal Distribution of Family Income: Percentage of National Money Income Received by Family Quintiles

Year	1st Quintile (lowest)	2nd Quintile	3rd Quintile	4th Quintile	5th Quintile (highest)
1947	5.0	11.9	17.0	23.1	43.0
1957	5.1	12.7	18.0	23.8	40.4
1967	5.5	12.4	17.8	23.9	40.4
1977	5.2	11.6	17.5	24.2	41.5
1987	4.6	10.8	16.8	24.1	43.7
1993	4.1	9.9	15.7	23.3	47.0
1999	4.3	9.9	15.6	23.0	47.2

Source: U.S. Bureau of the Census, "Table F-2. Share of Aggregate Income Received by Each Fifth and Top 5 Percent of Families (All Races): 1947 to 1999;" <http://www.census.gov/hhes/income/histinc/f02.html>

Visual 3
The Functional Distribution of Income (Percent)

	Wages & Salaries	Rental Income	Net Interest	Corporate Profits	Proprietors' Income
1959	68.3	3.7	2.4	13.0	12.6
1969	72.0	2.5	4.1	11.6	9.8
1979	72.3	1.2	6.9	10.7	8.9
1989	71.7	1.0	10.1	9.0	8.2
1999	72.0	2.0	6.4	11.1	8.5

Source: *Economic Report of the President, 2001.* Also available at *http://w3.access.gpo.gov/usbudget/index.html.*

LESSON ELEVEN
PUBLIC GOODS AND SERVICES

INTRODUCTION

Most goods and services produced in the marketplace are private goods and services. This kind of good or service is purchased by a consumer who desires it and can afford it, and then consumed only by that individual or anyone he or she gives it to. But some goods and services must be produced or provided by the public sector or government. Public goods and services are paid for through tax dollars and are available to everyone, even those who do not pay taxes. That means people have an incentive to use public goods, and try to get more of them produced, while shifting tax burdens to others. This is known as "free riding."

Public goods are characterized by shared consumption and nonexclusion. Nonexclusion means that it is difficult to exclude nonpayers from receiving the benefit of a good or service once it is produced. Shared consumption means that the consumption of a good or service by one individual does not reduce the amount available for others to consume. Although many goods and services are provided by the government, only those that exhibit these two characteristics, shared consumption and nonexclusion, are considered pure public goods and services.

CONCEPTS

Public goods and services
Taxes
Nonexclusion principle
Shared consumption
"Free riding" problems

CONTENT STANDARD

There is an economic role for government to play in a market economy whenever the benefits of government policy outweigh its costs. Governments often provide for national defense, address environmental concerns, define and protect property rights, and attempt to make markets more competitive. Most government policies also redistribute income.

BENCHMARKS

Public goods and services provide benefits to more than one person at the same time, and their use cannot be restricted only to those people who have paid to use them.

If a good or service cannot be withheld from those who do not pay for it, providers expect to be unable to sell it and therefore will not produce it. In market economies, governments provide some of these goods and services.

Governments provide an alternative method to markets for supplying goods and services when it appears that the benefits to society of doing so outweigh the costs to society. Not all individuals will bear the same costs or share the same benefits of those policies.

OBJECTIVE

♦ Students explain why the production of public goods and services is a role for government even in market economies, because of the concepts of shared consumption and nonexclusion.

LESSON DESCRIPTION

Students participate in a demonstration regarding the consumption of a private and public good and draw conclusions about their characteristics. Then they conduct a taxpayer survey and make generalizations about people's incentives to pay a share of the costs for goods and services they will receive whether or not they pay for them.

TIME REQUIRED

Two class periods. Day one – procedures 1-7. Day two – procedure 8 and Assessment.

MATERIALS

- Activity 1: Public Goods and Services Survey, three copies per student
- Activity 2: Public Goods and Services Survey – Group Work, one per student
- Activity 3: Newspaper Activity – Assessment, one per student
- Two small pieces of paper per student
- Visual 1: Economic Quiz with Answers, one printed copy

PROCEDURES

1. Explain to the class that most goods and services are produced by the private sector – private businesses. But some goods and services are provided by the public sector or government. The purpose of this lesson is to explain what public goods are and why government is involved in producing them, and most often use revenues from **taxes** to pay for them.

2. Begin Round 1 of a demonstration. Inform the class that there will be a surprise quiz today consisting of four questions. Show students a folded and stapled copy of Visual 1 which includes both the questions *and* answers to the quiz. Tell students that you are selling these for $1 each and you are willing to take an IOU. You will *not* let anyone who buys the quiz and answers share it with other students.

3. Distribute two small pieces of paper to each student. Instruct students to write their name on one of the sheets of paper and write "yes" below their name if they wish to purchase the quiz sheet, or "no" if they do not. Have students save the other sheet of paper for Round 2. Collect all sheets and tally the results. Write the results on the chalkboard under the heading, Round 1.

4. Now tell the class that you have decided it would be easier for you and require less paper – which is in short supply at school – if you put Visual 1 on a transparency. Display the title of Visual 1 on the overhead for all students to see.

5. Inform students that you are still willing to sell this information for $1, by displaying the transparency before passing out the quiz. Instruct students to write their name on the second sheet of paper and "yes" if they wish to purchase the information on the transparency, or "no" if they do not. Collect all the sheets and tally the results. Place the results on the chalkboard under the heading, Round 2.

6. Lead a class discussion on the following questions and points:

A. Why were more students willing to buy the "Economic Quiz with Answers" in Round 1 than in Round 2? (*The information was available only to students who paid for it in Round 1. In Round 2, some students should have recognized that if one person pays to have the transparency displayed, the teacher will not be able to prevent others from viewing it.*)

B. Explain that private goods and services are those that can be purchased and consumed by one individual at a time, and that individuals who do not pay for a private good can be excluded from using it. Ask students for examples of private goods. (*Hamburgers, cars, pizzas, movie tickets, and just about everything else a teenager buys.*) Ask students in which round the "Economic Quiz with Answers" was like a private good, and explain why. (*Round 1*)

C. Explain that **public goods and services** are those that, once available, can be enjoyed or used by numerous individuals at the same time without reducing the amount of the good available for others to use (**shared consumption**). Also, public goods cannot be withheld from those who don't pay for them (**nonexclusion principle**). With public goods, individuals will often not volunteer to pay as much for a product as they really value it, because they can "**free ride**" and use the goods or services even if other individuals pay for them. Have students explain how the transparency of Visual 1 was a public good.

D. Ask students to identify other examples of public goods. (*They are likely to suggest roads, dams, national defense, public education, the court system, lighthouses, weather forecasts, street lights, police and fire protection, national forests, and wilderness areas.*) Point out that not all government-produced goods and services are pure public goods and services, because crowding and congestion often mean that some peoples' use of the products will keep others from using them, and in some cases it is possible to keep those who do not pay for products provided by government from consuming them. Only products with the two characteristics of shared consumption and nonexclusion are considered *pure* public goods and services.

E. What happened to your incentive to pay for the quiz information when it was available to you whether you paid for it or not? (*Students had less incentive to pay – this is the "free rider" problem.*)

F. What happens to consumers' incentive to pay for public goods and services, such as dams, national defense, roads and police protection, when they can obtain these goods and services whether they pay for them or not? (*There is less incentive to pay.*)

G. If consumers have little incentive to pay for goods and services, what happens to the amount of the goods and services produced? (*There is less incentive and wherewithal to produce them, even though consumers may really want them.*)

H. If individual consumers are unwilling to pay for these goods and services, who is going to pay for them? (*Government must arrange for the production of goods and services that involve shared consumption, or when it is difficult to exclude those who are unwilling to pay for a product from using it.*)

I. How does government do this? (*Through taxation, government can require citizens to help pay for the products. In this way, the "free rider" problem can be solved, or at least reduced.*)

7. Distribute three copies of Activity 1 to each student. Tell them to survey at least three adults.

8. Once surveys are complete, divide students into groups and distribute Activity 2 to the class. Instruct students to tally their findings from the survey and use this information to answer the questions. As a class, have groups share their conclusions and generalizations.

CLOSURE

Review the key points of the lesson. Ask:

1. In a market economy, most goods and services are produced by the private sector. Why don't we depend on the private sector for all the goods and services we desire? (*Some goods and services are marked by two characteristics – shared consumption and nonexclusion. Good and services with these characteristics are demanded by people but the private sector lacks sufficient incentives to produce the right amount.*)

2. What is an example of a pure or nearly pure public good or service? (*Dams, national defense, the court system, lighthouses, weather forecasts, street lights, and police and fire protection are examples.*)

3. What is an example of a pure or nearly pure private good or service? (*Accept a variety of answers such as boats, scooters, vacations, computers, personal clothing, cars, and so forth.*)

4. What is an example of a good or service paid for by tax dollars that may not be a pure public good? (*Roads and public education might be examples offered. Both roads and public schools share the feature of shared consumption but non-payers can be excluded. Imposing tolls is one way of excluding non-payers from roads. Imposing certain kinds of school polices, such as rigorous attendance rules or strict discipline polices, allows public schools to exclude students who are unwilling to "pay" by conforming to school rules.*)

ASSESSMENT

Distribute Activity 3 to the class. Instruct students to locate two newspaper articles on public goods and services and attach the articles to the handout. They are to answer the six questions on Activity 3 for each article.

Activity 1
Public Goods and Services Survey

All the public goods and services listed below are currently paid for by taxes. For each good or service, place a check mark in the appropriate column that best expresses your viewpoint.

Column 1 – Check Column 1, "Pay for as used," if you believe that this good or service should not be paid for with tax dollars. People should pay for this good or service individually when they use it. Individuals who do not pay will do without this good or service.

Column 2 – Check Column 2, "Pay for with tax dollars," if you feel this good or service should continue to be provided with tax dollars.

Public Goods and Services	Column 1 Pay for as used	Column 2 Pay for with tax dollars
National defense		
Public schools		
Highways and roads		
Dams		
Police protection		
State universities		
National forests		
Weather forecasts		

Activity 2
Public Goods and Services Survey – Group Work

Working with a group, combine your survey results and record the information below.

SURVEY TOTALS		
Public Goods and Services	**Column 1** **Pay for as used**	**Column 2** **Pay for with tax dollars**
National defense		
Public schools		
Highways and roads		
Dams		
Police protection		
State universities		
National forests		
Weather forecasts		

Use this information to answer the following questions:

1. In general, how do people feel about paying for public goods and services as they use them rather than paying for them with tax dollars? Are they more willing to pay for some public goods and services through taxes than others? Which ones? How do you explain this behavior?

2. What would happen if the public goods and services on the survey list were produced and distributed based on the results of your survey?

3. Why would it be difficult to provide some of the public goods or services using the private sector, making those who use the goods and services pay for them?

From *Focus: High School Economics*, © National Council on Economic Education, New York, NY

Activity 3
Newspaper Activity – Assessment

Locate two newspaper articles on public goods and services. Attach the articles to this handout. For each article, answer the six questions below.

1.   What is the public good or service discussed in this article?

_____

_____

_____

2.   Is this a pure public good or service, or something produced by the government that might be produced and sold by private businesses? Explain.

_____

_____

_____

3.   Why is this good or service provided using tax dollars?

_____

_____

_____

4.   What level of government provides the good or service?

_____

_____

_____

5.   How does this public good or service benefit your community and you personally?

_____

_____

_____

6.   What would happen if government stopped using tax dollars to provide this good or service? How would this affect your community and you personally?

_____

_____

_____

Visual 1
Economic Quiz with Answers

1. **Who wrote, "In this world nothing is certain but death and taxes"? (Benjamin Franklin)**

2. **Who was the author of *The Wealth of Nations*? (Adam Smith)**

3. **Who wrote *The General Theory of Employment, Interest, and Money*? (John Maynard Keynes)**

4. **What does TNSTAAFL mean? (There's no such thing as a free lunch.)**

From *Focus: High School Economics*, © National Council on Economic Education, New York, NY

LESSON TWELVE
THIRD-PARTY COSTS AND BENEFITS

INTRODUCTION

If some of the costs or benefits entailed in either the production or consumption of a product "spill over" to people other than the producers and consumers of the product, and if the costs of collecting for those costs and benefits are substantial, private markets will fail to account for these third-party effects. As a result, too much of the product will be produced when spillover costs (also known as negative externalities) are present, because producers will not have to pay to cover those costs. Too little will be produced when there are significant spillover benefits (also known as positive externalities), because the people who receive the spillover benefits didn't pay to get them. If they had paid, the producers of these goods and services would have been willing to produce more of them.

To correct these market failures, the government can regulate or tax the production and/or consumption of products that generate spillover costs, and subsidize the production and/or consumption of products that generate spillover benefits. Or it can try to lower the costs of collecting for the benefits and costs in private markets, by defining and enforcing property rights to the resources affected by the spillover costs and benefits.

CONCEPTS

Market failures
Externalities (spillover benefits and costs)
Transaction costs

CONTENT STANDARDS

There is an economic role for government to play in a market economy whenever the benefits of a government policy outweigh its costs.

Governments often provide for national defense, address environmental concerns, define and protect property rights, and attempt to make markets more competitive. Most government policies also redistribute income.

BENCHMARKS

Markets do not allocate resources effectively if (1) property rights are not clearly defined or enforced, (2) externalities (spillover effects) affecting large numbers of people are associated with the production or consumption of a product, or (3) markets are not competitive.

Externalities exist when some of the costs and benefits associated with production and consumption fall on someone other than the producers or consumers of the product.

When a price fails to reflect all the benefits of a product, too little of the product is produced and consumed. When a price fails to reflect all the costs of a product, too much of the product is produced and consumed. Government can use subsidies to help correct for insufficient output; it can use taxes to help correct for excessive output; or it can regulate output directly to correct for over- or under-production or consumption of a product.

OBJECTIVES

♦ Students distinguish between cases where there are, and are not, market failures related to external costs or external benefits.

♦ Students evaluate the effectiveness of individual vs. governmental remedies for externalities, under conditions of both high and low transaction costs.

♦ Students illustrate government policies dealing with externalities using a supply and demand model, and identify the over- and underproduction and consumption associated with this kind of market failure.

LESSON DESCRIPTION

Students participate in a role-playing exercise that initially depicts a situation that may appear to involve externalities but does not. They then act out further developments involving external costs in cases where transaction costs are first very low, and then much higher. Through discussion questions on this activity, students should understand how these different circumstances may call for different kinds of public policy remedies.

A worksheet activity requires students to look at both external benefits and external costs in the context of a simple supply-and-demand model. Another activity sheet is used for assessment purposes.

TIME REQUIRED

Two class periods. Day one – procedures 1-7. Day two – procedure 8 and Assessment.

MATERIALS

- Activity 1: Life on Dismal Lake, one copy for each student
- Activity 2: Externalities Worksheet, one copy for each student
- Activity 3: What Would You Do?, one copy for each student
- Visual 1: Externalities

PROCEDURE

1. Explain that the purpose of this lesson is to examine problems where the decisions of producers and consumers in markets for some products result in costs or benefits for third parties, who do not produce or consume these products. Economists call these problems positive and negative **externalities**, or spillover benefits and costs, and suggest various kinds of remedies for these problems.

2. Display Visual 1. Explain **market failure** and externalities. Ask the students to predict whether the examples provided are positive or negative externalities:

- Contributions to public radio or television: positive externality
- Car exhaust: negative externality
- A barking dog in a city neighborhood: negative externality
- Apartment dwellers who buy fire extinguishers: positive externality
- Crying babies on crowded airplanes: very negative externality

3. Announce that the following group activity, Life on Dismal Lake, (procedures 4 – 6) demonstrates what is, and what isn't, an externalities problem.

4. Select four students to act out Part I of the scenario on Activity 1 as you or a student read it to the class. One student takes the role of Mama Smith, another the role of Papa Smith, and two students play the Smiths' teenage children. Read the passage slowly, with frequent pauses so that students can act out the events that are described. Or, if you prefer, simply distribute copies of Activity 1 to students, and have them read the material and answer the questions.

5. Pick one more student to play the role of Snively Whiplash, and continue with Part II of the scenario.

6. Bring 15 more students up to participate in the role-playing scenario, and read Part III.

7. Distribute copies of Activity 1 to students so that they will have the text of the scenario to work with, and debrief the Life on Dismal Lake activity by answering the discussion questions. Ask:

A. Was there any externality problem when only the Smith family lived on Dismal Lake? If so, how should this problem be solved? *(Although some may argue that the Smith teenagers imposed external costs on their parents, if we treat the family as a single economic unit, as economists usually*

From *Focus: High School Economics,* © National Council on Economic Education, New York, NY

do, then there is no externality problem because there is no third party being hurt by the pollution. The Smiths bear all of the costs whether they decide to carry the garbage out to the road for pickup, or to pollute the lake and live with the dirty, smelly, lake. They eventually choose not to pollute the lake, which is usually – but not always – the case when people think about trashing their own property and home.)

B. Was there an externality problem when Snively Whiplash and the Smiths were the only people living on the lake? If so, how should this problem be solved? *(There is an external cost here, because the Smiths bear some of the costs of Whiplash's garbage "disposal." Most students are likely to say that the Smiths should get the county police and courts to threaten Whiplash with fines or a jail sentence if the pollution continues, and that may be sufficient to resolve the externality problem. However, note the costs incurred by the Smiths and the county, for police, courts, monitoring the lake for pollution, and so forth.)*

C. Suppose it is decided either that Whiplash has the legal right to keep throwing trash in the lake because he owns almost all of the lake anyway, or that the lake is too far away from any county enforcement agencies to effectively stop the pollution. What can the Smiths do now, if anything? *(They can clean the lake up themselves, or offer to take Whiplash's garbage out to the road for pickup themselves, or even pay Whiplash to stop polluting. Under this possibility it is true that the Smiths pay more, but remember they are the ones who want the clean lake, and point out that there wouldn't be an externality problem if they didn't live on the lake and Whiplash owned it all. In that case Whiplash would bear all of the costs of*

any pollution or of taking out the garbage, just as the Smiths did before they sold most of the land to Whiplash. If they offer to pay Whiplash not to pollute, Whiplash will bear some costs by polluting, so at least part of the external cost has been internalized. Surprisingly, then, whether property rights are defined so that the Smiths have the right to clean water, or Whiplash has the right to pollute it, we can end up with no pollution if the Smiths are willing to pay Whiplash enough to stop. Or, Whiplash might pay the Smiths enough to make them willing to accept the pollution. So we may well end up with the same amount of pollution in the lake either way, and the only thing that changes is whether the Smiths or Whiplash end up paying for what they want.)

D. What incentives did Whiplash have to stop polluting before he sold the land around Dismal Lake? *(Not polluting would make property values higher, which would let Whiplash charge a higher price for the lots.)*

E. When the pollution begins with 16 families living on the lake, can the Smiths (and the other nonpolluters) deal with the problem the same way they might have when just Whiplash and the Smiths lived on the lake? *(No. It is now much more difficult to identify who is polluting, to determine how much they are polluting, and to monitor whether they have stopped or continue to pollute. Moreover, with so many families involved, it will be much more difficult to work out financial agreements between all of the families, either to stop the pollution or for the polluters to compensate the non-polluters. In other words, with more people involved the transaction costs are much higher, and it becomes much more likely that direct government rules and enforcement will be required to deal with the problem. Finally, point out that most externality problems occur where property rights are poorly defined and enforced, and often where it is very difficult to define and enforce those rights. For example, most pollution problems involve air, rivers and streams, or oceans, which nobody really owns. Similarly, public parks are more often littered than people's front yards, especially in neighborhoods with single-family homes.)*

8. Distribute copies of Activity 2 to students. When they have completed the sheet, review it. Suggested answers for the questions in Column 1 of Activity 2:

A. Define negative externality or third-party costs. *(Externalities exist when some of the costs or benefits associated with the production or consumption of a product spill over to third parties other than the direct producers and consumers of the product. Negative externalities are spillover costs.)*

B. Give three examples of third-party costs. *(The classic example of third-party costs, or negative externalities, is pollution. For example, paper mills emit chemicals that can increase the risk for some cancers. Other examples include the costs of alcohol consumption borne by the nondrinking victims of DWI accidents, and the costs paid by those with medical insurance when their premiums are raised because hospital charges are raised to cover the care provided to those who do not have insurance and can not pay their bills.)*

C. Draw a new supply curve, and use it to show the new equilibrium price and quantity for steel if the external costs of

pollution were also counted as costs of production.

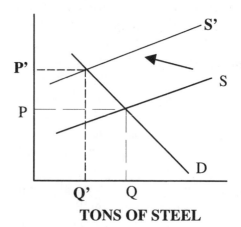

TONS OF STEEL

D. Would more or less steel be produced according to the new supply curve? *(less)*

E. Would the price be higher or lower? *(higher)*

F. Why may products that entail third-party costs be over-produced? *(If producers don't have to recognize third-party costs, they will produce on the supply curve that lies too far right, with a lower price and higher output level.)*

Answers for the questions in Column 2 of Activity 2:

G. Define positive externality or third-party benefits. *(Externalities exist when some of the costs or benefits associated with the production or consumption of a product spill over to third parties other than the direct producers and consumers of the product. Positive externalities are spillover benefits.)*

H. Give three examples of third-party benefits. *(Examples of external benefits include higher housing values neighbors enjoy when someone in their neighborhood restores and landscapes their property; or the benefits from vaccinations against contagious diseases, which lower chances of catching the disease even among those who are not vaccinated; or benefits to an entire community such as lower unemployment payments and crime rates, which are associated with raising the average educational attainments of people who live in low-income neighborhoods.)*

I. Change the graph to show the new demand curve for education if all the third-party benefits to the community were counted as part of demand. Show the new equilibrium price and quantity.

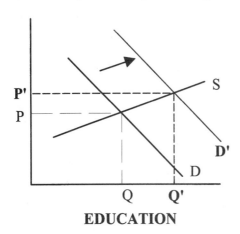

EDUCATION

J. Would more or less education be purchased according to the new demand curve? *(more)*

K. Would the price be higher or lower? *(higher)*

L. Why may products that yield third-party benefits be under-produced? *(If the external benefits aren't recognized, production takes place on the demand curve based only the private benefits received by those who do pay for the product [not those who benefit without paying], at a lower equilibrium price and output level.)*

CLOSURE

Remind the class that market prices usually reflect the benefits and the costs received by the producers and consumers involved in an exchange. However, sometimes markets work imperfectly. This is a kind of market failure. It occurs when market prices fail to reflect all the costs and all the benefits involved. Ask:

1. What is an externality? *(An externality exists when some of the costs and benefits associated with production and consumption fall on someone other than the producers or consumers of the product.)*

2. What will happen when a price fails to reflect all the benefits of a product? *(Too little of the product will be produced.)*

3. What will happen when a price fails to reflect all the costs of a product? *(Too much of the product is produced.)*

4. Why might government officials be justified in using tax dollars to subsidize (i.e., lower the price of) vaccines against contagious diseases? *(Private markets will not produce enough of these vaccines. This is a type of market failure. The market price for these vaccines fails to reflect all the benefits – specifically the benefits from those who are less likely to be infected by those who have paid for the vaccination, but choose not to get the vaccinations themselves.)*

5. Why might government officials be justified in placing a tax on businesses that allow dangerous chemicals to get into a river or lake? *(Pollution is also a type of market failure. Imposing a tax on pollution is one way to help correct for excessive output of dangerous chemicals.)*

ASSESSMENT

Distribute copies of Activity 3 to students, and review their evaluations of the three proposals in both scenarios.

(As shown in the debriefing for the Dismal Lake activity, there is something to be said for both Proposals 1 and 3 in the first scenario, even though Dismal Lake is an example of an external cost problem, not an external benefit as suggested in Proposal 1. The second proposal violates the economic way of thinking by looking only at the costs of the pollution, and not considering the economic costs of reducing pollution. Typically, as pollution controls and clean-up procedures are implemented, the benefits are initially high but fall off as the air or water becomes cleaner and cleaner, while clean-up costs for each "unit" of pollution are initially low, but become higher and higher as it becomes harder to find and remove the pollution once a lot of it has already been cleaned up. From an economic standpoint, then, the optimal amount of pollution is almost never zero, except in cases where a pollutant is extremely toxic. Effluent taxes and market-based programs such as public auctions for pollution permits are often suggested by economists as effective ways to get the right amount of pollution produced at the lowest possible cost.

In the second scenario, if no additional business will be brought into the city either by the baseball team or the new stadium, and if all of the spending is simply reallocated away from existing firms in the city, there is little rationale for the public investment in the program. That supports Proposal 1, especially if there are substantial external costs such as traffic jams and falling property values. If there are extensive opportunities for new businesses to be created and to attract higher spending in the city, then the stadium may well be a good infrastructure investment, supporting Proposal 3. The idea that those who use public services and facilities should pay for them certainly supports the user fee in Proposal 2. However, it is unlikely that the city will be able to recover all of the cost of the stadium with such fees – or similar taxes on hotel rooms, and so forth – in less than a decade or so. If that were true, private businesses would be likely to build the stadium *in the first place, as they already have in some cities.)*

Activity 1
Life on Dismal Lake

Part I.

The Smith family owns all of the land around 100-acre Dismal Lake, and builds its home on the eastern edge of the lake. Life is very pleasant for the first year. Then, unknown to Mama and Papa Smith, when the Smith children take out the family garbage once a week, they begin throwing it in the Lake because that is easier than carrying the bags all the way out to the road for the county trash trucks to pick up. A few months later the lake begins to stink, and Mama and Papa Smith discover where the garbage has been going. The Smith children are now dismal, because they have to clean up the lake instead of going out with their friends for the next four weekends.

Part II.

When the Smith children go off to college, Mr. and Mrs. Smith sell all of the land around Dismal Lake except their one-acre homestead to Snively Whiplash, an unscrupulous land developer. Whiplash builds a home on the western edge of the lake, and immediately starts throwing garbage into the lake instead of taking it out to the road for the county trash service.

Part III.

One year later, Whiplash stops throwing trash in Dismal Lake, subdivides the land around the lake, sells homestead plots to 15 families for $100,000 each, and moves away. The 15 new owners each build large houses on their lots. Then, after a few months, garbage starts to show up on and around Dismal Lake again – this time from at least two families. The Smiths call a neighborhood meeting to discuss the problem. At the meeting, four of the families accuse five other families of throwing their garbage in the lake. The accused families deny the charges, accuse other families instead, and the meeting breaks up with everyone shouting at everyone else. Dismal Lake continues to be a smelly, dismal place.

Discussion Questions:

    A. Was there any externality problem when only the Smith family lived on Dismal Lake? If so, how should this problem be solved?

    B. Was there an externality problem when Snively Whiplash and the Smiths were the only people living on the lake? If so, how should this problem be solved?

    C. Suppose it is decided either that Whiplash has the legal right to keep throwing trash in the lake because he owns almost all of the lake anyway, or that the lake is too far away from any county enforcement agencies to effectively stop the pollution. What can the Smiths do now, if anything?

    D. What incentives did Whiplash have to stop polluting before he sold the land around Dismal Lake?

    E. When the pollution begins with 16 families living on the lake, can the Smiths (and the other nonpolluters) deal with the problem the same way they might have when just Whiplash and the Smiths lived on the lake?

Activity 2
Externalities Worksheet

A. Define negative externality or third-party costs. _____

_____

B. Give three examples of third-party costs.

   1. _____
   2. _____
   3. _____

C. In the supply and demand graph below, only the private costs and benefits have been accounted for. Draw the new supply curve, and show the new equilibrium price and quantity for steel if the external costs of pollution were also counted as costs of production.

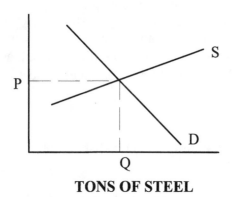

TONS OF STEEL

D. Would more or less steel be produced according to the new supply curve?

_____

E. Would the price be higher or lower?

_____

F. Why may products that entail third-party costs be over-produced? _____

_____

_____

G. Define positive externality or third-party benefits. _____

_____

H. Give three examples of third-party benefits.

   1. _____
   2. _____
   3. _____

I. In the supply and demand graph below, only the private costs and benefits have been accounted for. Change the graph to show the new demand curve for education if all third-party benefits to the community were counted as part of demand. Show the new equilibrium price and quantity.

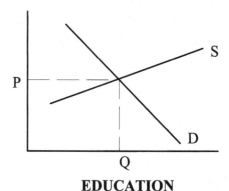

EDUCATION

J. Would more or less education be purchased according to the new demand curve? _____

K. Would the price be higher or lower?

_____

L. Why may products that yield third-party benefits be under-produced? _____

_____

_____

Activity 3
What Would You Do?

1.   A manufacturing plant pollutes a nearby river, much to the displeasure of the residents downstream. At a town meeting, residents discuss three proposals for solving the pollution problem. Based on your understanding of externalities, choose the proposal you think is best and defend your selection.

Proposal 1 – Because the downstream residents will receive the benefits of pollution control, they should pay for it. This is a clear case of external benefits or positive externalities. A property tax should be placed on the residents downstream.

Proposal 2 - The government should force the plant to close. That is the only way to stop all the pollution. There is no reason for the downstream residents to suffer. Any other solution still leaves some dirty water.

Proposal 3 - The company is not counting all of its costs of production. Keeping the river clean should be one of these costs. A tax, called an effluent tax, should be placed on the company for each cubic foot of polluted water it releases into the river.

2.   The National League has awarded a new franchise for a baseball team to be established in Indianapolis, Indiana, but only if the new team, the Indiana Racers, has a major league stadium designed specifically for baseball. Indianapolis will have to build a new stadium if a team is to be awarded a franchise in that city. Proponents argue that the team will generate new business, provide jobs, increase tax revenues, and promote tourism in Indianapolis because of the greater national exposure. Opponents argue that most of the money spent on baseball games will be by Indianapolis residents, who will simply reduce their spending on other things. Thus, there will be no net job creation or tax revenues, and few new tourists coming to Indianapolis in the summer. Others say that the stadium, wherever it is located, will cause property values to go down and create traffic and parking problems and noise pollution. Voters have three proposals before them. Using your knowledge of externalities, write a paragraph in support of each proposal. What assumptions concerning external costs and benefits does each proposal make?

Proposal 1 - No city money should be used in the construction of the stadium.

Proposal 2 - The city should place a tax on each ticket sold to pay for the stadium.

Proposal 3 - The city should build the stadium and lease the right to play there to the baseball team, at a subsidized rate.

Visual 1
Externalities

Market prices usually reflect the benefits and the costs received by the producers and consumers involved in an exchange. A kind of *market failure* occurs when market prices fail to reflect all the costs and all the benefits involved. This kind of market failure is called an *externality* problem.

- *Externalities* exist when some of the costs or benefits associated with the production or consumption of a product "spill over" to third parties, who do not produce or pay to consume the product.

- *Positive externalities* are *benefits* enjoyed by someone who does not produce or pay to consume a product.

- *Negative externalities* are *costs* paid by someone who does not produce or pay to consume a product.

Discuss whether the following are examples of positive or negative externalities:

- Contributions to support public radio or television
- Car exhausts
- A barking dog in a city neighborhood
- Apartment dwellers who buy fire extinguishers
- Crying babies on crowded airplanes

LESSON THIRTEEN
PUBLIC CHOICE: ECONOMICS GOES TO WASHINGTON AND INTO THE VOTING BOOTH

INTRODUCTION

Economist James Buchanan won the Nobel prize in economics in 1987, for pioneering work he had done with Gordon Tullock and others in the new field of public choice economics. This approach applies the basic economic way of thinking to group decisions made through the electoral process or by some government body. That means thinking of voters, elected officials, and government employees as people who pursue their own self-interest, rather than pursuing the public good even when that entails personal sacrifices. Before Buchanan's work, most philosophers, political scientists, and many economists, had not systematically applied an economic way of thinking to the public sector, except to decry individual cases of corruption or bribes.

Although this lesson focuses on applying public choice theory to voting and elections, these same ideas can also be used to explain the day-to-day actions of both ordinary government employees and politicians.

Public choice ideas are increasingly common in economic courses at the college as well as the high school level. But because this material may be new to many teachers, a brief appendix of background material is included at the end of this lesson.

CONCEPTS

Self-interest
Expected benefits and costs of voting
Information and search costs
Special interest effects
Government failure

CONTENT STANDARD

Costs of government policies sometimes exceed benefits. This may occur because of incentives facing voters, government officials, and government employees, because of actions by special interest groups that can impose costs on the general public, or because social goals other than economic efficiency are being pursued.

BENCHMARKS

Citizens, government employees, and elected officials do not always directly bear the costs of their political decisions. This often leads to policies whose costs outweigh their benefits for society.

Incentives exist for political leaders to implement policies that disperse costs widely over large groups of people and benefit relatively small, politically powerful groups of people.

OBJECTIVE

♦ Students critically assess the actions of voters, elected officials, and government employees, based on the assumption that individuals in each of these groups will follow their own economic self-interest.

LESSON DESCRIPTION

Students participate in a series of classroom elections to analyze special interest effects, and see how the costs of voting and acquiring information about candidates or propositions on a ballot can affect whether or not people vote, and if so how informed they will be. Finally, students examine the causes and consequences of logrolling and similar kinds of collusion by elected officials.

TIME REQUIRED

One to two class periods.

MATERIALS

- Activity 1: Student Information Sheet for Elections 1 & 2 (Cut apart so that individual students receive only the information for their own group. There are five groups.)
- Activity 2: Classroom Money (Duplicate one sheet for every two students in the class, and cut up money so that each student begins with a $5 bill and five $1 bills. Prepare 10 additional $5 bills and 10 additional $1 bills for each student participating in the elections, to be distributed as directed in the activities. Later, if possible, allow students to purchase inexpensive products or classroom privileges with the money they earn in the activities.
- Visual 1: Public Choice Theory 101
- Visual 2: The Costs and Benefits of Voting: Elections 1 & 2
- Visual 3: Logrolling Across the Land

PROCEDURES

1. Explain that the purpose of this lesson is to examine the behavior of voters and elected officials from an economic perspective. Here is an example of how an economic perspective works when it comes to voting and politics: Imagine that a U.S. Senator from a northwestern state, known and respected for long years of service to the voters of the state, votes for a bill that will increase the demand and therefore the price of lumber grown in the U.S. – a product used to help build new homes. Experts agree that passing this bill will increase the price of new homes. Senators from the midwest oppose the bill, but eventually it passes. What might lead this respected Senator from the northwest, and a majority of the Senate, to pass a bill that will increase the price of new homes? (Accept a variety of answers at this point.)

2. Display Visual 1. Explain that even though elected officials usually try to serve their constituents, not all of their constituents are very interested in the laws and policies adopted by

elected officials. To stay in office, however, elected officials have to get a majority of votes from the groups of their constituents who are interested enough in what they do to vote in the next election. Explain that a U.S. Senator might decide to vote in favor of a bill that increased the price of new homes if the Senator was persuaded that enough constituents would benefit from the higher demand and price of lumber to remember this bill, but few constituents who were home buyers would be hurt enough to resent the bill and vote against the Senator. That can happen. For example, a Senator from a northwestern state might favor an increased tariff on imported lumber to protect U.S. timber companies from Canadian competitors. Unfortunately, the amount of harm incurred by all U.S. homebuyers because of the price increase is typically much more than the amount of benefits gained by this Senator's interested constituents. But the benefits to U.S. timber companies and workers are concentrated among a small group of people, who are likely to remember and vote for (or send campaign contributions to) the Senator who supported this policy. The higher costs of new homes is widely spread out, across millions of families all around the country, who may well not realize that the increased tariff has caused the higher prices. So they aren't likely to vote or actively campaign against the Senators who voted for this policy, or vote for and support the Senators who voted against the policy. Explain to the class that this kind of outcome (policies that produce more public costs than benefits) constitutes a **government failure**. Specifically, in this case the failure results from what is called a **special interest effect**.

3. Tell the class that you will now use a series of simulated elections to see how outcomes that are not in the public interest can sometimes happen, even in democratic political systems. Divide the class into five groups with equal numbers of students in each group. If there are one or two students left over, have them help you count the votes and make the

cash payouts after the elections. Or you can have some students work as a voting pair or household, sharing one vote.

4. Explain that in both of the elections students will vote for one of two options. Each option offers differing amounts of overall benefits to society at large, which in this case is all of the students in the classroom. But explain that the most important rule for these elections is that all students are to vote according to their own **self-interest**. To simplify that idea in these elections, the payouts of classroom money are assumed to fully value each person's personal benefits and satisfaction from voting for and perhaps electing a candidate or policy. In other words, everything they care about in this election is reflected in the payout schedules. Therefore, make sure students vote in each election in the manner that will earn them the most money. Also, announce that payouts of classroom money will be made after each election, based on the schedule of the policy that is chosen by the majority of voters.

5. Before conducting the first election, give each student one $5 bill and five $1 bills, for a total of $10. Then distribute the information sheets for Activity 1. Give the portion of Activity 1 marked Group 1 to each student in Group 1, the portion of Activity 1 marked Group 2 to each student in Group 2, and so on for all five groups. Note that each student should receive information only about his or her own group's benefits from options A and B, not about the benefits for students in other groups. Give the students a minute to review the information. Check with several students to make sure that they are reading the information sheets correctly in terms of their expected benefits from the different election outcomes.

6. Conduct Election 1. Ask the students to raise their hands to indicate if they are voting in favor of option A or option B. Record the election result on the chalkboard. Make the "cash" payouts as shown on the information sheets. You should pay *each* student (or student

pair) in each group the payoff that is indicated for the winning option on the student information sheets, and in Visual 2.

7. Direct students' attention to the results of Election 1 you recorded on the chalkboard and Display Visual 2. Ask:

A. What are the total benefits paid out to one representative from each of the five groups if option A is chosen? (*$11*)

B. What are the total benefits paid out to one representative from each of the five groups if option B is chosen? (*$10*)

C. If each of the five groups has the same number of voters, will option A or option B be chosen? (*Option A will be chosen because the students in groups 3, 4, and 5 should vote for A.*)

D. Why did option A defeat option B in Election 1? (*When everyone votes their own self-interest option A defeats option B because students in groups 3, 4, and 5 earn more money by voting for option A, and students in groups 1 and 2 earn more money by voting for option B.*)

E. Did Election 1 result in the greatest amount of social benefits? (*Yes. In Election 1 the total social benefits of $11 – $5 for each student in group 5 and $3 for each student in groups 3 and 4 – were chosen over total social benefits of $10, which would be paid out to the students in groups 1 and 2 if option B won. But sometimes elections can result in outcomes that do not provide the greatest amount of social benefits. If you want to take the class time to demonstrate and discuss that, conduct the election described in optional procedure 15.*)

8. Explain the procedures for Election 2. The same payouts used in Activity 1 will be

used again. In Election 2, however, you will charge each voter $4 before they can vote. Explain that this does not represent a poll tax, which is illegal in the United States. Instead, the $4 represents real **costs of voting** that, although often overlooked, are really paid by those who choose to vote. These $4 costs include **information and search costs**, such as any time voters spend gathering information about the effects of option A and option B so that they may cast an informed vote. They also include the cost of driving or walking to the polling place, and the time it takes to vote.

9. Conduct Election 2. Ask the students to stand if they are going to vote, and collect $4 from each student (or pair of students if they are sharing a vote) who stands. Then have students raise their hands to vote for option A or option B. Only the students who are standing and paid the $4 get to vote. Record the election result on the chalkboard. Make the "cash" payouts to the winning voters as shown in the column for the winning option on the information sheets, and on Visual 2.

10. How should Election 2 turn out? If students followed the rules correctly, individuals in groups 3 and 4 should choose not to vote. If they did vote, point out that they are spending more than they can expect to gain – not a good way to earn classroom money. Individuals in groups 1, 2, and 5 may or may not choose to vote, depending on how optimistic they are about winning the election. If the students in group 5 vote and students in groups 1 and 2 do not, announce the outcome (option A still wins). Repeat Election 2 with the benefits to groups 1, 2, and 5 doubled, but the benefits to groups 3 and 4 remaining the same, as do the costs of voting for all students/groups. Continue raising these benefits and offering hints to groups 1 and 2, if necessary, until the students in these two groups vote together to defeat group 5, or until group 5 does not vote and either group 1 or 2 does vote to win the election. Make the appropriate payoffs to all students (including those who choose not to vote) and collect the $4

from voters in each election you hold. Record the result that option B defeats option A on the chalkboard or overhead transparency.

11. Discuss the results of Election 2. Direct the attention of the students to the results of Election 1 and 2 on the chalkboard. Display Visual 2. Ask:

A. Why did option B defeat option A? (When voters recognized the costs of voting, it changed the outcome. Voters are now more likely to vote only if they expect to get a higher financial return from casting a winning vote, or if they put more value and derive more personal satisfaction from the act of voting itself.)

B. Did Election 2 result in the greatest amount of social benefits? (No. In Election 2 when option B won, the total social benefit of $10 was paid out to one representative from each of the five groups – $5 for group 1 and $5 for Group 2. The total social benefit of $11 for option A was defeated – $3 for Group 3, $3 for group 4, and $5 for group 5.)

12. Explain that choosing B over A in Election 2 illustrates a special interest effect – differences in the distribution of costs or benefits associated with an election outcome give small groups of people strong incentives to organize, campaign, and vote, while a large portion of the electorate chooses not to vote, or at least not to vote as a block for or against some candidate or issue. Remind the class that people incur both time and money costs in getting to the voting place, and to different degrees in getting information to make an informed vote. These costs have the same effect in leading some people not to vote as the $4 charged in these simulated elections.

13. Discuss examples where the special interest effect is at work in U.S. elections or other public policies – e.g., farm subsidies

despite the fact that only 3 percent of the population works on farms; or trade protection in the form of tariffs, quotas, and voluntary export restraints provided to U.S. automobile and textile companies. Also discuss cases where voters or political leaders took a position that was not in their own self-interest – e.g., defenders at the Alamo, President Eisenhower signing the amendment limiting presidential terms, or see John F. Kennedy's chapter on John Quincy Adams in *Profiles in Courage*.

14. Explain that public choice economics assumes people follow their self-interest in making political decisions, and to the extent that they do not, that represents a limitation of the ability of public choice theory to predict the behavior of individuals and groups. You may have encountered that sort of behavior in Election 2, if some students choose to vote despite the fact that the voting costs are higher than their expected gains. If it occurs, note the number of people who did follow their own self-interest.

15. Optional Extension. Ask students if democratic elections not facing special-interest problems will always result in choosing the outcome that provides the greatest amount of social benefits. The answer is no, as shown in the following table.

Optional Election, Visual, or Handout

Group #	Benefits of Electing:	
	Option A	Option B
1	$0	$10
2	0	10
3	3	0
4	3	0
5	5	0

Use a transparency or handout of this table to demonstrate to students that, in this case, the option that provides the greatest overall level of social benefits will not be chosen in a democratic election where everyone votes their self-interest. Or if you prefer, first prepare slips for the five groups of students as in the earlier

elections, and conduct this as a separate election. The key point to stress here is, as Winston Churchill once said, "Democracy is the worst system in the world, except compared to everything else." Or as has also been said about democracy, the belief is that a majority of people will be right a majority of the time. When benefits and costs are distributed more evenly, as on Visual 2, democratic outcomes are more likely to result in choosing the outcome with the highest-valued outcome to the overall society.

16. Explain that understanding the basis of public choice economics helps to illustrate other types of common political behavior. Display Visual 3[1] to the class. Have students note the total costs and benefits of the Defense Contract and the Farm Subsidies. Discuss the questions. Ask:

A. Which of these programs is economically efficient – i.e., the benefits exceed the costs? (*Neither the defense contract nor the farm subsidy program is efficient, because the costs for both are $60 billion and the benefits are only $50 billion.*)

B. If only these three Senators are voting in a key Senate subcommittee and if majority voting is used, which of these programs is likely to be approved? (*A majority vote will result in both programs being defeated if the Senators vote strictly on what is best for their own constituents, because the costs are greater than the benefits for both programs for the constituents of two of the three Senators. Specifically, the Midwestern and Western Senators would both vote against the defense contract, and the Eastern and Western Senators*

---

[1] Developed by Jeffrey Blais and Raymond J. Pouliot, and originally published in *The Senior Economist* by the National Council on Economic Education in 1992.

would vote against the farm subsidies.)

C. If you were the Eastern Senator, what could you do to try and get one of the other Senators to vote for the defense contract? (*The Eastern Senator might approach the Midwestern Senator and offer to vote for the farm subsidy program if, and only if, the Midwestern Senator agrees to vote for the defense contract. Or the Midwestern Senator might propose the same arrangement to the Eastern Senator. If that happens, the benefits to the constituents in both the East and the Midwest will be $45 billion, and the costs $40 billion.*)

17. Explain that this "logrolling" could lead to both programs passing, despite the fact that the costs are greater than the benefits for both of them. The Western Senator can try to call attention to the "back room deals" and "pork barrel" politics, to try to defeat the programs when a vote is taken in the full Senate. Or, she can try to find a project that will benefit people in her district, and "trade" her vote in support of one or both of these projects in return for the Eastern and/or Midwestern Senators' votes. And so the log rolls on.

CLOSURE
Review the key points of the lesson. Explain that many factors, including special interest effects, voting costs that lead many people not to vote in elections, information costs that lead most voters to be rationally ignorant about at least some of the things they vote on, logrolling by elected officials, and other kinds of problems identified by public choice economists can lead to systematic inefficiencies in government policies and programs. Note that all of these problems stem from the fact that voters, elected officials, and government employees often pursue their own self-interests. That doesn't mean there is no economic role for the government to play in a market economy. But it does add large costs to many kinds of government programs, and in that sense

supports the idea of a limited role for government in a democratic market system.

ASSESSMENT
Ask your students to read the following true story and answer the questions that follow.

In 1995, the State of Wisconsin created the Southeast Wisconsin Professional Baseball Park District. This is a local unit of government that governs the stadium for the Milwaukee Brewers Baseball Club. The District issued bonds to build the Milwaukee baseball stadium. It collects a 0.1 percent local sales tax in five counties (population of over 1.6 million people) in southeastern Wisconsin, which will eventually pay off the bonds.

The stadium, named Miller Park, opened in April 2001. Miller Park is a baseball fan's dream. It has a natural grass playing field, seating for 43,000 fans, several luxury boxes, great restaurants, and a fan-shaped retractable roof that can be opened or closed in 10 minutes. Best of all, the seating is designed so that fans nearly everywhere are close to the action on the field.

Approval of the state law authorizing the tax to help pay for Miller Park came after intense lobbying of the State Legislature by several groups including the governor, representatives of professional baseball, Brewers' baseball fans, hotel owners, tavern owners, and restaurant owners. These groups argued that the social benefits of keeping professional baseball in Milwaukee were greater than the social costs. Economists, by and large, were skeptical of these claims. Several economists argued that Miller Park was a classic case of public choice economics. To explore that idea, have students discuss the following questions:

1. Who benefits from the State Legislature's decision to use a tax to pay for part of the construction costs of Miller Park? (*The benefits go to the Brewers' professional baseball organization, Brewers' baseball fans,*

hotel owners, tavern owners, and restaurant owners in the Milwaukee area. State legislators who voted for the tax received political and financial support from the groups that had large financial interests in the stadium.)

2. Are the benefits concentrated among relatively few people? (*Yes. The benefits go to the Brewers' organization, fans, some Milwaukee businesses, and some politicians.*)

3. Who is hurt by the state decision to use a tax to pay for part of the construction costs of Miller Park? (*People who pay the higher local sales tax in the five Wisconsin counties. They pay taxes to support a stadium that most will never visit.*)

4. Are the costs spread out over many people? (*Yes. The population in the five counties is over 1.6 million people.*)

5. Do you think most of these taxpayers were deeply interested in the stadium issue? Is a tax revolt or anti-incumbent political backlash likely? (*To be sure, some taxpayers grumbled about paying for a service that they do not use. But most voters are not very concerned one way or another. After all, the 0.1 percent local sales tax is a small part of their overall tax bill, and their total budget.*)

6. Is Miller Park a good example of public choice theory in action? (*It appears that it is. The State Legislature responded to pressure from interest groups to deliver the stadium. The analysis of the costs and benefits suggests that the social benefits derived by the fans and businesses are less than the social costs (the tax) paid by thousands of taxpayers, few of whom will ever visit Miller Park.*)

Activity 1
Student Information Sheet for Elections 1 & 2

GROUP 1

If option A is elected, you will receive $0.

If option B is elected, you will receive $5.

GROUP 2

If option A is elected, you will receive $0.

If option B is elected, you will receive $5.

GROUP 3

If option A is elected, you will receive $3.

If option B is elected, you will receive $0.

GROUP 4

If option A is elected, you will receive $3.

If option B is elected, you will receive $0.

GROUP 5

If option A is elected, you will receive $5.

If option B is elected, you will receive $0.

From *Focus: High School Economics,* © National Council on Economic Education, New York, NY

Activity 2
Classroom Money

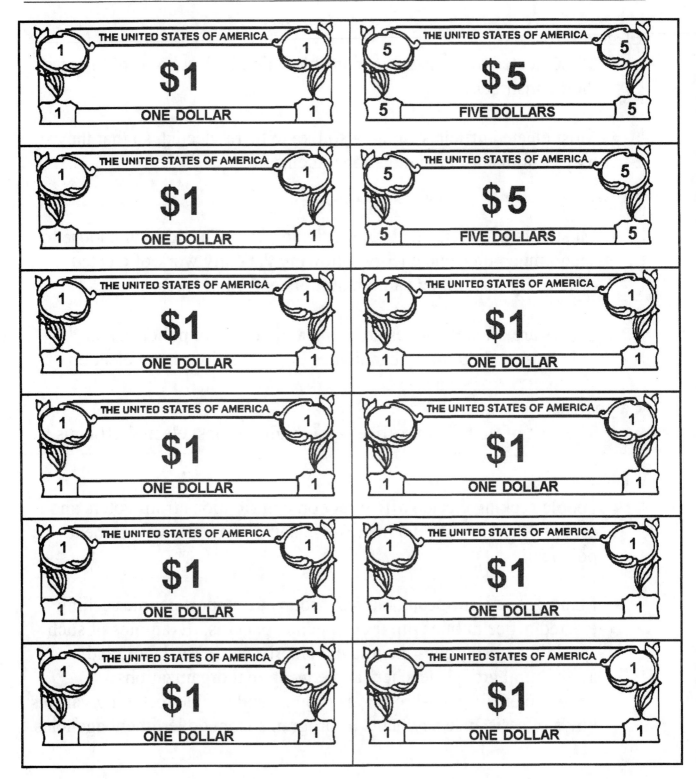

Visual 1
Public Choice Theory 101

Elected Officials

- Most elected officials are responsible individuals who want to serve their constituents.

- Most elected officials would also like to be re-elected, so that they may continue to serve their constituents.

Voters

- Most voters are busy with their private lives. They do not choose to spend much time and energy following the daily work of elected officials or government administrators and employees.

- Voters are often uninterested in most government policies, and uninformed about many candidates or propositions in an election.

Campaigns

- The cost of running for office is too high for most elected officials to pay personally.

- People seeking elected office rely on contributions from voters and groups who have special interests in some particular government policies.

- Many voters join special interest groups to support people seeking elected office in line with their special concerns. Examples of such special interest groups include the elderly; business, labor, and agricultural groups; teachers and educational organizations; environmental groups; religious groups; and people receiving various kinds of assistance payments or programs from government agencies.

Visual 2
Costs and Benefits of Voting: Elections 1 & 2

Group #	Benefits of Electing: Option A	Option B
1	$0	$5
2	0	5
3	3	0
4	3	0
5	5	0

1. What are the total benefits if option A is chosen?

2. What are the total benefits if option B is chosen?

3. If each of the five groups has the same number of voters, will option A or option B be chosen?

Visual 3
Logrolling Across the Land

	(Dollar values in billions)			
	Programs:			
	1) Defense Contract		**2) Farm Subsidies**	
Voter	Benefits to Constituents	Cost to Constituents	Benefits to Constituents	Cost to Constituents
Eastern Senator	$40	$20	$5	$20
Midwestern Senator	5	20	40	20
Western Senator	5	20	5	20

1. Which of these programs is economically efficient – i.e., the benefits exceed the costs?

2. If majority voting is used and only these three Senators vote (perhaps in a key Senate subcommittee), which of these programs is likely to be approved?

3. If you were the Eastern Senator, what could you do to try to get one of the other Senators to vote for the defense contract?

4. What role does the Western Senator play in this election?

Source: Blais, Jeffrey and Raymond J. Pouliet. *The Senior Economist,* National Council on Economic Education, 1992.

Appendix
Background Material on Public Choice Economics

Many people and writers have long adopted a cynical view of government and the political process. For example, some of Dickens' characters come to mind, as does Henry Adams' novel, *Democracy,* Joseph Heller's *Good as Gold,* and historian Charles Beard's famous work, *An Economic Interpretation of the Constitution.*

What is really different about public choice economics is the rigorous study of how people in the public sector systematically respond to the economic incentives they face. Admittedly, that still seems like a very simple idea. In fact, when the idea was summarized in the press after James Buchanan's Nobel prize was awarded, many people wondered how such a simple idea could merit such a prestigious award. The answer is that while the basic idea is very simple, it is often difficult and complex to trace the many different ways the idea shows up in real world settings. That is especially true because allegations of self-interested behavior by public officials are frequently denied and the evidence of such behavior is normally covered up by those who want to keep it hidden from the electorate.

Self-interest is a very powerful idea, however, and can lead to surprising insights when used by economists as skilled as Buchanan. He and other public choice economists, and some political scientists, used it to identify many additional concepts and issues, such as special-interest effects, "rational ignorance" on the part of voters, declining voter registration and turnout levels, inconsistencies in election results and voter preferences, the importance of controlling agendas when inconsistent outcomes are possible, models of how candidates try to package themselves to be most successful in various elections, and how they bargain to get the things they want once they are elected. Taken together, all of these ideas build up to a theory of "government failure" that often parallels economists' work on market failures, when problems such as public goods and externalities occur. (Lessons 11, 12, and 14 deal with market failures.)

Government policies are often suggested as ways to deal with market failures, so the idea of systematic government failure raises a fundamental question: Can we really depend on government actions to correct for market failures? Economists' answer to that question is a firm "It all depends." It depends on whether the expected benefits of a policy are greater than the expected costs. Public choice models show that those costs must include regular and often substantial provisions for government failures. They also force us to recognize that the very reasons markets fail to provide the right amount of certain goods and services are often likely to make it difficult for the government to determine and implement the right policies to deal with those same goods and services.

Appendix
(Continued)

Public choice models therefore provide a modern argument for maintaining a limited role of government in a market economy on the one hand, while encouraging searches for legal and constitutional arrangements to limit some kinds of government failure on the other. Debates over constitutional amendments imposing term limits and requiring a federal balanced budget are often promoted on these grounds; but of course there is a great deal of debate about the economic and political desirability of such reforms.

Longer treatments of public choice economics can be found in most college principles of economics textbooks, particularly those written by James Gwartney, Richard Stroup, and Russell Sobel (*Economics: Private and Public Choice*, 9th ed., Harcourt, 2000), and Robert Ekelund and Robert Tollison (*Economics*, 4th ed., Addison-Wesley Education, 1997).

LESSON FOURTEEN
WHEN THERE ISN'T PURE COMPETITION

INTRODUCTION

Most markets do not fit the strict assumptions of perfect competition: many sellers selling identical products in a market that is relatively easy to enter and exit. Imperfectly competitive markets can differ from perfect competition in terms of one or more of these factors, and in varying degrees. In most markets, products are *not* identical, but there may be several close substitutes. Many markets are not easy to enter because of high capital costs and the difficulty of competing with established producers selling well known, heavily advertised brands. And many important markets are characterized by a few large sellers rather than many small ones. For example, among the U.S. producers of such products as motor vehicles, cereal breakfast foods, chewing gum, cigarettes, photocopying equipment, and sewing machines, the four largest firms account for more than three-fourths of the total industry sales to U.S. firms. In many local markets, there are sometimes only a few competing firms even when there are more firms competing at the national or regional level. For example, even though there may be many sellers of gasoline in a large city, vigorous competition may exist only between a few sellers in a specific neighborhood. Therefore, it is important for students to understand the following characteristics and consequences of imperfectly competitive markets:

1. Firms in imperfectly competitive markets are often interdependent, with the actions of one firm greatly affecting business conditions for its competitors.

2. Large firms competing with other large firms often try to avoid direct price competition, because of the uncertainty concerning how their competitors will react, and a joint interest in keeping prices above the level that would prevail in perfect competition.

3. Both large and small firms in imperfectly competitive markets emphasize nonprice competition, especially advertising that stresses real or imagined differences in the quality of goods and services provided to customers.

4. In markets dominated by a few large firms, there are strong pressures supporting price collusion, although the collusion must often be tacit rather than explicit in countries such as the United States, where such price fixing is illegal.

Competition between many small firms producing identical products is desirable because it results in lower prices for consumers and a more efficient use of scarce resources. Imperfect competition typically leads to less output and higher prices. But sometimes these negative results are offset because large firms are able to take advantage of economies of scale, which lower production costs and prices. And there is clear evidence that consumers like the greater variety of product styles and features that are associated with some degree of imperfect competition.

Evaluating any specific imperfectly competitive market involves a careful weighing of these costs and benefits. Public policy should undoubtedly be directed toward eliminating extreme concentrations of market power and flagrant cases of collusive behavior in order to maintain an effective degree of competition. But such policies should stop far short of breaking up large firms just because a market isn't perfectly competitive.

CONCEPTS

Competition and market structures
Interdependence in imperfect competition
Nonprice competition
Collusion

Antitrust policy and regulation of natural monopolies

CONTENT STANDARD

Competition among sellers lowers costs and prices, and encourages producers to produce more of what consumers are willing and able to buy.

BENCHMARKS

Sellers compete on the basis of price, product quality, customer service, product design and variety, and advertising.

The level of competition in a market is influenced by the number of buyers and sellers in the market.

The level of competition in an industry is affected by the ease with which new producers can enter the industry.

Collusion among buyers or sellers reduces the level of competition in a market. Collusion is more difficult in markets with large numbers of buyers and sellers.

OBJECTIVES

♦ Students define perfectly competitive and imperfectly competitive markets.

♦ Students evaluate the role of nonprice competition in imperfectly competitive markets.

♦ Students explain the tendency toward price collusion in imperfectly competitive markets.

♦ Students assess government's role in dealing with imperfectly competitive markets.

LESSON DESCRIPTION

A series of activities are used to explore: 1) demand and pricing decisions facing imperfectly competitive firms, 2) interdependence in situations where actions by one firm have a large effect on the remaining competitors in a market, 3) the tendency for firms with formal or informal pricing agreements to go through phases of colluding and then cheating on the collusive agreement, and 4) public policy decisions over mergers when it is not clear whether a merger will result in more or less effective competition in an already concentrated industry.

TIME REQUIRED

Three class periods – Day one: procedures 1-7. Day two: procedures 8-16. Day three: procedure 17 and Assessment.

MATERIALS

* Activity 1: Perfectly and Imperfectly Competitive Markets, one per student
* Activity 2: The Prisoners' Dilemma, one per student
* Activity 3: Dueling Gas Stations, one per student
* Activity 4: We're All in This Together…Aren't We?, one per student
* Activity 5: The Airlines Case: Is Big Better?, one per student
* Buyer and seller cards, student score sheets, and one class tally sheet for the Classroom Market for Crude Oil (Lesson 3 of this volume).
* Several different brands of two or three different flavors of soft drinks (colas, lemon-lime, orange, etc.); several blindfolds; paper drinking cups; and a bag of ice.

PROCEDURES

1. Explain that this lesson will examine the causes and consequences of imperfect competition, and some strategies frequently employed by imperfectly competitive firms.

2. Distribute a copy of Activity 1 to each student. After discussing the major characteristics of perfectly and imperfectly competitive markets, ask the students to answer the questions on the activity sheet:

Considering these characteristics of perfectly and imperfectly competitive markets, imagine that you are a seller in each of the following markets. Explain what you think would happen to your sales levels if you raised or lowered the price of your product. Specifically, how much do you think sales would change, and why?

A. Wheat farmer. (*Agricultural products are probably the best example of a perfectly competitive market* – except for the presence of government price controls, as discussed in Lesson 6. *If you raise your price above the market price, your sales will be zero because wheat buyers can buy the identical product at the market price from any one of many other sellers. If you lower your price, your sales will not increase. You can sell all you want at the market price, so it doesn't make sense to lower your price below the market price.*)

B. Local electric company. (*This is an example of a natural monopoly, the most extreme form of an imperfectly competitive market. The product has no close substitutes, and there is only one seller in the market. If you increase your price your sales will fall, but quite possibly very little because the demand for electricity is inelastic. Similarly, if you lower your price, your sales will increase only slightly.*) See Lesson 7 on elasticity of demand.

C. U.S. automobile manufacturer. (*This is an example of an oligopoly – a market with a few large sellers. These markets are characterized by a high degree of* **interdependence**. *If you raise your price you may well lose a lot of sales* **if** *your competitors do not increase their prices, too, because many consumers consider different brands of cars to be close substitutes. If you lower your price you may capture some of your competitors' sales* **if** *they do not also lower their*

prices. If they do match your price decrease, the number of cars you sell will probably increase very little. You can't be sure what will happen if you raise or lower your price, because the results depend upon what other sellers do.*)

D. Flower shop. (*In this market, as with automobile manufacturers, the products of different sellers are close substitutes, and changes in prices at one flower store can affect sales at other stores where flowers are sold. But there are many more places where people can buy flowers in most U.S. cities than there are U.S. automobile manufacturers. The imperfectly competitive markets for flowers and other retail items are examples of the market structure that economists call monopolistic competition. In these markets, if you raise your price you will lose some sales, and if you lower your price you will gain some sales. But the actual results depend upon how many sellers are in the market, the extent to which consumers consider the products and support services of the competing shops to be close substitutes, and how sensitive customers are to the price changes.*)

3. If you did not use the "Classroom Market in Crude Oil" activity to demonstrate market clearing or equilibrium price and quantity in Lesson 3, or to demonstrate changes in supply and demand in Lesson 4, conduct the market game as described in Lesson 3, to establish a competitive market price and quantity. If you did use the activity, either remind the students of what the competitive price and quantity was (using the buyer or seller decks from Lesson 3), or conduct the activity again, using the buyer and seller decks from Lesson 3, establishing a market price of about $34 a barrel for crude oil.

4. Conduct the Classroom Market for Crude Oil again, using the buyer and seller decks from Lesson 3, but this time conduct one round with only four sellers. Assign one seller to each corner of the trading area, to keep the sellers separated. Allow each seller to make trades only when he or she is standing in the assigned corner. Instruct both buyers and sellers to make only one trade with each card, drawing a new card before they make another trade. Keep a class tally sheet as explained in Lesson 3, and when the new market clearing price is established (usually in five to 10 minutes) stop the trading.

5. Now bring the four sellers together in the middle of the trading area, tell them that they will stand next to each other in the next trading round, and give them a few minutes to discuss a joint strategy. You may want to let them discuss this outside of the classroom, while you discuss the market price and market structure of the last round with the rest of the class. When the sellers have their strategy set, conduct another round of trading until a new market price is clearly established, as recorded on the class tally sheet.

6. Debrief the activity, pointing out that when the market became less competitive as the number of sellers was decreased, equilibrium price increased and quantity decreased, even though the deck of seller cards (representing the firms' costs of producing and selling crude oil) did not change. Supply decreased (shifted to the left – see Lesson 4) because the number of sellers decreased. This is basically what happened to the world crude oil market in the 1970s, as a market that had been competitive became imperfectly competitive. Production cutbacks and price increases for crude oil and petroleum-based products were initiated by the Organization of Petroleum Exporting Countries (OPEC), the most famous current example of a cartel. The **collusion** to raise prices among sellers was probably much more explicit and effective in the second round, when sellers could easily meet to set a joint strategy, and

more easily keep track of what other sellers were doing during the trading round. This probably resulted in an even higher price and lower quantity sold.

7. Point out that oil and gas prices decreased sharply (adjusted for inflation) through the 1980s and most of the 1990s, then rose again around 2000 as a result of several factors, including increased global and U.S. demand, capacity constraints at U.S. refineries, higher production costs associated with producing environmentally "cleaner" gasoline in some parts of the United States, and renewed efforts by OPEC and some other oil producers to limit production and increase prices.

8. Briefly discuss why firms in imperfectly competitive markets must make price and output decisions under conditions of interdependence and a high degree of uncertainty. The key issue is that, with a smaller number of firms, when one firm changes its output and price levels (price competition), or when one firm introduces a new product, launches a new advertising campaign, or adopts some other competitive strategy (**nonprice competition**), that will affect the price, sales, and quite possibly profits of other firms producing similar products. Announce that the class will now consider a case of interdependence in decision making in a situation that may, at first, seem to have little to do with economics. Later, they will see how imperfectly competitive firms face exactly the same kinds of situations.

9. Distribute copies of Activity 2, The Prisoners' Dilemma. After the students have read the activity, review the payoffs facing both prisoners carefully, to make sure that students understand them.

10. Have students answer questions A through D on Activity 2, and then discuss their answers. A student who says "I would not confess and just take the one year in jail" probably doesn't understand the dilemma. Individually, for both Curly and Moe,

confessing is the best solution – offering the shortest jail term *regardless* of what the other crook does. But if the crooks are able to collude or cooperate, the total amount of jail time served by both of them will be minimized if they both refuse to confess. Despite that Curly and Moe should not confess *only* if they are absolutely certain that the other person will not confess, or if they are afraid that the other person (or that person's "associates") will somehow retaliate if they do confess. And remember, they both start out knowing that the other person is a crook!

A. 1. What would you do if you were Curly and you expected Moe to confess? Why? *(Curly should confess because in this case he expects to go to jail for 10 years if he doesn't confess, but only five years if he does.)*

2. What would you do if you were Curly and you expected Moe not to confess? Why? *(Curly should still confess because in this case he expects to go to jail for a year if he doesn't confess, but only three months if he does.)*

B. 1. What would you do if you were Moe and you expected Curly to confess? Why?

2. What would you do if you were Moe and you expected Curly not to confess? Why?

(The answers for Moe are exactly the same as for Curly. Therefore, the incentives they face may lead both Curly and Moe to confess, even though that way they both spend five years in jail, rather than only one year if they both refuse to confess.)

C. What would you do if you were Curly or Moe? Are there things other than the jail terms you should consider?

(Curly and Moe should consider the following possibilities:

1. Confess, because you serve less time that way whether the other person confesses or not, and the worst that can happen by confessing is a five-year term, while the worst that can happen by not confessing is a 10-year term.

2. Don't confess if you absolutely trust your partner not to confess. That way the total amount of time your both serve is minimized – two years total rather than 10 years if they both confess, and 10 years and three months if one confesses and one doesn't.

3. Don't confess, because you fear that if you confess and your partner doesn't, your partner or some of his other business associates will commit violent acts on various parts of your body, or against your family.)

D. Under what circumstances would Curly and Moe not confess?

(As explained in C, either because of complete trust in the partner, or complete fear. Trust is more likely if Curly and Moe have a long history of working together, and plan to work together for many years to come.)

11. To demonstrate the Prisoners' Dilemma operating in a business setting, distribute a copy of Activity 3 to all students. Allow time for them to answer questions A – C, individually or in small groups. This activity will reinforce students' understanding of the interdependence of firms in imperfectly competitive markets. It is a prisoners' dilemma problem again, because although both firms make more money if they cooperate and set higher prices, individually they both face incentives to lower price, no matter what price they believe the other seller will charge.

A. Mac is considering raising his price because he thinks that people will buy about the same amount of gasoline even if the price is raised a little. He figures that he can more than make up for the few sales he will lose with the higher price for the sales he makes. Would you advise Mac to do this? Explain your answer. *(No. Mac is correct that the overall demand for gasoline is relatively inelastic, but if he raises the price at his station and Charlie doesn't, he will lose a lot of sales.)*

B. Charlie is considering lowering his price because he thinks that he can take business away from Mac if his price is a little lower. He believes that he can more than make up for the small decrease in revenue from each gallon sold by selling a lot more gallons. Would you advise Charlie to do this? Explain your answer. *(No. Charlie is correct that he would draw business from Mac only if Mac doesn't lower his price, too. In fact, Mac may lower his price even more than Charlie does. They are both likely to wind up selling only a little more gasoline at a lower price, and making lower profits.)*

C. Can you think of any other actions that Mac or Charlie might take to increase the profitability of their businesses? *(They might try to sell more by advertising or by providing better service, clean restrooms, and free coffee, maps, or other "giveaways." These strategies are also costly, however, and may be matched by their competitors.)*

From the individual viewpoint of either Mac or Charlie, they will both expect to sell more gas by charging a lower price, regardless of whether they expect their competitor to charge a higher or lower price. But jointly, their best solution is to enter into an agreement to charge the same, relatively high price. (Note, however, that the threat of someone else opening a new gas station in the town, and the price of gas at the closest stations along the interstate highway, limit the price they can charge.) A mutual price agreement takes advantage of the fact that demand for gasoline is relatively inelastic, and reduces the risk of the competitor charging a lower price. Fortunately for U.S. consumers, such collusive agreements are illegal in this country. However, collusion can be difficult to identify and prove when the agreement is simply a tacit understanding.

In debriefing this activity, explain that prices in most imperfectly competitive markets tend to be "stickier" than in competitive markets, changing less frequently. One reason for this is the great uncertainty created by the interdependence between competitors. In some cases, however, it isn't practical to change prices very often. For example, paper catalogs and menus with price information have to be reprinted and distributed every time prices change, and that is expensive.

12. Distribute a copy of Activity 4 to each student. This activity can be conducted by collecting a pricing decision from each student, or the class may be divided into ten small groups that each make a pricing decision. The table shows clearly that what happens to a firm's profits depends upon what other firms in the industry do.

13. Ask students to read Activity 4 and, *without talking to other students – or to other groups if you are using small groups –* to decide whether to implement the price increase.

14. Collect the copies of Activity 4 and count the number of yes and no responses.

Announce the results. (If more than ten sheets are counted, the results can be interpolated from the data shown in Activity 4. If half the students raise the price, the results will be as shown for five firms; if 70 percent raise the price, the result will be as shown for seven firms, etc.) In debriefing this activity, stress that collusion can definitely benefit sellers in imperfect markets, but it is difficult to maintain collusive agreements. Again, a discussion of OPEC's problems in setting prices and maintaining production quotas in the 1980s and 1990s can be used to illustrate these points. As in many other cartels that have existed in earlier decades and centuries, firms in OPEC have a strong incentive to collude to raise prices and profits, but also face strong incentives to cheat on the cartel agreement, lowering their price (often secretly) to sell more than they are assigned to sell by the cartel.

15. To review the importance of nonprice competition, ask students to list their favorite brand of soft drink, blue jeans, automobile, and athletic shoes. Ask them to list the features that make their brand "special," and ask how much they would pay to get those special features, compared to the price they might pay for a competing brand. Estimate how much it is worth to the company that produces these brands to maintain this brand loyalty. Suggest that a rough estimate of this amount might be the price difference students were willing to pay times the number of items the company sells each year, minus the advertising and other costs associated with maintaining the brand loyalty and identification.

16. Ask students how much they are influenced by: a) advertising campaigns for their favorite products, and b) the popularity of these brands with their friends and other classmates. To investigate whether these differences are real or simply perceived, conduct a blind taste test of soft drinks, and see whether students can choose their brand from a selection of three or four competing brands of the same kind of sodas.

17. Distribute copies of Activity 5 to illustrate public policy concerns relating to imperfectly competitive markets. The purpose of the case study is to have students understand that many **antitrust policies** designed to prohibit collusion and limit firms' market power are not clear cut. Have the students read the case study and then write answers to the questions. Ask some students for their recommendations on the case, and then discuss the answers with the students, stressing the following points:

- The airline industry is an imperfectly competitive market, and the actions of one seller definitely affect other firms in the market.

- Brand loyalty associated with high advertising costs, frequent-flyer programs, and long-term safety and performance records are significant barriers to entry, as are high purchase, maintenance, and operating costs for airplanes; labor costs for highly skilled workers (pilots, mechanics, etc.); and computerized international ticketing and reservations systems.

- In general, owners of resources in a market economy are free to use these resources in whatever manner they choose. However, an important economic function of government in a market economy is to maintain competition. Therefore, the government limits property rights in certain circumstances, including prohibiting mergers of large firms in some highly concentrated industries.

- Often, the more firms in a market, the greater the degree of competition, which results in lower prices and increased output. Many markets are inherently imperfect, however; and big doesn't always mean bad if large-scale operations are required to minimize production costs. That is especially true if it is easy for some competitors to enter markets where economic profits are being earned. Note that airlines can often reroute their planes to different cities quite easily – unless gate space at airports is unavailable. On the other hand, in extreme cases such as natural monopolies – including the public utilities that provide electric, water, and sewerage service – where it is too expensive to have even two companies providing the same service, the government typically takes over these companies, or regulates the prices and/or profits of privately owned companies.

The airline case in this activity is certainly not clear-cut. A major point of difference among those evaluating this situation will be whether they believe the two companies can survive without merging. Another key point is that the two airlines are now generally serving different markets/cities.

CLOSURE

Review the characteristics of imperfectly competitive firms listed in the Introduction to this lesson, and the conclusions that immediately follow that list.

ASSESSMENT

1. Ask students to evaluate the following statement in a one or two-page essay:

"Most progress in the last century occurred in markets that are, or were, imperfectly competitive, not perfectly competitive. That progress included developing new products and lowering prices for established products. We would be better off if the government quit trying to keep markets so competitive, and let them become oligopolies or even monopolies if that's what happens in the marketplace. That's what other countries are doing already, and look how successfully their companies have been

competing with U.S. firms in recent decades."

Or

2. Have students read about a recent antitrust case, such as the case against Microsoft. You may want to start by having them check the Webpage at *http://www.usdoj.gov/atr/cases/ms_index.htm*. Let some students support the antitrust case, representing attorneys or economists at the Department of Justice; have other students oppose the case, representing attorneys or economists working for the company or companies involved in the case.

Activity 1
Perfectly and Imperfectly Competitive Markets

A perfectly competitive market is one in which many sellers produce identical products in a market that is relatively easy to enter and leave. In these markets, sellers have no control over the price of their products. They have to accept the market price and they can sell as much or as little as they want at that price.

If these conditions do not exist, the market is said to be imperfectly competitive. There are several possible kinds of imperfectly competitive markets depending upon: 1) the number of sellers, 2) the types of products produced (especially the availability of close substitutes), and 3) whether the market is easy to enter.

Considering these characteristics of perfectly and imperfectly competitive markets, imagine that you are a seller in each of the following markets. Explain what you think would happen to your sales levels if you raised or lowered the price of your product. Specifically, how much do you think sales would change, and why?

A.   Wheat farmer

       Increase your price

       Decrease your price

B.   Local electric company

       Increase your price

       Decrease your price

C.   U.S. automobile manufacturer

       Increase your price

       Decrease your price

D.   Flower shop

       Increase your price

       Decrease your price

Activity 2
The Prisoners' Dilemma

Curly and Moe are crooks. They have been caught stealing auto parts and are now sitting in separate rooms in the city jail. The District Attorney is delighted to have finally caught Curly and Moe in the act of committing a crime. The DA knows that Curly and Moe are guilty not only of this crime, but also of several other burglaries that have occurred during the past year. She *knows* they are guilty of these crimes, but she can't prove that in court.

The DA decides to try to persuade Curly and/or Moe to confess by offering them a deal. She talks to each one separately and says: "I have enough on both of you to send you to jail for a year. But if you alone confess to the other robberies, which carry a 10-year sentence, you will get off with three months and only your partner will serve 10 years. If you both confess to the other robberies, you will both get five years."

Don't worry here about whether the constitutional rights of Curly and Moe are being violated, or whether they would actually serve these exact sentences if convicted. Those are interesting and important issues, but they can be dealt with in another activity or course. For now, accept the four following propositions:

1. If Curly confesses and Moe doesn't, Curly goes to jail for three months and Moe for ten years.

2. If Moe confesses and Curly doesn't, Moe goes to jail for three months and Curly for ten years.

3. If both Curly and Moe confess, they both go to jail for five years.

4. If neither Curly nor Moe confess, they both go to jail for one year.

Given those results, answer the following questions:

A. 1. What would you do if you were Curly and you expected Moe to confess? Why?

    2. What would you do if you were Curly and you expected Moe not to confess? Why?

B. 1. What would you do if you were Moe and you expected Curly to confess? Why?

    2. What would you do if you were Moe and you expected Curly not to confess? Why?

C. What would you do if you were Curly or Moe? Are there things other than jail terms you should consider?

D. Under what circumstances would Curly and Moe not confess?

Activity 3
Dueling Gas Stations

Mac and Charlie each own and operate gasoline stations across the street from each other on the edge of town, near an interstate highway. There are no other service stations in this town. They are now selling their gasoline for exactly the same price and they both have large signs listing their price.

A. Mac is considering raising his price because he thinks that people will buy about the same amount of gasoline even if the price is raised a little. He figures that he can more than make up for the few sales he will lose with the higher price for the sales he makes. Would you advise Mac to do this? Explain your answer.

B. Charlie is considering lowering his price because he thinks that he can take business away from Mac if his price is a little lower. He believes he can more than make up for the small decrease in revenue from each gallon sold by selling a lot more gallons. Would you advise Charlie to do this? Explain your answer.

C. Can you think of any other actions that Mac or Charlie might take to increase the profitability of their businesses?

Activity 4
We're All in This Together. . . Aren't We?

Imagine that you represent one of the 10 largest soft-drink companies in the nation, and that you are attending a meeting of the American Soft Drink Producers Association. During an afternoon session the association economist presents evidence showing that, at current prices, the demand for all soft drinks (not one particular brand) is inelastic. This means that if prices are lowered, consumers will buy more soft drinks, but the increase in sales will be relatively small. If prices are raised, consumers will buy fewer soft drinks, but the decrease in units sold will be relatively small. The economist presents evidence showing that if all of the 10 largest companies increase their prices 15 percent, each company's profits would increase 12 percent. Each company would sell a little less than now, but at higher prices. An off-the-record motion is made (after all, you wouldn't want the Justice Department to bring charges of illegal price fixing) that each firm raise its prices by 15 percent. The unofficial motion passes unanimously.

Returning to your office, you must decide whether to send out a memo announcing a price increase. Having had some training in economics, you realize that the effect of a price increase on your profits depends on how many other firms really go along with the price increase.

The following table shows the change in your profits under the different possible outcomes. Under these circumstances, would you raise your price?

Number of firms raising price	Number of firms not raising price	Percent change in profits for firms raising price	Percent change in profits for firms not raising price
10	0	+15	—
9	1	+12	+100
8	2	+9	+75
7	3	+6	+50
6	4	+2	+30
5	5	0	+18
4	6	-5	+10
3	7	-15	+6
2	8	-30	+4
1	9	-50	+2
0	10	—	0

_____ Yes, I would raise the price of my product.
_____ No, I would not raise the price of my product.

Explain your decision. _____

_____

Activity 5
The Airlines Case: Is Big Better?

Imagine that it is 10 years from now and you have been hired as a consulting economist for the Antitrust Division of the Department of Justice. The following case is given to you for review. Use what you know about markets plus the information in the case to suggest a policy to the assistant attorney general in charge of antitrust actions.

Two relatively new airline companies, Gigantic Airways and Nationwide Airlines, have announced plans to merge. The leading airline companies and their respective shares of total U.S. ticket sales over the past year are:

United	17%
American	15%
Delta	14%
Gigantic	11%
Northwest	10%
Nationwide	9%
Southwest	8%
All others	16%

During the past five years, the airline industry has become more concentrated as smaller airlines have gone out of business or merged with larger companies. Note that the four largest airlines now account for 57 percent of total sales.

Arguments against the merger: Some staff attorneys at the Justice Department believe the merger should be opposed. They believe the merger of the fourth and sixth largest airlines will continue what they regard as an unhealthy trend toward larger airlines, a higher concentration of sales, and less competition. The newly merged airline will be the largest in the nation, with more sales than the leading firm now has. Aggressive advertising campaigns by the large airlines are raising

significant barriers to the entry for potential new competitors.

Arguments for the merger: Attorneys for the companies involved have filed papers arguing that the merger would not materially affect competition in the industry. Most of Gigantic Airlines' business consists of coast-to-coast flights using very large aircraft. Nationwide Airlines specializes in shorter flights using smaller planes and the hub concept. Only four cities are now served by both airlines. Furthermore, the attorneys argue that neither airline can survive in the long run without the merger, because of heavy competition from the largest firms in the industry today. The merged company would have a larger advertising budget and could realize substantial economies in their reservation and ticket sales operations. The company attorneys state that if either of these two companies fail, the lost sales will go primarily to the largest three airlines, and thus increase concentration in the market even more. The attorneys argue that one strong competitor is better than two smaller companies going out of business.

Question: Should the Justice Department announce that it will oppose the merger? What is your recommendation? Explain your position.

_____ Support the merger.

_____ Oppose the merger.

Why? _____

_____

_____

LESSON FIFTEEN
UNTIL THE LAST UNIT EQUALS. . .

INTRODUCTION

Marginalism is an important concept in both personal and social decision-making. Choices are rarely all-or-nothing propositions, but instead usually deal with incremental (marginal) changes – giving up a little of one thing to get a little more of something else. Should a firm produce a few more or a few less units of output? Should a consumer buy a bit more of this and a bit less of that? Are the additional revenues generated by hiring another worker equal to or greater than the additional cost? Should the government increase taxes to hire a few more teachers so class sizes can be lowered by three to five students? All of these decisions are made "at the margin" – with clear marginal costs and marginal benefits to be compared. And surprisingly, comparing marginal benefits and costs turns out to be an effective and relatively easy way to maximize a consumer's total level of satisfaction, or a business' level of total profits, or the net benefits of a government program or policy.

Nevertheless, the marginalist way of thinking isn't widely taught or appreciated, and it takes some practice to master. In fact, although marginalism is now one of the cornerstones of economic analysis and the economic way of thinking, not even economists understood the approach until the late nineteenth century, more than a century after the development of economics as a formal and separate discipline.

CONCEPTS

Marginalism
Diminishing returns
Marginal product
Marginal cost

Marginal utility
Diminishing marginal utility

CONTENT STANDARD

Effective decision making requires comparing the additional costs of alternatives with the additional benefits. Most choices involve doing a little more or a little less of something; few choices are all-or-nothing decisions.

BENCHMARKS

Marginal benefit is the change in total benefit resulting from an action. Marginal cost is the change in total cost resulting from an action.

As long as the marginal benefit of an activity exceeds the marginal cost, people are better off doing more of it; when the marginal cost exceeds the marginal benefit, they are better off doing less of it.

To produce the profit-maximizing level of output and hire the optimal number of workers and other resources, producers must compare the marginal benefits and marginal costs of producing a little more with the marginal benefits and marginal costs of producing a little less.

OBJECTIVES

♦ Students apply marginal analysis in economic decision making.

♦ Students define marginal product as the additional output produced by each successive unit of an input.

♦ Students explain that as one input increases (keeping others the same), the marginal product of the input will eventually decrease (i.e., the law of diminishing returns).

♦ Students explain that marginal cost is the extra cost of producing an additional unit of output.

♦   Students explain that marginal cost increases as more labor is added because of diminishing returns.

♦   Students explain that for most, if not all, goods and services, the additional satisfaction or marginal utility a consumer gets from purchasing each additional unit of a product will eventually decrease.

LESSON DESCRIPTION

Several students participate in an activity in which they purchase and consume marshmallows up to the point where the value they place on the additional satisfaction they receive from eating one more marshmallow is less than what they must pay for it. Students share examples from their own experiences in which they have used marginal analysis as consumers. Then they participate in a Left-Foot Pattern Factory production simulation, and use marginal analysis to decide what number of workers to hire to maximize profits (or minimize losses). Finally, they use marginal analysis to discuss whether they will be hired for a summer job.

TIME REQUIRED

One-and-a-half class periods. Day one (half day) – procedures 1-7. Day two – procedures 8-27 and Assessment.

MATERIALS
- Large bag of marshmallows
- 45 nickels
- A large supply of 8 1/2" × 11" scrap paper
- One pencil
- Masking tape
- Activity 1: Left-Foot Pattern Production Table, one per student, and a transparency.
- Activity 2: Assessment, one per student.

PROCEDURES

1.   Explain that the purpose of this lesson is to show that people, businesses, and the government make decisions at the margin.

Producers (including government agencies) must decide whether to produce a few more or a few less units of the goods and services they provide. Consumers must decide whether to buy a few more or a few less units of hundreds of different goods and services. The government must decide how many miles of streets and highways to pave, how many schools and military aircraft to build, etc.

2.   Ask for three volunteers to participate in an activity that involves eating marshmallows.

3.   Give each of the three volunteers 15 nickels. Tell them they may purchase marshmallows to eat at a price of $.05 per marshmallow. They must immediately eat each marshmallow they buy, and once they stop buying marshmallows they can not start buying them again. They can keep any nickels they do not spend on marshmallows.

4.   Begin selling marshmallows, one at a time, to the students. After they eat each marshmallow, ask them if they would like to purchase and eat another one. Continue selling marshmallows until each student decides not to purchase another one. The volunteers will probably consume different amounts of marshmallows.

5.   Ask: Why did each of you stop buying marshmallows? (*Most students will stop before eating 15 marshmallows, but some may not. Point out that different people have different tastes and preferences – and different stomach capacities. Also, some students may not have eaten as much at breakfast or lunch as others. For almost everyone, however, after eating several marshmallows, the next marshmallow won't be as appealing as the first ones they ate. Eventually, buying one more marshmallow isn't worth it.*) Ask the three students, "How many more marshmallows will you eat at a price of zero?" (*Some may eat a few more marshmallows at the lower price, but eventually they will stop even at a price of zero.*)

6. Explain to students that their decision to purchase additional marshmallows depended on the additional satisfaction, or **marginal utility,** they expected to gain from each marshmallow. Their total satisfaction increased with each one they bought, but at some point the additional satisfaction began to diminish with each additional marshmallow. This illustrates the law of **diminishing marginal utility**. Because of that economic law, people stop buying an item when the value of the satisfaction from the next unit of the same item becomes less than the price they must pay for it. (Note that for some products, such as houses, cars, or smallpox vaccinations, this usually happens after only one or two units are purchased. For other kinds of products, such as shirts or french fries, people usually buy many more units. Both price and marginal utility are important in determining how many units are purchased.)

7. Ask students for examples of where they have used marginal analysis when buying goods or services. (*Examples may include deciding whether to buy one more soda at a ball game on a hot day; to super size an order of fast food; or to take advantage of a "buy one, get one at half price" offer*.) Suggest other examples, such as selling newspapers from vending machines that allow people to take more than one paper – but one reason they usually don't is because the marginal utility of a second paper is very low, and maybe even zero or negative. Contrast that with vending machines for candy and chewing gum, which do not let people take "seconds" unless they put in more coins. Note that for these products, the marginal utility of a second unit of the product is usually higher than it is for a second newspaper.

8. Tell students that like consumers, producers use marginal analysis when making production decisions. Announce that to illustrate this point they are going to participate as workers in the Left-Foot Pattern Factory.

9. Use masking tape to mark off an area on the floor approximately 36" square. Tell students that this space represents the Left-Foot Pattern Factory, in which the class will produce left-foot shoe, boot, and sandal patterns. Demonstrate by standing inside the square, placing your left foot on a piece of 8 1/2" × 11" scrap paper, and tracing your foot with a pencil.

10. Place a large supply of scrap paper inside the factory with a pencil. Select one student to produce left-foot tracings. Inform the class that you will be the quality control inspector, who ensures left-foot pattern standards. Instruct the student worker to produce as many left-foot patterns as possible in three minutes.

11. Begin the production period. Stop after three minutes and inspect each left-foot pattern. Keep and count only those of good quality.

12. Distribute a copy of Activity 1 to each student. Using a visual of Activity 1, show students how to complete the table for zero workers and for one worker. Discard all left-foot patterns produced in round 1.

13. Select a second student worker to join the first worker in the Left-Foot Pattern Factory. Instruct both workers to produce as many left-foot patterns as possible in three minutes. They may only use the scrap paper, one pencil, and the factory work space.

14. Begin production. After three minutes, stop production and inspect the left-foot patterns. Discard those that fail to meet quality standards. Instruct students to fill in the new information in column 2 on Activity 1.

15. Repeat the same procedure adding one more worker for four more rounds. Remind students to complete column 2 on Activity 1 after each round. Remind students that they must work inside the factory walls (the masking tape).

16. After six rounds, stop production and ask the class to fill in column 3 with the number

of additional left-foot patterns produced in the **Marginal Product** column. Explain that this column shows how many additional left-foot patterns were produced each time one more worker was hired. For example, using data from the sample, you might say, "The first worker produced 7 left-foot patterns; therefore, the additional left-foot patterns produced compared with no workers at all is 7. Hiring a second worker brings the total number of left-foot patterns to 15. Thus, the second worker accounts for the production of 8 more left-foot patterns than when only one worker is used. The marginal or additional product is 8." Continue along these lines as shown in the table following procedure 21. Substitute numbers from the class simulation in column 3, Activity 1.

17. Ask and discuss the following questions:

A. What happened to the total number of left-foot patterns produced as additional workers were hired? (*increased*)

B. What happened to marginal product as additional workers were hired? (*It probably increased initially, then decreased.*)

C. Why do you think this occurred? (*At first, having more workers may increase efficiency as they help each other and specialize. Soon, however, there is not enough space, tasks, or capital equipment (pencil and factory space) to keep all workers busy all of the time. Marginal product begins to diminish.*) Point out to students that this is an example of the law of diminishing returns.

18. Explain that the law of **diminishing returns** states that as more units of a variable input are added to one or more fixed inputs, eventually the number of additional units of output produced will begin to fall. This occurs because the fixed input is spread more and more

thinly across the growing number of variable inputs.

19. Divide the class into management teams of four to five students each. Ask each team to decide how many workers it will hire and to prepare a justification for its decision.

20. After allowing time for the students to reach decisions, ask each group to announce its decision and give its justification. (Many times, groups will stop hiring workers as soon as marginal product starts to diminish. Later, they will see that this decision is incorrect.)

21. Tell the groups that you have additional information for them that might make them change their decisions. Tell them to label column 4, "Value of Additional Left-Foot Patterns Produced." Explain that each left-foot pattern is worth $.02. Thus, the "Value of Additional Left-Foot Patterns" produced is the marginal product of the last worker hired times $.02. For example, the value of the second worker to the firm is that worker's marginal product times $.02, and so on. Have students label column 5, "**Marginal Cost** of Labor (3 min. worked)." Tell students that workers earn $.12 for each three minutes worked. Therefore, the additional labor cost of the first worker compared to having no workers at all is $.12. In fact, the marginal cost of each worker (for three minutes of work) is $.12.

LEFT-FOOT PATTERN PRODUCTION
TABLE (SAMPLE)

# of Workers (1)	Left-Foot Patterns Produced (2)	Marginal Product (3)	Value of Additional Left-Foot Patterns Produced (4)	Marginal Cost of Labor (3 min. worked) (5)
0	0	—	0	0
1	7	7	$.14	$.12
2	15	8	.16	.12
3	23	8	.16	.12
4	30	7	.14	.12
5	33	3	.06	.12
6	34	1	.02	.12

22. Allow the management teams time to decide how many workers to hire. Then ask each team for its new decision and justification. Teams should stop hiring workers at the point where the marginal cost of hiring the next worker exceeds the additional (marginal) value of what that worker produces. In the sample, four workers should be hired.

23. Explain the hiring rule: "Additional workers will be hired as long as the additional (marginal) value of the output of the next worker employed exceeds the additional (marginal) cost of hiring that worker." Ask students to discuss why this happens. (*With a set wage rate and falling marginal product, it eventually costs more to hire an additional worker than the worker adds to revenues. Note that additional workers are not as productive because they have less equipment and space to work with, not because the later workers hired are less motivated or diligent than those hired earlier. In fact, in terms of doing this kind of simple job, we can assume the workers are essentially identical and interchangeable – we could switch the first and last workers hired and* still see the same general production patterns – which is why they are all paid the same wage.)

24. Ask students how many workers should be hired if labor costs increase to $.15 per three minutes of work. (*Using the sample data, three workers should be hired.*)

25. Ask students what happens to the per unit costs of producing left-foot patterns, once the law of diminishing returns sets in. (*With the constant wage rate per worker and diminishing returns in production, the per unit cost of producing additional left-foot patterns increases. You may want to show that by dividing the total costs of the workers hired by the number of left-foot patterns produced at each employment level after diminishing returns set in.*)

26. Because per unit production costs rise as output levels increase in the range of diminishing returns, what must happen to product price in order to make producers willing to produce and sell more units? (*The price must rise to cover the higher per unit costs. This is, in fact, a key rationale for the law of supply – quantity supplied increases as price increases – because the higher price allows producers to cover their higher per unit production costs as output levels increase.*)

27. Present this problem to the class: Three Service Club members work in the snack stand selling snacks for 30 minutes at half time during each high school basketball game. Because a large number of customers don't get served in 30 minutes, the club has decided that nine members should work at the next home game. Do you believe that, with three times as many workers, the club will be able to serve three times as many customers? Explain. (*Probably not, because the work space and equipment remains the same, so diminishing returns will likely set in.*)

CLOSURE

1. What is marginal utility? (*The additional satisfaction a consumer receives from purchasing or using an additional unit of a product.*)

2. What is diminishing marginal utility? (*For most goods and services, the extra satisfaction a person gets from consuming one more unit of a product will eventually become lower and lower.*)

3. How does diminishing marginal utility affect consumer decision making? (*Because satisfaction decreases as more and more units of a product are used, consumers reach a point where the additional satisfaction or marginal utility received from one additional unit of a product is less than the price of the additional unit.*) Give an example. (*No matter how satisfying the first chocolate candy bar is, satisfaction received from additional candy bars eventually declines. For example, at a price of $.70 per candy bar, you buy four candy bars. The value you place on the additional satisfaction of the fifth candy bar is less than $.70, so you use the $.70 to buy something else that will give you more satisfaction.*)

4. What is marginal product? (*the extra or additional output produced by each additional unit of input*)

5. What is the law of diminishing returns? (*The law of diminishing returns states that the marginal product of a variable input will eventually fall when at least one other input is held constant, or fixed.*)

6. What is marginal cost? (*the additional cost of producing one additional unit of output*)

7. What eventually happens to marginal cost as production levels continue to increase? (*At first it may decrease, but ultimately it increases*) Why? (*Even though they are paid the same wage rate, eventually, additional workers are not as productive as workers hired earlier because of the law of diminishing returns. Therefore, the cost of producing additional products increases.*)

ASSESSMENT

1. Distribute copies of Activity 2 to each student. Instruct students to use marginal analysis to answer the questions.

2. Assessment Answer: As shown in the table below, the student will be hired, but the friend will not. The additional (marginal) cost of hiring the friend – the fifth worker who applied – would exceed the value of the additional (marginal) product produced by the fifth worker.

# of Workers (1)	# of Rolls of Grip Tape Produced Each Day (2)	Marginal Product (Additional Rolls of Grip Tape Produced Per Day) (3)	Value of Additional Grip Tape Rolls Produced Per Day (4)	Marginal Labor Cost Per Day (5)
1	20	20	$60	$40
2	50	30	90	40
3	70	20	60	40
4	85	15	45	40
5	95	10	30	40
6	100	5	15	40

3. Answers will vary but most students will purchase less than five pairs of jeans, because at some point the additional satisfaction they receive from one more pair of jeans will be less than $15. They will choose to save the remaining money or spend it on something else.

Activity 1
Left-Foot Pattern Production Table

# of Workers (1)	Left-Foot Patterns Produced (2)	(3)	(4)	(5)
0				
1				
2				
3				
4				
5				
6				

Activity 2
Assessment

1. SUMMER JOBS IN THE SKATEBOARD GRIP TAPE FACTORY

You and your friend have applied for a summer job at RAD SPORTS. RAD manufactures Skateboard Grip Tape. RAD has selected a pool of six qualified applicants from which to choose summer employees. Summer employees are hired from this pool of applicants on a first come, first serve basis. You were the fourth applicant to apply and your friend was the fifth.

RAD's Skateboard Grip Tape is manufactured by people working with two machines. RAD sells its grip tape for $3 a roll and can sell as many rolls as it can produce at that price, but very few rolls if it increases price even a little. It pays its workers $40 per day. The following table shows how many rolls of grip tape are produced per day with each additional summer employee hired, up to six workers.

# of Summer Employees	# of Rolls of Tape Produced Per Day
0	0
1	20
2	50
3	70
4	85
5	95
6	100

Will you and your friend be hired by RAD SPORTS this summer? Explain your answer.

2. HOW MANY TO BUY?

You have received $75 as a birthday gift and plan to buy a pair of blue jeans. When you go to purchase these jeans, you discover the store is having a super sale on your brand and style of jeans, for $15 per pair. How many pairs would you buy and why? Use what you have learned about diminishing marginal utility to explain your answer.

LESSON SIXTEEN
THE CIRCULAR FLOW(S)

INTRODUCTION

The circular flow of economic activity is a simplified model of the basic economic relationships in a market economy. This model gives students an overview of how households, businesses, and the government interact in different markets by exchanging goods and services, productive resources (also known as inputs or factors of production), and money.

CONCEPTS

Productive resources (human resources, natural resources, capital)
Resource payments (wages and salaries, rent, interest, profits)
Interdependence
Circular flow of goods, services, productive resources, and money payments

CONTENT STANDARDS

Markets exist when buyers and sellers interact. This interaction determines market prices and thereby allocates scarce goods and services.

Income for most people is determined by the market value of the productive resources they sell. What workers earn depends, primarily, on the market value of what they produce and how productive they are.

BENCHMARKS

A market exists whenever buyers and sellers exchange goods and services.

Market prices are determined through the buying and selling decisions made by buyers and sellers.

To earn income, people sell productive resources. These include their labor, capital, natural resources, and entrepreneurial talents.

Employers are willing to pay wages and salaries to workers because they expect to sell the goods and services those workers produce at prices high enough to cover the wages and salaries and all other costs of production.

OBJECTIVES

♦ Students analyze the economic relationships that exist between households and businesses in a market economy.

♦ Students illustrate the economic relationship among households, businesses, and government by using a circular flow diagram.

♦ Students identify the three types of productive resources (inputs) and the kind of income each factor earns.

LESSON DESCRIPTION

In this lesson, students read about market interactions and participate in a simulation titled Econoland, which involves transactions between businesses and households in two kinds of markets – product markets and factor (or input) markets. They also learn how government fits into the circular flow of economic activity in a market economy.

TIME REQUIRED

Two class periods. Day one – procedures 1-8. Day two – procedures 9-12 and Assessment.

MATERIALS

- Activity 1: Earning a Living in Econoland, one per student.
- Activity 2: Business Cards, duplicate and cut apart 2 copies per student for half of the students in the class, but initially distribute only one Business card and ten $100 bills. Prepare a few extra sheets and cut all of the sheets apart. Cut out 10 ECONO slips for each student in half of the class, but do not

distribute these slips until the appropriate time in the simulation (see procedure 6).

- Activity 3: Household Cards, duplicate and cut apart enough copies of the productive resource sheet to give each student in the class a total of 15 resource cards. The same total number of each type of resource should be distributed but do *not* give individual students the same number of each type of resource. For example, one student might get 8 capital resource cards, 5 human resource cards, and 2 natural resource cards.
- An 8½" × 11" (or larger) sheet of paper on which you have written "ECONO FACTORY."
- Masking tape or straight pins.
- Activity 4: The Circular Flow of Economic Activity, one per student.
- Visual 1: The Circular Flow of Productive Resources, Goods and Services, and Money Payments
- Visual 2: Government in the Circular Flow

PROCEDURES

1. Explain that people participate in the economy in a variety of ways. People make decisions as consumers when purchasing goods and services. They make decisions as producers when providing human and natural resources they own to businesses, or through savings that allow businesses to borrow to make investments in capital goods. They also make decisions as citizens – especially as voters – that influence the economic decisions made collectively in the economy.

2. Explain that students will engage in a simulation called "Econoland" to improve their understanding of the interrelationships between households and businesses in a market economy.

3. Give each student a copy of Activity 1. Tell students to read the Overview. Review the roles of households, three categories of productive resources, and the roles of business firms.

4. Divide the class in half. Students in one group will represent business firms and students in the other group will represent households. Each business firm should receive ten $100 bills and a Business badge to wear during the simulation (Activity 2). Each household should receive 15 Household Resource cards (Activity 3).

Note: Approximately equal numbers of Natural Resources, Human Resources, and Capital Goods cards must be distributed among the households as a whole. However, it is not necessary or desirable to give a household five of each type of card. For example, you can give one student 15 Natural Resources cards and another student 10 Human Resources and five Capital Goods cards. The total number of resource cards distributed to each household must be 15.

5. Tell students to read the instructions for the Econoland simulation. Be sure that households know they must sell their cards for money and use the money to buy ECONOs. Businesses must pay money for the productive resource cards and then sell ECONOs to households.

6. Tape the ECONO FACTORY sign at the place in the classroom where the businesses are to exchange sets made up of one Natural Resources card, one Human Resources card, and one Capital Goods card for one ECONO. ECONOs represent goods and services that will be sold to households. The teacher or a student may staff the ECONO FACTORY.

7. Review the instructions for the Econoland simulation and answer any questions. Students may take up to 20 minutes to engage in exchange activities, but usually finish in less time. After one-fourth to one-third of the households have sold all their cards, announce that exchanges will end in five minutes. Students must know in advance when the exchanges will end so they can plan for the sale

of their remaining productive resources and products.

8.   Conduct the simulation. It is possible that some households may try to circumvent the business process by bringing their resource cards directly to the ECONO FACTORY. Explain that they lack a Business badge and are unable to produce ECONOs.

9.   Distribute a copy of Activity 4 to each student. Instruct students to read Parts I and II and then complete Part II, using the information they gained from Activity 3 and from participating in the simulation. The answers are:

1. *Money payments*
2. *Finished goods and services (ECONOs)*
3. *Productive resources (human resources, natural resources, capital goods,)*
4. *Money income payments (wages and salaries, rents, interest, profit)*
5. *Product market*
6. *Productive resource (or input) market*
7. *Money payments*
8. *Finished goods and services (ECONOs)*
9. *Productive resources (human resources, natural resources, capital goods,)*
10. *Money income payments (wages and salaries, rents, interest, profit)*

You may wish to point out that, from the perspective of businesses, line 1 is sales revenue, line 2 is its output, line 3 represents inputs (the productive resources it buys), and line 4 represents payments for productive resources (expenses and profit).

10. Discuss the students' answers regarding the flow chart. Choose one student to put his or her version of the completed flow chart on the chalkboard and have other students evaluate it. Project a transparency of Visual 1 and explain the **circular flow** of **productive resources** (factors of production), goods and services (products), and money payments shown on the

diagram. Ask students to describe how households and businesses are interdependent.

11. Tell students to read and complete Part III of Activity 4. Discuss the answers:

From Households to Government:
  1. productive resources;
  2. money payments (mainly taxes)
From Businesses to Government:
  1. goods and services;
  2. money payments (mainly taxes)
From Government to Households:
  1. government goods and services;
  2. money income payments and transfer payments
From Government to Businesses:
  1. government goods and services;
  2. money payments for purchases of goods and services and some subsidies.

12. Project a transparency of Visual 2 and ask students to compare the visual to their diagrams on Activity 4. Discuss all the ways the circular flow model was altered to incorporate the government sector, and suggest that even more changes would be needed to show international trade relationships (imports and exports).

Note: Transfer payments are government payments for which recipients do not currently perform productive services. Significant transfer payments in the United States today include Social Security benefits, Medicare and Medicaid, government employee retirement benefits, unemployment compensation, and public assistance (such as food stamps).

CLOSURE

Explain to the class that the United States economy is organized around a system of private markets in which prices for goods and services are determined by the interaction of buyers and sellers. This form of economic activity creates a type of **interdependence** between people in households and people in businesses. Ask:

1. How do individuals and families in households depend on people in businesses? (People in households buy the goods and services they desire from businesses. They sell the productive resources they own to businesses in order to earn income. Note that households own capital and natural resources, too.)

2. How do businesses depend on individuals and families in households? (Businesses sell goods and services to households to earn revenue and profits. They purchase productive resources from households in order to produce the goods and services consumers desire.)

3. What is the role of government in the circular flow of economic activity? (Government imposes taxes on businesses and households to pay for the productive resources its uses to provide certain kinds of goods and services to households and businesses. See Lessons 11 and 12 for more on the economic role of government in a market economy.)

ASSESSMENT

Explain that there are three basic economic questions that must be answered in any society: (1) what to produce? (2) how to produce? (3) for whom to produce? Have students use the circular flow model to write a brief paper on how those decisions are made in the United States. If students have studied supply and demand analysis, they should incorporate those ideas into their papers.

Activity 1
Earning a Living in Econoland

OVERVIEW:

The Roles of Households (Individuals and Families)

Individuals function as both consumers and producers. In the U.S. economy, households act as consumers when they buy goods and services that businesses produce. These exchanges take place in product markets. Buying food at a local grocery store is an exchange in a product market.

As resource owners, individuals function as producers by supplying productive resources to businesses, which use these resources to produce goods and services. These exchanges take place in factor markets (or productive resource or input markets). Examples of the transactions that occur in factor markets are businesses paying wages to workers, rent to landowners, or interest on loans for plant and equipment.

There are three categories of **productive resources** used to produce goods and services: human resources, natural resources, and capital.

Human resources are the number of people available for work and the skills and motivation of these individuals. Businesses pay wages and salaries to households for their labor services. Entrepreneurship refers to a special type of human resource that assumes the risk of organizing other resources to produce goods and services. The payment to entrepreneurs is called profit.

Natural resources are gifts of nature. They include undeveloped land, oceans and rivers, virgin forests, oil and mineral deposits, and climatic conditions.

Capital refers to the manufactured or constructed items used by businesses. They include buildings, machinery, and equipment used in the production process. (In everyday speech, people commonly refer to money as capital; but in economics, the term capital refers to the real productive resources – buildings, machines, and tools – used to produce other goods and services.)

The Roles of Business Firms

Like households, businesses function as both consumers and producers. Businesses supply goods and services in the product market. They are the buyers, or consumers, of the productive resources (human resources, natural resources, and capital resources) used to produce goods and services. Businesses try to sell their products for more than their costs of production, thereby earning profits. If a business is not successful, it will incur losses. In order to earn profits, businesses must supply products that households want to buy, and supply them at competitive prices. If a business doesn't produce what households want to buy, or if it doesn't keep costs of production low enough to compete with other producers, it will incur losses. A firm will eventually go out of business if it continues to incur losses.

Activity 1
(Continued)

INSTRUCTIONS FOR THE ECONOLAND SIMULATION:

In this simulation, you will play the role of either a household or a business. Read carefully about both roles, then your teacher will assign your role.

Households: Your first goal is to sell to businesses the human resources, natural resources, and capital goods they use to produce a product. Then, with the income you earn from selling those productive resources, you will purchase from businesses the goods and services your household wants to consume. In this simulation, these goods and services are called ECONOs. Your success as a household will be measured by the number of ECONOs you accumulate. You will be given 15 Productive Resource cards. You may not want to sell all your resources immediately because their prices may change as the game goes on. However, in general, the more resources you sell, the more money you will earn to acquire ECONOs. Be sure to sell all your resource cards before the activity ends, because at the end of the simulation only the ECONOs you have will count.

Business Firms: Your goal is to earn a profit by supplying the goods and services households want. In this activity, the only products households want to buy are ECONOs. To produce one ECONO, you must acquire 1 unit of human resources, 1 unit of natural resources, and 1 unit of capital goods. You must buy these resources from households at the best price you can negotiate. Once you have accumulated 1 unit of each resource, you may turn the set of three cards in at the ECONO FACTORY, which will produce 1 ECONO for you. You are then free to sell the ECONO to any household for the best price you can negotiate. To earn a profit, you must sell the ECONO for more than your costs of production, which in this game includes the wages and salaries paid for human resources, the rent paid for the use of natural resources, and the interest paid for the use of capital. You can then use the money you receive to buy more productive resources in order to produce and sell more ECONOs. You have $1000 to start the game. Your business success will be measured by the dollars of profit you are able to earn during the activity. Try to sell all your products by the end of the activity. If you run out of money and have no ECONOs to sell, announce publicly that you are bankrupt and return to your seat.

A Word about Pricing: Only $100 bills are used in this activity. It is possible to arrive at prices other than $100, $200, $300, etc., by combining several items in a single transaction. For example, two Productive Resources cards could be sold for $300, which is the equivalent of $150 each. Five cards could be sold for $300, which is the equivalent of $60 each. However, you must agree on a price for which an exchange can take place using the denominations of money provided in the simulation. The suggested price range for Productive Resource cards is $50 to $300, but any price that buyers and sellers agree to and can complete using $100 bills is acceptable.

Activity 2
Business Cards

Activity 3
Household Cards

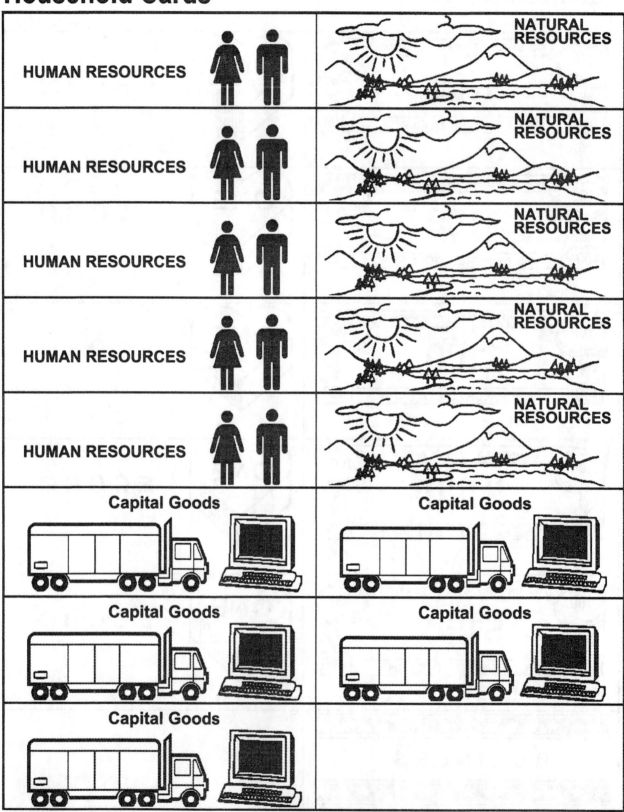

From *Focus: High School Economics,* © National Council on Economic Education, New York, NY

Activity 4
The Circular Flow of Economic Activity

Part I:

Households supply the natural resources, human resources, and capital they own to businesses in exchange for money income payments – wages, salaries, rents, interest, and profits. These income payments are used to purchase the finished goods and services supplied by businesses. Business firms use the proceeds from these sales to purchase more productive resources from households, to make more goods and services to sell. This is how the circular flow of productive resources, goods and services, and money income payments, is established and maintained.

Part II:

In the circular flow chart shown below, the curved lines with arrows show the direction of payments and products that flow between households and businesses. The outer set of lines shows the flow of income (money payments). The inner set of lines shows the flow of finished products and productive resources for which the payments are made. Label each line or empty box to complete the circular flow model of a simple economy. (One label, for the flow of finished goods and services [ECONOS], has been provided to help you get started.)

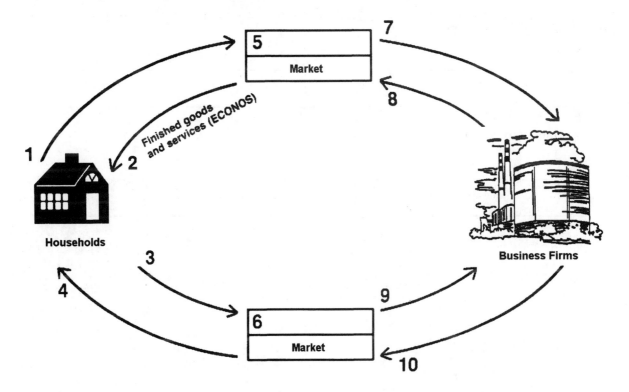

Activity 4 (cont.)

Part III:

Now expand the circular flow chart to include government. Households sell some of their productive resources to the government as well as to businesses, and businesses sell some of their finished goods and services to the government as well as to households. The government collects money (mostly taxes) from both businesses and households, and also makes money payments to both of these groups. In the space below, list all the appropriate flows you can think of.

From Households to Government

1. _____

2. _____

From Businesses to Government

1. _____

2. _____

From Government to Households

1. _____

2. _____

From Government to Businesses

1. _____

2. _____

Visual 1
The Circular Flow of Productive Resources, Goods and Services, and Money Payments

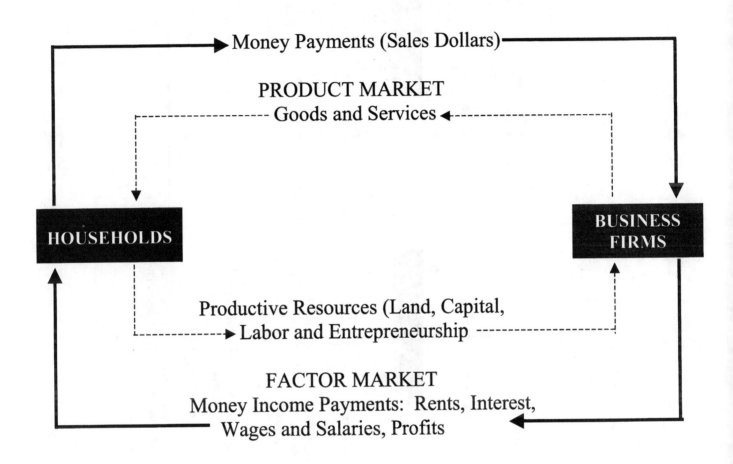

Visual 2
Government in the Circular Flow

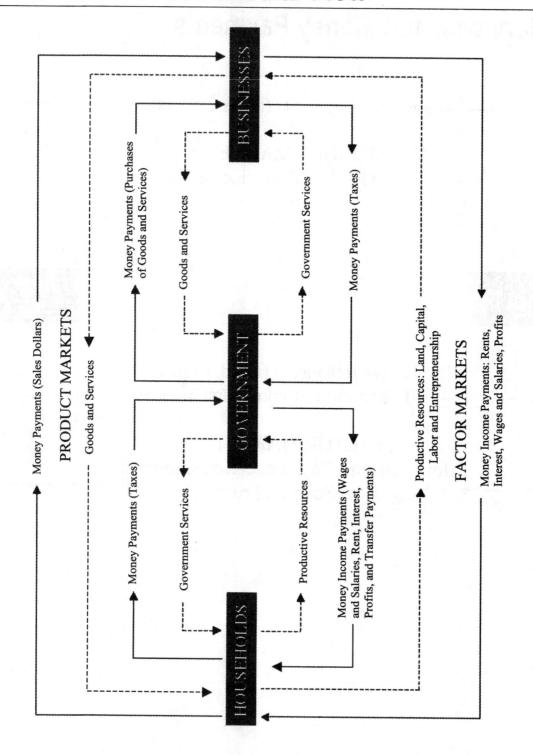

From *Focus: High School Economics,* © National Council on Economic Education, New York, NY

LESSON SEVENTEEN
SAVING, INVESTING, AND THE INVISIBLE HAND

INTRODUCTION

This lesson explains how financial institutions in a market economy channel savings into economic investments. How much people save and how effectively those savings are transformed into good investments are directly related to a nation's economic growth. Historically, economic growth has been the primary way market systems reduce poverty and raise standards of living. Economic growth results from several factors, including technological change that stems from research and development on the one hand, and investments in new capital goods that embody those new technologies on the other hand. Economic growth also depends on how successfully individuals and nations invest in education, training, and other forms of human capital, which also requires saving and a reduction in current consumption levels. Most saving and investment decisions in market systems are made by individuals and businesses.

CONCEPTS

Saving
Investment
The stock market
The bond market
Primary and secondary markets for financial securities
Banks
The circular flow of income with financial intermediaries
The "invisible hand"

CONTENT STANDARDS

Institutions evolve in market economies to help individuals and groups accomplish their goals. Banks, labor unions, corporations, legal systems, and not-for-profit organizations are examples of important institutions. A different kind of institution, clearly defined and well enforced property rights, is essential to a market economy.

Investment in factories, machinery, new technology, and the health, education, and training of people can raise future standards of living.

BENCHMARKS

Banks are institutions where people save money and earn interest, and where other people borrow money and pay interest.

Saving is the part of income not spent on taxes or consumption.

Banks and other financial institutions channel funds from savers to borrowers and investors.

Economic growth is a sustained rise in a nation's production of goods and services. It results from investments in human and physical capital, research and development, technological change, and improved institutional arrangements and incentives.

Historically, economic growth has been the primary vehicle for alleviating poverty and raising standards of living.

OBJECTIVES

◆ Students recognize that saving means not consuming all current income, and investment refers to the production and purchase of machines, buildings, and equipment that can be used to produce more goods and services in the future.

◆ Students explain that personal investments in stocks, bonds, and other financial securities may or may not fund additional real investments in capital goods, depending on whether those personal investments involve the purchase of new issues of stocks and bonds, or purchases of previously issued securities in the secondary markets (such as the New York or American Stock Exchanges, or NASDAQ – the National Association of Securities Dealers Automated Quotations System).

♦ Students identify institutional arrangements that connect saving and investment including banks, the bond market, and new issues of stock sold through the investment banking process.

♦ Students analyze the economic incentives that encourage saving and investing.

♦ Students recognize that self-interested decisions about saving and investment can also have important social benefits.

LESSON DESCRIPTION

Students learn the distinctions between saving and investment, and between primary and secondary markets for financial securities. They apply their understanding in a brief activity. Then they study how financial institutions channel household savings to businesses investments. The financial institutions discussed in this lesson include the stock market, the bond market, banks, and other saving and lending institutions. After examining how financial institutions help to promote economic growth, students see that saving and investment decisions in a market economy are yet another example of Adam Smith's "invisible hand" at work.

TIME REQUIRED

One class period.

MATERIALS

- Activity 1: Saving, Investment, or Personal Investing?, one per student and a visual
- Activity 2: Saving and Investing in Market Economies, one per student
- Visual 1: Saving and Investing

- Visual 2: Two Kinds of Markets for Financial Securities
- Visual 3: Channeling Savings to Investment
- Visual 4: The Circular Flow of Income with Financial Intermediaries
- Visual 5: Adam Smith and the Invisible Hand

PROCEDURES

1. Explain to the class that the purpose of this lesson is to explain how the financial institutions of a market economy help channel savings to economic investment. This is a key linkage that affects a nation's rate of economic growth. Historically, economic growth has been the primary way market systems reduce poverty and raise standards of living. Economic growth results from several factors including research and development and technological change. It also depends on the levels of saving and investment in physical and human capital, which determine how widely and rapidly new technologies will be used in the economy.

2. Explain that when people save, they do not consume all of their current income. Instead, they set some of it aside. Discuss why people often save. Ask:

A. What are some reasons that some people save? (*Accept a variety of answers. People often save because they wish to purchase something expensive in the future, such as a car, house, vacation, or college education. They also want protection against unforeseen events, such as health problems or being laid off. Most adults also try to save for their retirement years.*)

B. When people save, they are usually trying to make themselves better off in the future. But can this saving help others as well? How? (*Again, accept a variety of answers, such as one person's savings being loaned to someone else who wants to buy a car or house.*)

From *Focus: High School Economics*, © National Council on Economic Education, New York, NY

Explain that the social benefits of saving will be discussed later.)

3. Note that in economics, a distinction is made between the terms "saving" and "investment." Display Visual 1. Explain that saving means not consuming all of your current income. **Investment** is the production and purchase of capital goods, such as machines, buildings, and equipment that can be used to produce more goods and services in the future. When individuals make **personal investment decisions** by purchasing stocks and bonds – which are riskier than deposits in savings accounts, but in many cases pay considerably higher returns than the interest on savings accounts – that decision may or may not provide additional funds for real investments in capital goods, such as factories and machines. Whether the decision results in direct real investment depends on the kind of personal investment, and where and how people buy the securities.

4. Explain that people commonly do not understand that the stocks and bonds traded on markets like the New York Stock Exchange are actually secondary (in effect, used or second-hand) securities. Explain that a distinction is made between new issues of stock made through investment banks and the reselling of these shares in the **stock markets**. Similarly, people can buy new issues of bonds from corporations or brokers who are selling those bonds for the corporations, or they may buy a bond that is being sold by an individual, bank, or other firm that purchased the bond earlier, and has now decided to resell it in the **bond market**. The key point for students to understand is that new issues of stocks and bonds generate additional investment funds for the business that issues them (or for the government, if it issues new bonds). But stocks and bonds that are resold in secondary markets do not provide additional funds to the company or organization whose stocks and bonds are traded. Rather, the seller of the stocks and bonds receives the funds paid by the buyer of the securities.

5. Display Visual 2. Explain that new corporations that want to raise money to begin operations, and sometimes existing corporations that want to expand, offer new issues of stock to investment bankers in the **primary market**. These companies use the primary market to raise financial capital. Investment banks purchase these new securities and then sell these shares to the public at a somewhat higher price than the banks paid the issuing companies – if the investment banks earn a profit. From that point on the securities will be traded in the **secondary markets**. The investment banking process saves time and reduces risks for the corporations that issue new shares of stock, and provides an orderly way to bring the shares to the market.

6. Distribute copies of Activity 1, and display the transparency. Allow time for the students to indicate their responses, working individually or in small groups. Then review the distinctions between saving, investment, and personal investments by discussing the eight examples listed on Activity 1. Answers are indicated below: (I = investment; P = personal investment, S = saving, N = neither saving nor investment)

A. (*I*) Katiwe borrowed $25,000 from a bank to purchase a computer and other equipment and supplies to open her new Internet home page business.

B. (*P*) Aunt Bonnie buys 100 shares of America Online hoping the price per share will increase.

C. (*N:* consumption) Uncle Mike dies and leaves his estate of $100,000 to his five children. They use it to take an around the world once-in-a-lifetime, one-year cruise.

D. (*I*) Sam Sun, the head of Sunshine Computer Systems, issues new shares of stock in his company through an investment banker, and uses those funds to build a new assembly line to produce the world's fastest microprocessors.

E. (*S*) Amanda takes a new job and has $20 a week deducted from each paycheck, to be deposited directly into a savings account at her bank.

F. (*I* for Ford, *P* for Granny Sara) Ford Motor Company issues a $5,000 bond, which is purchased by Granny Sara.

G. (*I*) Medical Systems, Inc. builds a new plant to produce experimental pacemakers.

H. (*P*) Cousin Mark quits his job to go back to school to study economics, hoping to earn more money with a college degree.

7. Explain that market economies have developed several different institutional arrangements that channel savings to investment. Display Visual 3. Discuss the following points, stressing how each participant expects to gain from the transactions. The anticipated gains are the financial incentives that encourage savers and investors to voluntarily cooperate with each other.

A. In the stock market, the buyers of stocks are purchasing shares of ownership in a corporation, hoping that their share of the corporation's future profits will make the stocks a good personal investment. People who buy shares of stock hope that the share price will increase, resulting in a financial gain. Many companies also pay out part of their profits to stockholders each year or quarter, as dividends. Corporations issue new shares of stock when they are formed, in order to raise funds to start the business. Some companies also issue new shares of stock when they want to expand the business by constructing new plants or purchasing new equipment. However, most routine sales of stock, such as those made on the New York Stock Exchange or NASDAQ, do *not* generate funds for the companies whose stocks are traded there. Instead, these are secondary markets where existing shares of stock are bought and sold. New issues of stock are sold through investment bankers. Refer back Visual 2.

B. In the bond market, those who buy new issues of bonds loan their savings to businesses in exchange for a promise that the amount loaned will be repaid, with interest, by a specified date. Many corporations issue bonds to raise funds when they expand by constructing new plants or purchasing new equipment. Federal, state, and local governments also issue bonds to finance various projects, such as building new schools, jails, or bridges.

C. **Banks** accept and compete for deposits from savers. Savers expect their deposits to earn interest. Banks use these deposits to make loans to other people and businesses who wish to borrow. The borrowers agree to repay the loans, with interest, at a specified time. Banks pay a lower rate of interest to savers than they charge to borrowers. The difference between the interest paid to savers on deposits and the interest charged on loans to borrowers is one source of income that banks use to pay their costs of operating and (they hope) to earn a profit.

8. Display Visual 4. Use the circular flow diagram to review how business owners borrow savings from households, using banks or other saving and lending institutions as financial

intermediaries. Explain that the situation is somewhat more complex than the one illustrated in Visual 4, because some businesses as well as households provide savings to the market for loanable funds. Also, consumers and governments compete with businesses to borrow the available savings. But over the past 75 years in the U.S. economy, only households have been net savers in the U.S. economy. Both business and government have been net borrowers – and businesses actually borrow much more than government. In some years, however, the federal government has run a surplus; and in 2001 it was projected to run a surplus over the next decade or more.

9. Distribute Activity 2. After students have completed the reading, ask:

A. Who makes most decisions about how much to save and invest in a market economy, and about how to save and invest? (*Business owners and individual households.*)

B. Why are banks and financial markets important to economic growth? (*Banks and other financial intermediaries lend money to help people start and expand businesses. Financial markets such as bond markets and stock markets also play a critical role in channeling personal savings to businesses that use these funds to make investments.*)

C. Why are individuals in households and businesses more likely to make saving and investment decisions that advance their own economic interests more effectively than decisions made by government officials? (*A key assumption of a market economy is that individuals in households and businesses have better information about their own circumstances and objectives than government officials. They also have the strongest incentives to make good investment decisions, because they make money from good investments, and lose money with bad investments. However, some kinds of investment decisions relate to public rather than private goods – see Lesson 11 – and therefore must be made by government officials.*)

10. Remind students that market economies allow individuals to act in their own self-interest in making most economic decisions. Ask:

A. When savers in households decide to use some of their savings to buy stocks, how are they acting in their own self-interest? (*They hope to gain financially from such decisions. Specifically, they hope that the value of the stocks they purchase will increase, and that the total return from higher stock prices and any dividends paid on the stock will be more than they could earn in a savings account.*)

B. When business owners decide to borrow money or issue shares of stock, how are they acting in their self-interest? (*Business owners hope that their increased production will lead to increased revenues and profits.*)

11. Display Visual 5. After the students read the quotation, ask: How does Adam Smith's **invisible hand** apply to the decisions made by people who borrow and save using financial institutions? (*While pursuing their own financial self-interest, savers and investors are also making decisions that help a market economy grow, provide new jobs and income for workers, and expand the number and types of goods and services produced to sell to consumers.*)

CLOSURE

Pose the following questions for review. Ask:

1. What do economists mean by the term saving? (*not consuming all current income*)

2. What do economists mean by the term investment? (*the production and purchase of capital goods such as machines, buildings, and equipment that can be used to produce more goods and services in the future*)

3. What is the difference between primary and secondary markets for financial securities? (*Primary markets sell new issues of stocks and bonds. Secondary markets sell previously issued or "used" securities.*)

4. What is a bond? (*a legal promise to repay money loaned to a business or government agency, with interest, on a specified date or dates*)

5. What is a stock? (*a share of ownership in a corporation*)

6. What are the major types of markets for financial securities in the U.S. economy? (*the bond market and the stock market*)

7. What are financial intermediaries? (*banks and other financial institutions that lend deposits made by some people and firms to other people and firms, including businesses that are investing in factories, machinery, and other capital goods*)

8. How does Adam Smith's invisible hand apply to the decisions made by people who borrow and save using financial institutions? (*The saving and investment decisions of individuals and businesses are guided by Smith's invisible hand. While pursuing their own financial self-interest, savers and investors are also making decisions that help a market economy grow, provide new jobs and income for workers, and expand the number and types of goods and services produced to sell to consumers.*)

ASSESSMENT

Have one group of students contact a reputable local stockbroker, if possible one affiliated with a national brokerage company.

The students should explain they have learned that the nationally known stock and bond markets are actually "second-hand" or secondary markets, and ask the stockbroker to provide them with a recent example of a new issue of stocks, and a copy of the prospectus for that new issue. They should be sure to find out from the stockbroker:

1. Who issued the new stock? (Name the corporation.)

2. What investment banks originally purchased the new issue of stock from the corporation? (Name the investment bankers involved.)

3. How will individual buyers be able to purchase these shares? (Name the exchanges on which the stock is now being traded, if any. If the stock is from a privately held corporation, it may not be traded on any exchange.)

Have another group of students interview a local banker, and ask the banker to explain how deposits from the local community are channeled to those who borrow money (both businesses and individuals).

Have both groups report their findings to the entire class, pointing out how savings are channeled to investments, and how the local and national economy benefit from this activity.

    From *Focus: High School Economics*, © National Council on Economic Education, New York, NY

Activity 1
Saving, Investment, or Personal Investing?

Directions: In the blank space before each of the statements below, mark an S in the space if the situation involves saving, an I if the situation involves investing, P if the situation involves personal investing, and an N if the situation involves neither saving nor investing.

_____ A. Katiwe borrowed $25,000 from a bank to purchase a computer and other equipment and supplies to open her new Internet home page business.

_____ B. Aunt Bonnie buys 100 shares of America Online, hoping that the price per share will increase.

_____ C. Uncle Mike dies and leaves his estate of $100,000 to his five children. They use it to take an around-the-world, once-in-a-lifetime, one-year cruise.

_____ D. Sam Sun, the head of Sunshine Computer Systems, issues new shares of stock in his company through an investment banker, and uses those funds to build a new assembly line to produce the world's fastest microprocessors.

_____ E. Amanda takes a new job and has $20 a week deducted from each paycheck to be deposited directly into a savings account at her bank.

_____ F. Ford Motor Company issues a $5,000 bond, which is purchased by Granny Sara.

_____ G. Medical Systems, Inc. builds a new plant to produce experimental pacemakers.

_____ H. Cousin Mark quits his job to go back to school to study economics, hoping to earn more money with a college degree.

Activity 2
Saving and Investing in Market Economies

Saving and Investing in Market Economies

In a market economy, most basic economic questions about how to use resources are answered by millions of individuals in households and businesses. They decide what goods and services will be produced, how they will be produced, and who will consume the goods and services that are produced.

A key assumption in market economies is that households and business owners usually have better information for making saving and investment decisions that promote their own objectives and take into account their own circumstances than government planners do. After all, how could a relatively small number of government officials have sufficient information to make sound saving and investment decisions regarding thousands of firms and millions of households? Individual savers and investors also have stronger incentives to make good and careful decisions, because they hope to enjoy financial gains as a result of their decisions, and avoid losses.

In countries with market economies, banks provide essential financial services for individual households and businesses, and in the process facilitate economic growth for the overall economy. First, banks provide a safe place for individuals to keep their checking and savings accounts. Banks then lend out a large part of those deposits, to help some people start and expand businesses, and many other individuals purchase homes and expensive durable goods, such as refrigerators and cars. Other people borrow money to purchase expensive services, such as education for their children, or medical care, or a foreign vacation.

In developed market economies, financial markets such as stock markets and bond markets also play a critical role in promoting good investment and business practices. Millions of investors – usually working through brokerage firms that analyze thousands of large companies' past performance and plans for future operations and investments – compete to invest in the firms that will earn the highest profits at a reasonable level of risk. Over the long run, firms that are successful will experience rising stock prices. Firms that are unsuccessful or not managed as well as they could be will experience falling stock prices, and eventually go out of business or be taken over by other companies and managers.

Questions for Discussion

1. Who makes most decisions about how much to save and invest in a market economy, and about how to save and invest?

2. Why are banks and financial markets important to economic growth?

3. Why are individuals in households and businesses more likely to make saving and investment decisions that advance their own economic interests more effectively than decisions made by government officials?

Visual 1
Saving and Investing

Saving: Not consuming all current income.

Investment: The production and purchase of capital goods, such as machines, buildings, and equipment that can be used to produce more goods and services in the future.

Personal investment: Purchasing financial securities such as stocks and bonds, which are riskier than savings accounts because they may fall in value, but in most cases will pay a higher rate of return in the long run than the interest paid on savings accounts.

Visual 2
Two Kinds of Markets for Financial Securities

Primary markets: New issues of bonds and corporate stocks are offered for sale to the public by companies or investment banks.

Secondary markets: Markets where previously issued stocks and bonds can be bought and sold by individuals and institutions, including the New York Stock Exchange, the American Stock Exchange, and NASDAQ.

Visual 3
Channeling Savings to Investment

New issues of corporate stock: New corporations raising funds to begin operations, or existing corporations that want to expand their current operations, can issue new shares of stock through the investment banking process. People who buy these shares of stock hope to make money by having the price of the stock increase, and through dividends that may be paid out of future profits.

New issues of bonds: New issues of bonds are issued by companies that want to borrow funds to expand by investing in new factories, machinery, or other projects, and by government agencies that want to finance new buildings, roads, schools, or other projects. The bonds are a promise to repay the amount borrowed, plus interest, at specified times. Individuals, banks, or other companies that want to earn this interest purchase the bonds.

Borrowing from banks and other financial intermediaries: Companies (and individuals) can borrow funds from banks, agreeing to repay the loans, with interest, on a specified schedule. Banks and other financial intermediaries lend out money that has been deposited by other people and firms. In effect, banks and other intermediaries are just a special kind of "middleman," making it easier for those with money to lend to find those who want to borrow funds. Of course, banks also screen those who borrow money, to make sure they are likely to repay the loans.

Visual 4
The Circular Flow of Income with Financial Intermediaries

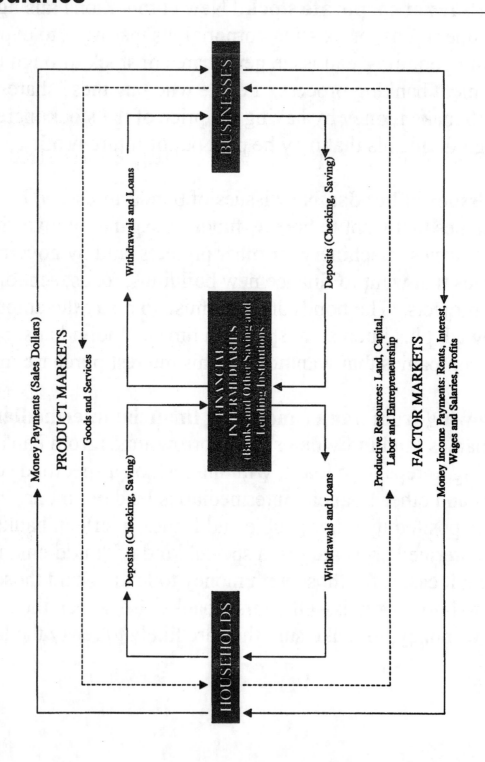

From *Focus: High School Economics*, © National Council on Economic Education, New York, NY

Visual 5
Adam Smith and the Invisible Hand

"Every individual . . . neither intends to promote the public interest, nor knows how much he is promoting it . . . . He intends only his own gain, and he is in this, as in many other cases, led by an invisible hand to promote an end which was not part of his intention. Nor is it always the worse for the society that it has no part in it. By pursuing his own interest he frequently promotes that of the society more effectually than when he really intends to promote it."

Adam Smith (1776) *An Inquiry into the Nature and Causes of the Wealth of Nations.* University of Chicago Press, 1976, page 477.

LESSON EIGHTEEN
ECONOMIC UPS AND DOWNS

INTRODUCTION

News reports about the economy often refer to data concerning economic growth, recessions, inflation, and unemployment. Students (and adults) should understand these data and how they both reflect and affect peoples' and companies' decisions to buy, save, invest, and produce. These data or measures of national economic performance have also become major topics in national elections and political debates.

Business cycles are the series of increases and decreases in real (inflation-adjusted) gross domestic product (GDP), a basic measure of national economic output. Business cycles typically consist of four phases: a period of expansion; a peak; a period of contraction; and a trough or bottoming-out period. Then another expansion begins, and the whole cycle is repeated.

During expansionary periods, productive capacity and GDP increase, employment levels increase, and wages and prices also tend to rise. During contractionary periods, the reverse is usually true: there is typically higher unemployment; underutilized productive capacity; stagnant or declining GDP; and falling, constant, or at least slowly increasing wages and prices.

There is no economic law that says these cyclical patterns of macroeconomic activity have to happen, and during the past century macroeconomic stabilization policies have been used to try to moderate, if not eliminate, these cycles. But history and current events suggest that the business cycle is still with us, and probably will be for the foreseeable future.

CONCEPTS
Business cycles
Gross domestic product
Unemployment
Consumer price index
Recession
Inflation
Economic growth
Fiscal policy

CONTENT STANDARDS

A nation's overall levels of income, employment, and prices are determined by the interaction of spending and production decisions made by all households, firms, government agencies, and others in the economy.

Unemployment imposes costs on individuals and nations. Unexpected inflation imposes costs on many people and benefits some others because it arbitrarily redistributes purchasing power. Inflation can reduce the rate of growth of national living standards, because individuals and organizations use resources to protect themselves against the uncertainty of future prices.

Federal government budgetary policy and the Federal Reserve System's monetary policy influence the overall levels of employment, output, and prices.

BENCHMARKS

Gross Domestic Product (GDP) is a basic measure of a nation's economic output and income. It is the total market value, measured in dollars, of all final goods and services produced in the economy in one year.

The unemployment rate is the percentage of the labor force that is willing and able to work, does not currently have a job, and is actively looking for work.

Unemployment can be caused by people changing jobs, by seasonal fluctuations in demand, by changes in the skills needed by employers, or by cyclical fluctuations in the level of national spending.

The consumer price index (CPI) is the most commonly used measure of price-level changes. It can be used to compare the price level in one year with price levels in earlier or later periods.

Inflation is an increase in most prices; deflation is a decrease in most prices.

The costs of inflation are different for different groups of people. Unexpected inflation hurts savers and people on fixed incomes; it helps people who have borrowed money at a fixed rate of interest.

Fiscal policies are decisions to change spending and tax levels by the federal government. These decisions are adopted to influence national levels of output.

Economic growth is a sustained rise in a nation's production of goods and services. It results from investment in human and physical capital, research and development, technological change, and improved institutional arrangements and incentives.

OBJECTIVES

♦ Students define real GDP, inflation, unemployment, and economic growth.

♦ Students analyze economic data for trends.

♦ Students describe the purpose of fiscal policy, and distinguish between automatic stabilizers and discretionary fiscal policy.

♦ Students explain how periods of economic growth and recession can influence peoples' lives, including students' career plans.

LESSON DESCRIPTION

Students use economic data to learn about business cycles; to determine the relationships between GDP, inflation, and unemployment; and to understand how expansions and contractions in the economy can affect their own career goals.

TIME REQUIRED

One class period.

MATERIALS

*   Activity 1(A): Gross Domestic Product 1975-1999; 1(B): U.S. Unemployment Rates 1975-2000; 1(C): Year-to-Year Changes in the Consumer Price Index 1975-2000, one per student and transparencies. (You can update all of the data in Activity 1 using the appendix of the *Economic Report of the President*, published every February by the Government Printing Office in Washington, DC. The report is also available on the Internet at *http://w3.access.gpo.gov/usbudget*.)
*   Activity 2: Economic Ups and Downs, one per student
*   Activity 3: U.S. Economic Growth Rates, 1959-1999, one per student and a transparency
*   Activity 4: If You Could Choose, one per student

PROCEDURES

1. Ask students how physicians measure people's health. (*take a pulse, check heart pressure, take an X-ray, or run blood tests*) Explain that the national economy is also measured in many ways to determine its health (performance). Ask for examples of statistics students have heard about in the media that may indicate how the economy is performing. (*Dow Jones Industrial Average, interest rates, unemployment rates, Consumer Price Index*)

2. Distribute copies of Activities 1 (A-C) and 2 to each student.

3. Display the transparency of Activity 1(A), and read the definition of real gross domestic product (GDP), emphasizing the following points:

A. Gross Domestic Product (GDP) is expressed in dollar terms. It is impossible to add up all the goods and services produced in our economy in physical terms, so the dollar value of what is produced is added. GDP is therefore a price times quantity (P × Q) figure. All final goods and services produced are multiplied by their prices and then summed.

B. Only the value of final goods and services are counted – not the value of inputs used to make these goods and services. The value of the inputs is included in the value of the final product, so adding both the value of the inputs and the final products would result in "double counting." For example, economists count only the value of a loaf a bread in calculating GDP, not the value of the bread and the value of the wheat and flour used to make the bread.

C. Only the goods and services produced within the borders of the United States are counted. If a U.S. company produces shoes in South Korea, then that output is not counted. If a Japanese company produces cars in Kentucky, that output is counted because it was produced within U.S. borders.

D. GDP is usually expressed as the annual value of output. GDP that is calculated as the output produced in a given year at the prices that prevailed in that year is called nominal GDP.

E. Because year-to-year changes in nominal GDP are affected by changes in the average price level, economists must eliminate the effects of price changes to determine changes in the level of output. Using nominal GDP, if output stayed the same but prices increased, it would appear that our economy grew, which would not be true. Therefore, economists and statisticians have developed ways to eliminate the price effects, to have a better account of how "real" output is changing – hence the term real GDP.

F. One key factor on which an economy is judged is its ability to provide jobs and produce goods and services. Therefore, increases in real GDP are generally viewed as good economic performance, and decreases as poor performance.

4. Display the transparency of Activity 1(B). Read the definitions of unemployment rate and labor force, emphasizing the following points:

A. The labor force is comprised of all people over the age of 16 who have jobs or who are not employed but have actively looked for a job in the past 30 days.

B. Some people choose not to enter the labor force for a variety of reasons, such as age, illness, or choosing to engage in household production (such as raising their children) rather than taking a paying job.

C. There are three major types of unemployment: 1) Some people are between jobs because of seasonal fluctuations in demand or simply because they are changing jobs. This is called **frictional unemployment**. Some agricultural and construction workers tend to be unemployed in the winter. And at any given time, some workers have quit one job to look for another job. 2) Some people are unemployed because of changes in the skills employers expect their employees to have. This is called **structural unemployment**. For example, the widespread use of computers in many different kinds of jobs has left some people who do not have computer skills out of work, and others in low-paying jobs. 3) In some periods, unemployment rates rise because of decreases in the level of national production, spending, and income (real GDP). This is called **cyclical unemployment**. If the economy experiences a downturn and consumers are buying fewer cars, then some autoworkers will lose their jobs.

D. Most adult workers depend on the income from their jobs to maintain their economic well-being. Low unemployment rates are desirable, and high unemployment rates undesirable. Full employment is said to occur when there is only frictional unemployment in the economy.

5. Display the transparency of Activity 1(C), and read the definition of the consumer price index (CPI), emphasizing the following points.

A. An increase in the overall price level (average prices) is called **inflation**; a decrease is called deflation.

B. In times of inflation, some prices rise, some stay the same, and some decrease; but *on average*, prices are rising.

C. Both inflation and deflation are undesirable because they arbitrarily affect different people's purchasing power in different ways, depending largely on how difficult or easy it is for the dollar level of their income to change as the price level changes. People on fixed incomes are hurt by inflation because they can buy less with their income when prices are increasing. Debtors are harmed by deflation because as prices fall, they must repay their debts with dollars that will buy more goods and services than the dollars they borrowed.

6. Put students in small groups, and tell them to use the information on the graphs in Activity 1 to answer Part I on Activity 2. Use the transparencies for Activity 1 to review the answers.

A. A recession is technically defined as a period when real GDP drops for six or more consecutive months. During which years did we have recessions? (*Recessions occurred during 1979-80, 1981-82, and 1990-91.*)

B. What happened to the unemployment rate during these recessions? (*The unemployment rate tends to increase.*)

C. What happened to the consumer price index (CPI) during and just after these recessions? (*The rate of inflation declined during each recession.*)

D. Real GDP increases during a period of economic expansion. During which years did the economy expand? (*Periods of expansion include 1975-79, 1980-81, 1982-90, and 1991 through at least 2000.*)

E. What was the longest period of economic expansion? What was the shortest period of economic expansion? (*The longest expansion was 1991-2000; 1980-81 was the shortest.*)

F. What usually happened to the unemployment rate during periods of economic expansion? (*The unemployment rate usually declined.*)

G. What usually happened to the CPI during economic expansion? (*The rate of inflation tended to increase more rapidly toward the end of expansion periods than at the beginning.*)

H. When did the highest rate of inflation occur? When did the lowest rate of inflation occur? (*The highest rate of inflation occurred in 1979, the smallest in 1981.*)

7. Display the transparency of Activity 1(A). Ask students why they think Activity 2 is titled "Economic Ups and Downs." Explain that the ups and downs shown on the graph are referred to as business cycles. The **business cycle** is a series of rises and falls in the overall level of economic activity, measured by real GDP. Although business cycles occur repeatedly, they do so at irregular and unpredictable intervals. Business cycles typically consist of four phases: a period of expansion in total economic activity; a peak or topping-out period; a contraction period, during which total economic activity declines; and a trough or bottoming-out period. A new expansion then begins, and the whole cycle of phases is repeated. Discuss the following.

A. What years was the economy in contraction? at a peak? in expansion? and at a trough? (*1975-1979: expansion; 1979: peak; 1979-1980: contraction; 1980: trough; 1980-1981: expansion; 1981: peak; 1981-1982: contraction; 1982: trough; 1982-1990: expansion; 1990: peak; 1990-1991: contraction; 1991: trough; 1991-2000: expansion*)

B. What happens to prices and unemployment during contractions and recessions? (*In rare occasions the price level actually declines, but usually the rate of increase simply slows down, and that effect is sometimes delayed. In the 1970s, the economy experienced aggregate supply decreases or "shocks" that lead to "stagflation" – inflation and higher unemployment at the same time. Unemployment increases during recessions.*)

C. What happens to prices and unemployment during expansions? (*Prices tend to increase, although less during the early stages of recovery than during the later stages. Unemployment usually declines.*)

8. Point out that Activity 1(A) shows that real GDP has generally increased over the years, which means that the economy has been growing, but not always smoothly or steadily.

9. Display a transparency of Activity 3 and give a copy to each student. Cover the definition of economic growth, emphasizing the following points.

A. **Economic growth** occurs when there is a *sustained* increase in real GDP; that is, in spite of periodic contractions, the output of the economy continues to increase over a substantial period of time.

B. In general, economic growth is considered beneficial because it can help to alleviate poverty and raise standards of living.

C. Activity 3 shows real GDP growth rates over time. The solid, straight line represents a zero economic growth rate. The dashed, straight line shows that the economy had an average growth rate of 3.5 percent from 1959 to 1999.

D. The solid line shows the short-run fluctuations of the economy. Although the average annual rate of growth was 3.5 percent during this period, the rate fluctuated considerably over this period.

10. Have students complete Part II of Activity 2. When they are finished, discuss the following.

    A. Did the U.S. economy always grow in the 1960s? (*Yes, the economy was growing because the growth rate was always positive; that is, greater than zero economic growth; but the growth rate fluctuated significantly from year to year.*)

    B. In what periods did the U.S. economy experience negative economic growth? (*The economy contracted – i.e., experienced negative growth rates – from 1973-1975, 1979-1980, 1981-1982, and 1990-1991.*)

    C. What is another name for periods of negative economic growth? (*A contraction is a period in which the economy has a negative growth rate; that is, real GDP is decreasing. If the contraction lasts six months or longer it is called a* **recession**.)

11. Point out that fluctuations in economic activity have real costs: especially higher unemployment during recessions, and sometimes higher inflation during expansions.

    A. Unemployment results in lower production (real GDP) and therefore lower income and consumption levels.

    B. Inflation has redistribution effects that may not be desirable. Some people are worse off during inflation (people on fixed incomes who can't buy as many goods and services), and some people are better off (people who own assets that are rising in value faster than prices are increasing).

12. Explain that the federal government tries to avoid these costs by minimizing the fluctuations in economic activity through two kinds of macroeconomic stabilization policies. The first is **fiscal policy** — changes in government spending and/or taxes. There are two basic forms of fiscal policy, automatic stabilizers and discretionary fiscal policy.

    A. Some government expenditure and tax revenues automatically rise or fall with changes in the level of national economic activity. For example, when the economy suffers a recession, government spending for unemployment compensation and welfare payments increases, while revenues from income and sales taxes fall. Economists refer to these kinds of programs as automatic stabilizers.

    B. The government can adopt countercyclical changes in spending and taxes – increasing spending or cutting taxes during recessions, and decreasing spending or increasing taxes during periods of high inflation. These actions are called discretionary fiscal policy.

13. Explain that it takes some time for both automatic stabilizers and discretionary fiscal policy to take effect in the economy. But the lags are considerably longer for discretionary policies. For those policies, first a problem must be recognized, then members of the legislative and executive branches of government must agree on what spending or tax changes to adopt, and then it still takes time for these actions to have an effect on the economy. During these lags, things may well have changed in the economy. In some cases, by the time discretionary policies are implemented they may have become unnecessary, or even harmful, rather than helpful.

14. In addition to fiscal policy, monetary policy is conducted by the Federal Reserve System to affect output, employment and prices in the economy. (See lesson 19.)

15. Given the economic fluctuations that have existed in our economy, tell students to use the information from Activity 1 to write a news flash on the state of the economy for the year of their birth.

CLOSURE

1. What is real gross domestic product? (*the total market value of the final goods and services produced within the borders of a country during a specific year, adjusted for price changes*)

2. Why is it important to adjust GDP for price changes when measuring the economy? (*Production, consumption, and income are ultimately determined by levels of real output, not prices.*)

3. Describe the three types of unemployment; that is, the percentage of workers in the labor force who are not working. (*Frictional: people out of work because of seasonal fluctuations in demand or because they are changing jobs. Structural: people out of work because of changes in the skills employers demand. Cyclical: people out of work because of decreases in total spending/demand in the economy.*)

4. Why is unemployment considered undesirable? (*It lowers production, consumption, and income levels.*)

5. What is inflation? (*an increase in the overall price level in the economy*) deflation? (*a decrease in the overall price level in the economy*)

6. Why are inflation and deflation considered undesirable? (*Both inflation and deflation arbitrarily redistribute income. This affects different people in different ways, depending largely on how difficult or easy it is for the dollar level of their income to change as the price level changes.*)

7. What is the business cycle? (*a series of*

rises and falls in the overall level of economic activity, measured by real GDP*)

8. What happens to unemployment during recessions? (*It increases.*)

9. What generally happens to prices as the economy approaches a peak? (*They increase.*)

10. What is fiscal policy? (*changes in the overall level of government spending and/or taxes designed to lower unemployment and inflation*)

11. What are the two types of fiscal policy. (*Automatic stabilizers are tax or government spending programs that increase or decrease when the level of national output/income changes, without requiring any new legislation by the government. Discretionary fiscal policy refers to changes in taxes or government spending programs enacted by the legislative and executive branches to deal with current or expected problems with unemployment or inflation.*)

12. Why does the federal government engage in fiscal policy? (*to reduce unemployment and inflation, and encourage economic growth*)

ASSESSMENT

Distribute copies of Activity 4 for students to complete, again referring to the graphs in Activity 1. Have students share their answers. (*High School Graduate 2 had a better chance of achieving his or her goals. The economy was in an expansionary period and the unemployment rate was declining. The 1982 graduate left high school during a recession, when unemployment was high.*)

Activity 1(A)
Gross Domestic Product 1975-1999 (in trillions of 1996 dollars)

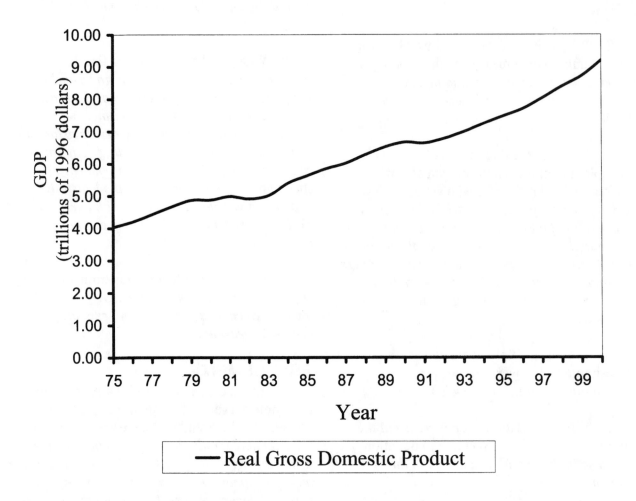

Real **gross domestic product** is the total market value of the final goods and services produced within the borders of a country during a specific year, adjusted for price changes from a base year (here, 1996).

Source: Table B-2, *Economic Report of the President, 2001*, United States Government Printing Office, Washington: 2001. Also at *http://w3.access.gpo.gov/usbudget*

From *Focus: High School Economics*, © National Council on Economic Education, New York, NY

Activity 1(B)
U.S. Unemployment Rates, 1975-2000

The **unemployment rate** indicates the percentage of the labor force that does not have a paying job. The **labor force** includes individuals 16 or older who have a job or who have actively looked for a job during the past 30 days.

Source: Table B-36, *Economic Report of the President, 2001*, United States Government Printing Office, Washington: 2001.

Activity 1(C)
Year-to-Year Changes in the Consumer Price Index 1975-2000 (December to December)

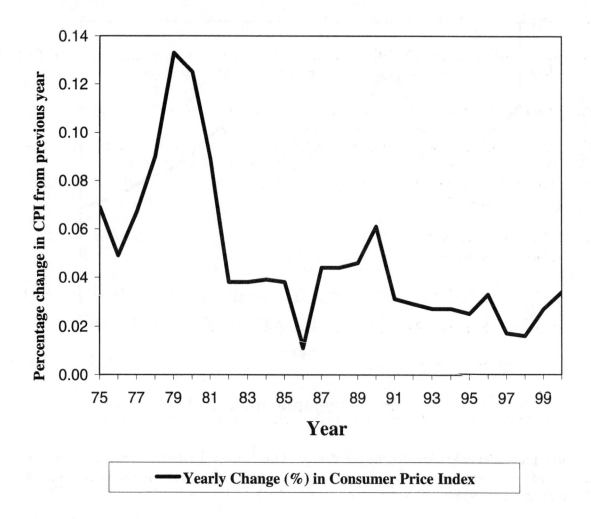

The **consumer price index (CPI)** is a measure of the average price level in the economy.

Source: Table-B-64, *Economic Report of the President, 2001*, United States Government Printing Office, Washington: 2001.

Activity 2
Economic Ups and Downs

Part I. Output, Unemployment, and Prices

Use the graphs from Activity 1 to answer the following questions:

A. A **recession** is technically defined as a period when real gross domestic product (GDP) drops for six or more consecutive months. During which years did we have recessions?

B. What happened to the unemployment rate during these recessions?

C. What happened to the consumer price index (CPI) during and just after these recessions?

D. Real GDP increases during a period of economic expansion. During which years did the economy expand?

E. What was the longest period of economic expansion? What was the shortest period of economic expansion?

F. What usually happened to the unemployment rate during periods of economic expansion?

G. What usually happened to the CPI during economic expansions?

H. When did the highest rate of inflation occur? When did the lowest rate of inflation occur?

Part II. Economic Growth
Use the graph from Activity 3 to answer the following questions:

A. Did the U.S. economy always grow in the 1960s?

B. In what periods did the U.S. economy experience negative economic growth rates?

C. What is another name for periods of negative economic growth?

Activity 3
Economic Growth Rates, 1959-1999

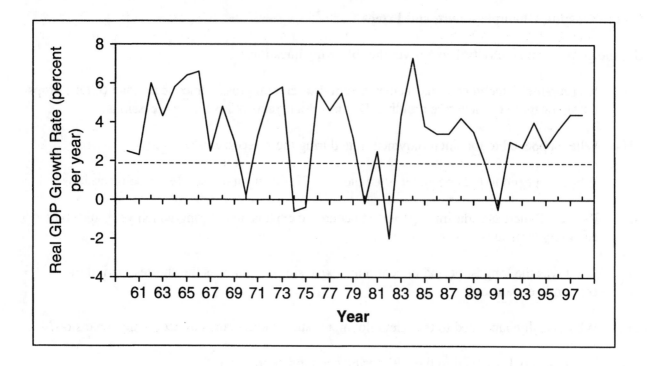

☐ — **U.S. Economic Growth Rate**

Economic growth is a sustained increase in real GDP.

Source: *Economic Report of the President, 2001*, United States Government Printing Office, Washington: 2001.

Activity 4
If You Could Choose

A. Read the situation for each high school graduate below. In which year would you prefer to have graduated? Which graduate had a better opportunity of achieving his or her economic goals? Explain why.

High School Graduate 1: The year is 1982. You have just graduated from high school. You want to work for 1-2 years to save money and then go to college.

High School Graduate 2: The year is 1986. You have just graduated from high school. You want to work for 1-2 years to save money and then go to college.

B. What do you predict will be the status of the economy one year after you graduate from high school? What evidence supports your prediction? How could this affect your career plans?

LESSON NINETEEN
MONEY, INTEREST, AND MONETARY POLICY

INTRODUCTION

Growth of the money supply is related to inflation. This lesson examines how money supply growth rates can lead to inflation when they outpace the growth in output. To maintain price stability and steady rates of economic growth, the Federal Reserve System (the Fed) tries to control the supply of money. Changes in the money supply lead to changes in interest rates which, in turn, affect the availability of credit and national levels of spending and output.

CONCEPTS

Money supply
Inflation
Open market operations
Reserve requirements
Discount rate
Interest rate

CONTENT STANDARD

Federal government budgetary policy and the Federal Reserve System's monetary policy influence the overall levels of employment, output, and prices.

BENCHMARKS

In the long run, inflation results from increases in a nation's money supply that exceed increases in its output of goods and services.

Monetary policies are decisions by the Federal Reserve System that lead to changes in the supply of money and the availability of credit. Changes in the money supply can influence overall levels of spending, employment, and prices in the economy by inducing changes in interest rates charged for credit and by affecting the levels of personal and business investment spending.

The major monetary policy tool that the Federal Reserve System uses is open market purchases or sales of government securities. Other policy tools used by the Federal Reserve System include increasing or decreasing the discount rate charged on loans it makes to commercial banks and raising or lowering reserve requirements for commercial banks.

OBJECTIVES

♦ Students describe how changes in the money supply can affect the average level of prices.

♦ Students explain how the Federal Reserve System uses the major tools of monetary policy to regulate the economy's money supply.

♦ Students explain the chain of events that occur in the economy when the Federal Reserve System engages in a specific monetary policy.

LESSON DESCRIPTION

Students participate in two simulations. In the first, they discover the effects of excessive money creation on product prices. In the second simulation, they learn how the Federal Reserve System uses different tools of monetary policy to adjust the amount of money in the economy. Then they learn how monetary policies affect the economy as a whole.

TIME REQUIRED

Two class periods. Day one – procedures 1-15. Day two – procedures 16-22 and Assesment.

MATERIALS

- Popcorn seeds and kidney beans – enough to give each student 10 seeds and 5 beans
- Three identical bags of candy
- Activity 1: Money Matters Simulation Questions, one per student
- Activity 2: Money Creation, 10 copies cut in thirds, and 10 additional copies of the $10,000 bill from this Activity

- A paper tent sign with the word "BANK" written on both sides
- Visual 1: Monetary Policy and the Demand for Loanable Funds

PROCEDURES

1. Ask students how many of them would be better off with more money. (Most will raise their hands.) Tell them that may be true for each of them, but it may not be true for everyone. Explain that the "fallacy of composition" (what's true for the individual is also true for the whole) is a common pitfall in economic thinking. Announce that you will conduct a simulation to determine if everyone is better off if everyone receives more money. You will hold three auctions for three identical bags of candy, one sold in each round.

2. Give each student five popcorn seeds, and explain that for this activity each seed is worth 10¢. Calculate the size of the classroom **money supply** (50¢ × number of students) and write it on the chalkboard. Sell the first bag of candy to the highest bidder, collect the "money" from the winning bidder, and write the price paid (in a dollar equivalent) on the chalkboard. Don't be concerned if some students pool their "money" during the bidding; this adds to the excitement of the auction.

3. Distribute the remaining popcorn seeds (5 per student), reminding students that each seed is worth 10¢, including any they did not spend in the first auction. Write the size of the money supply on the board ($1 × the number of students, minus the amount paid by the winner of the first auction). Conduct the second auction. Give the second bag of candy to the highest bidder, collect the price from the winning bidder, and write the price on the board.

4. Expand the money supply again to include the popcorn seeds students still have *and* the kidney beans that you distribute now (5 per student). The kidney beans are valued at $1 each. Calculate the money supply and write the number on the board. ($6 × the number of students, minus what was paid by the winners of the first two auctions.) Auction the third bag of candy to the highest bidder, and write the price on the board. Note that the rapid increase in the classroom money supply when the amount of goods available to be consumed in each period remained constant drove up the price of candy. Explain that the same thing would have happened if there had been more than one kind of good auctioned in each round, as long as the total quantity of goods in each round remained fixed while the money supply increased rapidly.

5. Ask students to explain the fallacy of composition in thinking that everyone will be better off if everyone has more money, based on their experience with the simulation. (*There was a larger money supply, but there was still the same amount of goods. The amount of money alone had no impact on the amount of goods available, only on the price of the goods.*) Ask for a term that students might have heard to describe this situation. (*inflation*)

6. Define **inflation** as an increase in the average price of goods and services in the economy. Explain that, during the second and third auctions, students witnessed the fundamental long-run source of inflation in an economy – the supply of money growing faster than the supply of goods and services available for purchase. This is often described as too much money chasing too few goods.

7. Distribute a copy of Activity 1 to each student to reinforce the understanding of inflation developed in the auctions. Have students complete the worksheet independently, and then discuss students' answers in class. (Answers are provided below.) Point out that the long-run growth in the production of goods and services in the U.S. economy averages 2-4 percent a year. A long-term growth in the money supply of about the same rate would have a neutral effect on prices, assuming people don't change their spending and saving behavior for other reasons. (Over the long run, however, people do change

their spending and saving behaviors as a result of institutional factors, such as being paid more or less frequently, and to some extent as a result of changes in other factors such as income levels and interest rates.)

Answers to Activity 1

A. What happened to the price of the item auctioned between the first and third auctions? (*increased*)

B. What happened to the amount of "money" in the classroom between the first and third auctions? (*increased*)

C. What gave the seeds and beans value? (*They could be used to buy something. The money's real value depended on the amount of goods it could buy.*)

D. When students had more money to spend, what happened in the successive auctions? (*Prices increased.*)

E. What do you think would have happened to the price if the number of items offered for sale in the third auction increased from one to 100? (*decrease in average price*)

F. Under what conditions is increasing the supply of money inflationary? (*when the increase in the money supply greatly exceeds the increase in the number of goods and services available*)

G. Under what conditions is increasing the supply of money not inflationary? (*when the increase in the money supply is not greater than the increase in the number of goods and services, or if people choose not to spend their larger money holdings*)

8. Summarize that when the money supply increases, it is important that it grow at an appropriate rate – not too fast, not too slow.

Explain that the students will participate in an activity to show how the Federal Reserve System (the Fed) can determine, at least to a large extent, how fast or how slowly the U.S. money supply grows. (Note to teacher: Students can learn more about the Federal Reserve System at *www.FederalReserveEducation.org*.)

9. Inform students that an independent agency of the federal government, the Federal Reserve System, is responsible for regulating the U.S. money supply. In doing this, the Fed influences **interest rates** (the price of loanable funds) in the economy. To demonstrate how the Fed regulates the money supply, divide the class into thirds. Using materials prepared from Activity 2, give each student in the first group a $10,000 U.S. Treasury bond; each student in the second group $10,000 in currency; and each student in the third group $10,000 in a checking account.

10. Explain that the students with bonds have each lent money to the U.S. Treasury. The Treasury bond is an IOU from the government, acknowledging the debt and promising to repay the bondholder, with interest, at a certain time. The bond is *not* money, however, because it can't be widely used to purchase goods and services from people or in stores. Students with $10,000 in a checking account or in currency have money that *can* be used to buy goods and services; only the forms in which they hold the money differ. Point out that students have probably seen people buy things with currency and checks, but not with bonds.

11. Ask all students with money (checking deposits or currency) to raise their hands. Count the number of hands and multiply by $10,000 to determine the initial amount of money in the classroom. Write this number on the chalkboard under the heading of "Money Supply."

12. Tell four students with bonds to assume that they want to buy something, so they must get money by selling their bonds. Tell four students with money (currency or checks) to assume that

they now want to buy bonds in order to earn interest. Have the eight students exchange their bonds and money. Ask the class if there has been any change in the amount of money in the classroom. (No – different people hold money and bonds, but the total amounts have not changed. Demonstrate with another show of hands, counting those who hold currency and checks.)

13. Tell four more students with bonds that they have decided they want to get money by selling their bonds. Announce that you will act as the Federal Reserve System in the rest of the activity. The Fed has decided to buy these four bonds. Give each of the four students $10,000 in currency in exchange for the $10,000 bond. Explain that the Federal Reserve System buys bonds when it engages in an expansionary monetary policy. Discuss the following.

A. What has happened now to the amount of money in the classroom? (*It increased by $40,000. Demonstrate with another show of hands*.)

B. Where did the money come from? (*the Federal Reserve*)

C. Where did the Federal Reserve get the money? (*The Fed created the money out of thin air, in effect printing money, although in practice it simply pays with a check, not by issuing additional currency.*)

D. When the Fed buys bonds, it engages in expansionary monetary policy. Why is it called "expansionary?" (*The money supply increases, or expands*.)

14. Reverse procedure 13; that is, have the Fed sell bonds to four students in exchange for money (currency or checks) from the students. Once again, ask all students with money to raise their hands. Count hands and multiply by $10,000 to show that when the Fed sells bonds, that reduces, or contracts, the money supply.

15. Tell students that the Fed buying and selling government bonds is called **open market operations**, and that this is the most important tool used by the Fed to regulate the money supply. Open market operations are used on a week-to-week basis to make both large and small adjustments to the nation's money supply.

16. Ask all students with checking account money to raise their hands. Multiply the number of hands by $10,000, and write this number on the chalkboard under the heading "Bank Deposits." Have a pile of currency equal to this amount with the sign marked "BANK" beside it. Tell the students that the bank has their money on deposit and would like to lend some of it.

17. Explain that the amount the bank can lend depends on the reserve requirements set for banks by the Federal Reserve. The **reserve requirement** is the amount of deposits that a bank must keep "on reserve." These funds may not be lent. Point out that if the reserve requirement were 100 percent, none could be lent; if it were 25 percent, 75 percent could be lent. Announce that in this simulation the Fed's reserve requirement for banks is initially 50 percent. (The actual reserve requirement is much less than 50 per cent.) Then lend half the bank's checking account deposits to a student, by giving the student that much money in a checking account. Have the student sign an IOU for the amount of the loan. Explain that banks don't keep every dollar deposited in the bank in the vault – they make loans to earn money for the bank and its depositors, charging interest on those loans. Because depositors don't all show up at the bank at the same time trying to withdraw their money, banks can use most of their deposits to make loans, subject to the Fed's reserve requirements and following sound banking practices, which are monitored by other state or federal banking agencies.

Ask the class the following questions:

A. How much money is in the classroom now? (*Count all currency and checking account balances.*)

B. By how much has the money supply increased? (*By the amount of the loan.*)

C. What action caused the increase in the money supply? (*The bank's loan.*)

D. If the Federal Reserve cut the reserve requirement, what could the bank do? (*Make more loans and expand the money supply even more.*)

Summarize by explaining that actions by the Federal Reserve that change the reserve requirement will influence the money supply. A decrease in the reserve requirement is an expansionary monetary policy. An increase in the reserve requirement is a contractionary monetary policy.

18. Announce that the bank made too many loans yesterday and is $500,000 short of meeting its reserve requirement. Explain that the Federal Reserve lends money to banks in these circumstances, so they can meet their reserve requirements; but it charges banks interest on these loans. The interest rate on these loans to banks from the Federal Reserve is known as the **discount rate**. Ask if the bank would borrow this money from the Federal Reserve if it had no better way to meet its reserve requirements? (Yes, although banks usually try to avoid such loans. But the higher the Federal Reserve sets the discount rate, the more it costs banks to borrow, and the greater their incentive to limit their lending to meet their reserve requirements. Therefore, raising the discount rate is a contractionary monetary policy; lowering the discount rate is an expansionary monetary policy.)

19. Tell students that although the reserve requirement and the discount rate are monetary policy tools the Federal Reserve System sometimes uses, open market operations are the monetary policy tool most frequently used by the Fed. By buying and selling government securities (bonds), the Fed changes the nation's money supply. Changes in the money supply affect the market for loanable funds.

20. Display Visual 1. Explain that this graph shows the effect of a change in the money supply on the quantity of loanable funds demanded by individuals, businesses, and government agencies (local, state, or federal) that want to borrow money. The interest rate is the price of loanable funds. Those who lend money receive interest; those who borrow pay interest.

21. Remind students that when the Fed buys bonds (as in the classroom simulation), the money supply increases. Discuss the following.

A. When the supply of loanable funds increases, what happens to the interest rate? (*It decreases.*)

B. Would people who want to buy cars, houses, and durable goods be more or less encouraged to borrow money? (*more*)

C. Would businesses that want to build factories or purchase equipment be more or less encouraged to borrow money? (*more*)

D. If people and businesses borrow more money at the lower interest rate, what will happen to the level of spending in the economy? (*It will increase.*)

E. If people are spending more money, what will businesses want to do? (*produce more goods and services*)

F. If businesses begin to produce more goods and services, what is happening in the economy? (*The real gross domestic product is increasing; that is, more output is produced and more people have jobs.*)

G. If the money supply increases faster than the rate at which output is growing, what will result? (*inflation*)

H. What happens if the Fed sells bonds? (*The money supply decreases, interest rates rise, spending and production of goods and services decrease.*)

22. When would the Fed want to conduct an expansionary monetary policy? (*When the economy is facing a recession, or not growing as rapidly as the Fed believes it should.*) When would the Fed want to conduct a contractionary monetary policy? (*When the economy is experiencing high rates of inflation, or growing more rapidly than the Fed believes it should.*)

CLOSURE

1. If the money supply is growing faster than the production of goods and services in our economy, what will be the result? (*inflation – too many dollars chasing too few goods*)

2. What is inflation? (*an increase in the average price of goods and services in the economy*)

3. What is the primary role of the Federal Reserve System? (*to regulate the money supply in order to keep inflation and unemployment low, and promote steady economic growth*)

4. What are open market operations of the Fed? (*buying and selling bonds or other financial securities issued by the federal government*)

5. If the Fed sells government bonds, what type of monetary policy is it pursuing? (*contractionary*)

6. If the Fed buys government bonds, what type of monetary policy is it pursuing? (*expansionary*)

7. What is the reserve requirement? (*the percentage of deposits commercial banks must keep "on reserve" with the Fed, which are not available for loans*)

8. Is a decrease in the reserve requirement contractionary or expansionary? (*expansionary*)

9. What is the discount rate? (*the interest rate paid by commercial banks if they borrow from the Fed*)

10. Which monetary policy tool does the Fed use most often? (*open market operations*)

11. Describe the chain of events in the economy when the Fed engages in an expansionary monetary policy using open market operations. (*The Fed purchases government bonds, the money supply increases, interest rates fall, people and businesses borrow and spend more money, the production of goods and services [real GDP] increases.*)

ASSESSMENT

1. Tell students to assume the role of members of the Federal Reserve Board. They are charged with controlling the nation's money supply to achieve full employment and stable prices in the economy. In groups of twelve students (corresponding to the size of the Fed's Open Market Committee, the FOMC), have the students prepare a proposal recommending monetary policy actions designed to correct problems with spending, employment, and average prices caused by high interest rates. Specifically, different groups should assume one of the following scenarios for the economy or, if time permits, have each group consider all three scenarios:

A. The national economy is sluggish as a result of tight (contractionary) monetary policies over the past two years.

B. The economy is growing rapidly. Many economists believe there will be shortages of skilled labor and key industrial inputs, such as steel and electric power.

C. The economy is experiencing 10 percent inflation per year.

Have each group identify and list the most likely problems with spending, employment, and average prices under the different scenarios. What monetary policy does each group propose? How does each group expect the monetary policy it proposes to solve the problems the group identified with spending, employment, and average prices? Have the groups present their recommendations to the full class, compare their reasoning, and try to agree on the most appropriate set of monetary policies for each scenario.

2. Have students read the business section of any large daily newspaper and find articles on interest rates. Have students, individually or in small groups, speculate on the actions that the Fed might have taken to produce the effect on interest rates described in the article. Have some students present the results of their investigations to the rest of the class for discussion.

Activity 1
Money Matters Simulation Questions

A. What happened to the price of the item auctioned between the first and third auctions?

B. What happened to the amount of "money" in the classroom between the first and third auctions?

C. What gave the seeds and beans value?

D. When students had more money to spend, what happened in the successive auctions?

E. What do you think would have happened to the price if the number of items offered for sale in the third auction increased from one to 100?

F. Under what conditions is increasing the supply of money inflationary?

G. Under what conditions is increasing the supply of money not inflationary?

Activity 2
Money Creation

$10,000

U.S. Treasury Bond

Face Value Will Be Paid on July 31, 2011

7 1/2% Interest Paid Quarterly

$10,000   THE UNITED STATES OF AMERICA $10,000

$10,000

$10,000   TEN THOUSAND DOLLARS $10,000

Your Name & Address		Check # 0001
		Date

Pay to the Order of _____ **YOU** _____ $ | 10,000.00 |

Ten thousand and no/100 ————————————————— dollars

Your Bank

For:_____

Signature

653276014   223600122   0001

Visual 1
Monetary Policy and the Demand for Loanable Funds

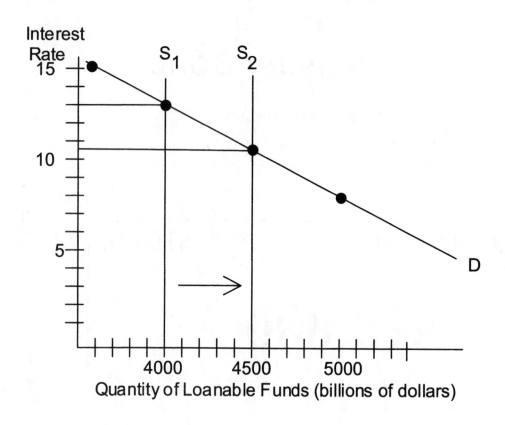

Quantity of Loanable Funds (billions of dollars)

LESSON TWENTY
AGGREGATE SUPPLY AND DEMAND: THE SUM OF THEIR PARTS, AND MORE

INTRODUCTION

Over the last two decades, the most dramatic pedagogical innovation in teaching introductory economics has been the use of aggregate supply and demand curves to illustrate key macroeconomic concepts and policy issues. There is still some debate about this development among university economists, but because these curves look and operate so much like the standard supply and demand curves featured at the heart of microeconomics, in some ways it is surprising that it took so long for aggregate supply and demand curves to become this popular.

Unfortunately, the conceptual underpinnings of aggregate supply and aggregate demand curves are quite different from those of the supply and demand curves for an individual product or productive resource. Therefore, an inherent problem in using the aggregate curves is to make sure students understand those differences. For that reason and others, some high school economics textbooks still do not feature aggregate supply and aggregate demand curves, even though virtually all college-level principles textbooks now do.

Because these models may not be familiar to some high school instructors, an appendix with background information is included at the end of the lesson. If the approach is new to you, or you are uncomfortable using it for any reason, read the appendix before you look through the following activities.

CONCEPTS
Aggregate demand
Aggregate supply
Gross domestic product (GDP)
Fiscal policy
Monetary policy

CONTENT STANDARDS
A nation's overall levels of income, employment, and prices are determined by the interaction of spending and production decisions made by all households, firms, government agencies, and others in the economy.

Federal government budgetary policy and the Federal Reserve System's monetary policy influence the overall levels of employment, output, and prices.

BENCHMARKS
Nominal gross domestic product (GDP) is measured in current dollars; thus, an increase in GDP may reflect not only increases in the production of goods and services, but also increases in prices. GDP adjusted for price changes is called real GDP.

The potential level of real GDP for a nation is determined by the quantity and quality of its natural resources, the size and skills of its labor force, and the size and quality of its stock of capital resources.

One person's spending is other people's income. Consequently, an initial change in spending (consumption, investment, government, or net exports) usually results in a larger change in national levels of income, spending, and output.

When desired expenditures for consumption, investment, government spending, and net exports are greater than the value of a nation's output of final goods and services, GDP rises and inflation occurs and/or employment rises.

When desired expenditures for consumption, investment, government spending, and net exports are less than the value of a nation's output of final goods and services, GDP decreases and inflation and/or employment decreases.

Fiscal policies are decisions to change spending and tax levels by the federal government. These decisions are adopted to influence national levels of output, employment, and prices.

Monetary policies are decisions by the Federal Reserve System that lead to changes in the supply of money and the availability of credit. Changes in the money supply can influence overall levels of spending, employment, and prices in the economy by inducing changes in interest rates charged for credit and by affecting the levels of personal and business investment spending.

OBJECTIVES

♦ Students define aggregate supply and aggregate demand, and identify the factors that can cause those schedules to shift over time.

♦ Students use the aggregate supply and aggregate demand model to analyze the effects of various macroeconomic events, including different stabilization policies.

LESSON DESCRIPTION

After an introductory lecture and discussion, students participate in two activities. In the first, competing in quiz show formats, students identify different components of aggregate supply and demand and determine whether the immediate impact of that component is to increase the level of a nation's aggregate supply or aggregate demand. In the second activity, individual students or small teams compete to identify the effects of various changes in the economy on the position of the aggregate supply curve or the aggregate demand curve.

TIME REQUIRED

An initial lecture and class discussion (procedure 1) requires one class period. The remaining activities take an additional three periods, covering procedures 2-4 on the first day, procedures 5-9 on the second day, and procedure 10 and the Assessment on the third day. Additional assignments are suggested that could be used for a few additional days, or for as long as two weeks in classes emphasizing macroeconomic theory and policy issues.

MATERIALS

- Activity 1: Which Side Are You On? transparency and one per student
- Activity 2: Shifting Shapes and Curves, transparency and one per student
- Visual 1: A Century of U.S. Macroeconomic Performance, one per student

PROCEDURES

1. Give an introductory lecture on aggregate supply and aggregate demand, based on the Appendix in this lesson or textbook treatments of these topics. Be sure to cover the components of aggregate supply and aggregate demand, noting how an increase or decrease in those components would shift the relevant curve. Also stress the differences between what is shown by aggregate supply and aggregate demand curves and by supply and demand curves for an individual product or productive resource.

2. Divide the class into two or more teams for a 20-question quiz show on aggregate demand and aggregate supply, called "Which Side Are You On?" Let students or teams earn points or "money" by answering questions correctly (as on the popular television show, *Who Wants to Be a Millionaire?*), or if you prefer eliminate teams or individuals who offer incorrect answers (as on the television show, *The Weakest Link*). Indicate at the outset that you will ask a total of only 20 questions, and the student or team with the most money, or the students or teams still surviving after 20

questions are asked, will be declared the winners.

For each of the 20 items listed in Activity 1, students must identify quickly (no more than 30 seconds – the time it takes to play the "Final Jeopardy" tune) whether the item is part of aggregate supply or aggregate demand. You will read out the 20 items in random order. Tell students they must indicate whether the *immediate* impact of the resource or activity should be classified as a component of aggregate supply or aggregate demand.

3. Play "Which Side Are You On?" announcing the correct answers after students have given their answers. Also indicate a dollar value for each question (which may vary or increase from question to question) if you are using that format for the game, or eliminate students or teams of students who answer incorrectly, if you are using that format. Do not explain or debate answers at this time, however. Hold those discussions for the debriefing, and maintain a rapid, game-show pace as you read out the 20 items. Congratulate the winners, and say "Goodbye" to those who do not win.

4. Distribute a copy of Activity 1, "Which Side Are You On?" to each student and debrief the activity. (If you plan to use this activity in multiple classes throughout the day, collect and reuse the sheets, to make sure a copy does not "leak" to students in later classes.) Review all of the classifications shown on Activity 1 with the entire class. Note that while the immediate impacts of the resources and activities can be assigned to either aggregate supply or aggregate demand, many of the classifications become far more ambiguous over time. For example, factories are primarily part of aggregate supply, but investment spending to build factories (or a new house) is part of aggregate demand. In the long run, all of the cases involving people as resources will impact both aggregate supply and aggregate demand. At a given moment in time, however, in their roles as workers and entrepreneurs, people are productive resources

acting as part of aggregate supply; as consumers their spending for goods and services is the largest single component of aggregate demand. This ambiguity in the long run is a natural part of the system-wide or general equilibrium nature of macroeconomics. Here, it will also make the students' discussion and your debriefing more interesting.

The key point is for students to understand the basic components of aggregate supply and aggregate demand (discussed more fully in the Appendix), and then the factors that shift these two curves, which are the focus of the second group activity.

5. Divide the class into groups of three to five students, including stronger and weaker students on each team. Announce that the teams will compete in a new game, "Shifting Shapes and Curves," to see who can identify the initial effect on aggregate supply or aggregate demand of several different events that you will announce. If you have more time to devote to this material, have the teams compete on the basis of which team gets the most correct answers when you announce all of the events, with each team recording its answers on paper.

6. *Important: Decide whether you will use optional procedure 8 before you begin this activity!* Explain that the events you are about to describe will initially cause aggregate supply or aggregate demand curves to increase or decrease, or lead to a movement along the aggregate supply and aggregate demand curves without causing them to shift. (When the price level changes we move along the aggregate supply and aggregate demand schedules, just as we move along a microeconomic supply or demand curve for a particular product when its price changes. See Lessons 3-5 for the microeconomic parallel.) As in the previous group activity, over time some of these events may also result in shifts in the other aggregate schedule, too – be sure students understand that once again you want them to identify the

immediate effect on aggregate supply or aggregate demand.

7.   Mixing the order of individual items and different categories on Activity 2, call them out to the class one by one. Team members should discuss their answers together before announcing or recording their final team answers. They should not talk with students in other groups. *If you use optional procedure 8, first announce the event from Activity 2, then announce whether the students should use the short-run aggregate supply curve, the long-run aggregate supply curve, or both, to identify the effects on the price and output/income levels*

8.   (Optional) As an extension of procedures 6 and 7, you may want to award additional points if students can identify the effects of the shifts in aggregate supply and aggregate demand depicted in procedure 7 on the equilibrium price level and the level of real national output. Recognize that, for shifts in aggregate demand, the effects on the price and output levels will depend on whether aggregate demand is shown as intersecting the short-run or long-run aggregate supply curve, as discussed in the appendix to this lesson. Therefore, before announcing each event, you should announce the relevant time period (short run or long run) students should use in determining the price and output effects (*not* in determining whether the immediate impact of the item affects aggregate supply or aggregate demand). You may want to determine the time period at random, by flipping a coin. If you want to be sure both aggregate supply curves are covered about the same number of times, simply choose the particular aggregate supply curve used in each situation yourself. Or, if you prefer, you can have students answer each question for both the long-run and short-run aggregate supply curve. However you choose to do this, remember to keep track of which aggregate supply curve (or curves) are used for each question.

9.   After all of the items from Activity 2 have been called out and the student responses

collected, distribute copies of Activity 2 to each student. (Once again, if you will use this activity in later classes during the day, collect and reuse these sheets, to make sure copies are not "leaked" to students in classes that meet later in the day. Debrief the "Shifting Shapes and Curves" activity. Review each of the factors and its impact on aggregate supply and aggregate demand, as shown on the sheet. In particular, note that price level changes in and of themselves will simply lead to movements along the aggregate supply and aggregate demand curves, not to shifts in either of these schedules.

If you conducted optional procedure 8, review the reasons for the different shapes of the short-run and long-run aggregate supply curves. An increase (decrease) in aggregate demand on the long-run aggregate supply curve will increase (decrease) the price level, but not change the level of output and employment. On the short-run aggregate supply curve, an increase in aggregate demand will increase price, output, and employment levels; a decrease in aggregate demand will have the opposite effects. Increases in aggregate supply will lower the price level and increase employment and output levels; decreases in aggregate supply will increase the price level and decrease employment and output levels.

10. Show the graphs and table in Visual 1 on overhead transparencies, or distribute copies to each student, working individually or in small groups. Ask them to identify periods of high inflation, high unemployment, or both. Use the information in the graphs and the following debriefing suggestions to help students discuss whether those periods seem to be primarily related to shifts in aggregate supply or aggregate demand. Make sure the students suggest a shift or simultaneous shift in these schedules that is consistent with the changes in the price, employment, and national income/output levels indicated in Visual 1. Relate these problems to the uneven, "business cycle" pattern of growth of the economy (see Lesson 18, on business

cycles) shown in the third graph and table, and suggest that the ideal role of macroeconomic stabilization policies (i.e., **monetary and fiscal policies**) is to make the pattern of growth smoother and, if possible, faster. Fiscal policies are decisions to change spending and tax levels by the federal government. Monetary policies are decisions by the Federal Reserve System that lead to changes in the supply of money and the availability of credit. Debrief the exercise.

(*Most of the periods of high inflation are associated with periods of war, when enormous increases in government spending and the nation's money supply sharply increased aggregate demand, leading to higher prices and output levels. Inflation during the two oil-price shocks of the 1970s is also notable – these shocks reduced aggregate supply, leading to higher price but lower output levels, with higher unemployment. The OPEC cartel accomplished this directly by reducing oil supplies, and indirectly because higher oil and energy prices also made much of the nation's capital stock of factories and machines inefficient or obsolete, because they had been designed to run on low-price oil, gas, or electricity.*

Unemployment rates were highest during the Great Depression, which President Roosevelt himself called a "failure of demand" – i.e., a period of falling prices and output. Most economists agree with Roosevelt's assessment, but suggest different reasons for the decrease in demand. For example, John Kenneth Galbraith blames the financial panic caused by speculation and the eventual crash of the stock market; Milton Friedman blames bad monetary policies adopted by the Federal Reserve System. Some economists have identified supply problems in agriculture and other key sectors in the late 1920s and the 1930s, but the strong consensus is that the Great Depression was primarily demand-induced. Other periods of high unemployment are related to the peacetime readjustments after the two World Wars, and to demographic changes during the late 1970s and 1980s when many women and "baby boomers"

first entered the labor force. To a large extent, those are both supply-side issues in labor markets, leading to lower wages and higher unemployment. By the 1990s, these demographic groups of once-new workers had become experienced, mostly middle-aged workers, who typically exhibit higher productivity and less turnover and unemployment.

Widespread use of computers and other new technologies may also have increased productivity and output during the 1990s, and stabilization policies that focused more on long-run target levels of inflation and unemployment may also have promoted the two longest peacetime expansions of the U.S. economy on record.)

Suggestions for Further Assignments on Aggregate Demand and Aggregate Supply

Aggregate supply and aggregate demand analysis deals with all of the productive resources in an economy; with all of the spending by households, businesses, and the government; with monetary and fiscal policies; and with international trade – all at the same time! It is difficult to capture fully all of those sectors in any detail using the kind of activities featured in this volume, so if class time and interest permit you may want to turn to more extensive sources and supplementary instructional activities. For example:

Running the U.S. Economy is a microcomputer simulation developed by Keith Lumsden and Alex Scott in 1992, and distributed by the National Council on Economic Education. The simulation is based on real historical data, but presented in a Year 1, Year 2, etc., framework that keeps the simulation from seeming dated to users. It features several scenarios that ask students to use monetary and fiscal policy to increase national economic welfare by reducing inflation, unemployment, and the federal deficit, while promoting economic growth.

Simulation of Macroeconomic Concepts, developed by Ronald L. VanSickle, Charles D. DeLorme, and Suzanne S. Wygal, includes several different versions of an aggregate supply-aggregate demand board game. It was published by The University of Georgia (Department of Social Science Education, Athens, Georgia, 30602) in 1990, with funding from the National Science Foundation.

The most widely used and available single source of macroeconomic data on the U.S. economy is the *Economic Report of the President,* prepared by the Council of Economic Advisers and published by the Government Printing Office in Washington, D.C., every February. Or, on the internet, go to *http://w3.access.gpo.gov/eop/*

For individual student worksheets that provide drill-and-practice exercises in shifting aggregate supply and demand curves, see the National Council on Economic Education's *Advanced Placement Instructional Package.*

CLOSURE

1. Referring to transparencies of Activities 1 and 2, review the components of aggregate supply and demand, and the reasons for the different shapes of the short-run and long-run aggregate supply curves.

2. Show the transparencies of the charts from Visual 1, and then draw graphs showing changes in aggregate supply or aggregate demand curves to illustrate the effects on the price level and the level of national output/income/employment for some of the historical periods discussed in procedure 10.

3. Relate stabilization policies (monetary and fiscal policies) and long-term public investment projects in education, infrastructure (roads, dams, etc.), and incentive structures in tax laws to changes in aggregate demand and aggregate supply. Ask students to identify some recently debated federal laws or policies that

will or would likely have an impact on aggregate supply or aggregate demand.

ASSESSMENT

Over a period of several weeks, have students identify reports on factors affecting aggregate supply or aggregate demand from the financial section of any large daily newspaper, *The Wall Street Journal, Business Week,* or stories carried on national nightly news broadcasts. Such stories appear frequently. For example, the Federal Reserve regularly tightens or loosens the growth of the money supply (see Lesson 19 on monetary policy) with an eye toward affecting aggregate demand, and consumer and investment spending in particular. Budget debates in Congress related to the annual budget bill prepared by the President are frequently reported as contractionary or expansionary. Consumer and business optimism indexes, related to planned consumer and investment spending, are often reported. Demographic trends affecting labor markets are frequently newsworthy, as are droughts, floods, OPEC production cuts or expansions, power shortages and new inventions – all factors influencing aggregate supply.

Appendix
Background Material on Aggregate Supply and Aggregate Demand

Aggregate demand is the total demand for goods and services in a national economy, which includes purchases of goods and services by domestic consumers, businesses, and government agencies, and by international consumers, businesses, and government agencies. **Aggregate supply** is all of the goods and services produced by all of the firms (including sole proprietorships) in an economy.

The nicest thing about using aggregate supply and aggregate demand curves to teach macroeconomics is that they are familiar to students who have already learned about supply and demand curves for an individual product in the introductory or microeconomic sections of an economics course. The mechanics of shifting the curves around and finding new equilibrium levels on the vertical and horizontal axes are, in fact, perfectly transferable. Therefore, once students understand what the aggregate supply and aggregate demand curves are they can use them to explain or predict the effect of some macroeconomic event or policy on the overall price level and the level of national output. But it is also important for students to understand that microeconomic and macroeconomic (i.e., aggregate) supply and demand curves depict very different things, and have the similar shapes they are normally shown as having for very different reasons.

The microeconomic demand curve for a particular good or service is downward sloping because of substitution and income effects. The *substitution effect* simply refers to the fact that, as the price of some product increases, it becomes relatively more expensive compared to other goods and services consumers might use to satisfy their wants. This increase in the relative price of the product leads people to buy less of it – or more of it in the case of a price decrease.

The *income effect* is based on the fact that people face budget constraints. That means that if the price of something they buy increases but the dollar value of their income does not, in real terms they are poorer and will have to buy less of most of the things they buy. In particular, the income effect associated with such a price increase will lead them to buy less of a product if it is a normal good, but more of the product if it is an inferior good. For example, they might buy less steak and more beans.

The macroeconomic or aggregate demand curve shows the relationship between the average price level for all goods and services and the quantity of all goods and services people are willing and able to buy. There is no direct parallel to the substitution effect that lies behind the microeconomic demand curve, because there obviously isn't any substitute for *all* goods and services.

Similarly, when the prices of all goods and services rise by some percentage, that does not imply that people's real incomes change. As the price level rises, the higher prices are paid out to households as income – in the form of wages and salaries, interest payments, rents, or profits. Or they are paid as taxes, which the government then uses to pay households for the goods and services it purchases, or to redistribute to other households as transfer payments, in either case increasing some households' incomes. Because every price increase also increases somebody's income,

Appendix (continued)

the real problem with unanticipated inflation is that it redistributes income, not that it directly lowers the average level of real income across all households. For that reason, the microeconomic idea of an income effect can't explain the typical shape of the aggregate demand curve, either.

Instead, the characteristic, downward-sloping shape of the aggregate demand curve is explained by:

- *The real balance or wealth effect.* As the average price level for all goods and services falls, the cash balances people are holding as currency and in their checking accounts will buy more goods and services. This isn't an increase in people's income but it is an increase in their wealth, which leads them to buy more goods and services when the price level falls. A rise in the overall price level has the opposite effect, decreasing wealth and the purchasing power of people's money holdings, which will reduce the amount of goods and services they buy.

- *The interest-rate effect.* As the overall price level rises (falls), the demand for money and interest rates will also tend to rise (fall), and that reduces (increases) investment spending, one of the most volatile components of aggregate demand. Once again, changes in the price level are inversely related to the amount of goods and services people want to buy – in this case capital goods such as factories and machines in particular.

- *The foreign-purchases effect.* As the price level for goods produced in a country rises, that tends to make those goods more expensive compared to

products produced in other countries, and so its net exports (exports minus imports) will fall. Net exports are a component of aggregate demand, so this is a rationale for the decrease in the quantity of all goods and services purchased as the price level increases. A decrease in the price level in a country will have the opposite effect, and increase its net exports.

At a given price level, the level of aggregate demand depends on the level of spending in four different categories: consumption expenditures, investment spending by businesses, government spending (by all levels of government), and net exports (exports minus imports). Factors that increase any of these components will shift the aggregate demand curve to the right; factors that reduce these components will shift it to the left.

The aggregate supply curve is a bit more complicated to explain, and has to be presented in two different situations or time horizons. To begin, the long-run aggregate supply curve is simply a vertical line, as shown in the first graph below, indicating the quantity of goods and services that a nation can produce using all its productive resources as efficiently as possible, given the current production technologies that are available to it. Developing more and better productive resources or technologies will shift the long-run aggregate supply curve to the right, but the curve will remain perfectly vertical.

In the long run, all resources brought to the factor markets where labor, capital, and natural resources are exchanged will be employed, because the fundamental economic problem of scarcity means that people want

Appendix (continued)

more goods and services than the economic system can produce. In the short run, prices for some resources may get out of line and lead to their unemployment or underemployment. But in the long run the owners of those resources have time to recognize their true market clearing prices, and must accept those prices (including wages) to keep the resources employed and thus contributing to their income and overall economic welfare.

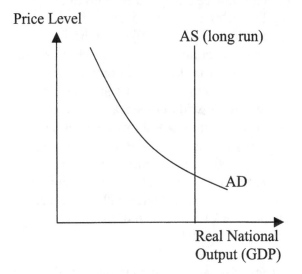

Price Level

AS (long run)

AD

Real National Output (GDP)

The short-run aggregate supply curve is typically shown with an upward slope, like the typical microeconomic supply curve for an individual good or service. But here, too, the reasons for the shapes of the aggregate supply curve and microeconomic supply curves are different. For the aggregate supply curve, if the overall price level decreases (perhaps because of a decrease in aggregate demand), but some wages and prices are "sticky" in the short run, output and employment levels will fall in the markets where wages and prices do not decrease enough to clear the markets of product inventories or unemployed workers.

Wages and prices can exhibit such "downward rigidity" because of long-term purchasing contracts between buyers and sellers of some products, multi-year

employment contracts between employers and unions, or legal wage or price floors (such as minimum wage laws and agricultural price supports). The same thing can happen when there are significant costs involved in lowering wages for workers and prices for products, even if there are not long-term contracts that prohibit such changes. (Examples of the costs of changing prices include such things as printing new catalogs and menus to notify employees and customers of these changes, or the costs of renegotiating contracts to establish new wage and price levels.) To avoid or at least reduce these costs, some firms will make adjustments in output and employment levels rather than price and wage changes, especially if there is a feeling that the decrease in demand is just a temporary phenomenon.

There are also cases in which informal, long-term agreements between buyers and sellers or employers and employees develop over years or decades, and come to have the status of implicit contracts that neither side wants to abandon because of a temporary slowdown. Initially, therefore, when there is a downturn in the economy that results in unsold products or too little work for the current labor force at such firms, the firms and unions may try to maintain current price and wage levels even though sales and employment fall, hoping that the economy and demand for their products will quickly rebound. Whatever the reason for the sticky wages and prices may be in particular markets, as the overall price level falls the real cost of using products and workers that exhibit sticky prices and wages goes up. That means the quantity of these products sold and the number of these workers employed falls, leading to a decrease in the overall level of output produced. If the lower level of demand, output, and employment continues long enough, wages and prices will eventually

Appendix (continued)

fall. But until that happens, the level of national output, employment, and national income fall, moving down along the short-run aggregate supply curve, as shown in the graph below.

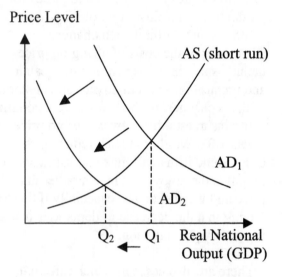

Another explanation for the positive slope of the short-run aggregate supply curve relates to situations where aggregate demand increases, starting from a level below full employment. When demand increases and output levels begin to rise, some key resources may reach full employment levels sooner than others, leading to production "bottlenecks" and upward pressures on wages and prices.

The exact shape and other characteristics of the short-run aggregate supply curve is a matter of some dispute among economists from different "schools" of macroeconomic thought. They disagree in particular about how flexible wages and prices really are, how costly it is to change wages and prices, and how important bottlenecks are in periods of increasing aggregate demand. They also disagree about the potential and historical effectiveness of stabilization policies adopted to deal with unemployment and lower levels of output, depending on their beliefs about the causes, pervasiveness, and persistence of the wage and price rigidities. Some economists (and politicians) favor using stabilization policies to help keep output and employment levels high even when the economy faces only moderate and relatively short downturns. Others believe that firms and workers will accept wage and price decreases quickly enough to make short-term stabilization policies unnecessary, and perhaps even ineffective or counterproductive if firms and workers anticipate the effects of the stabilization policies on wages and prices, and soon get back to the level of output established by the long-run aggregate supply curve, with or without the stabilization policies. If workers and firms expect the economy to return to full employment anyway, and the government increases spending to try to stimulate the economy, then the effect of those policies will be to increase the price level rather than output and employment levels.

These debates among macroeconomists date back at least to the Great Depression, and to the 1936 publication of the book that signaled the birth of modern macroeconomic theory and policy, John Maynard Keynes' *The General Theory of Employment, Interest, and Money*. Keynes' ideas have been loudly and actively debated since that time, and in recent decades the scope and conduct of stabilization policies have been modified sharply from what Keynes and his followers originally proposed. But to a large extent, the framework Keynes established, including his seminal work on aggregate demand, still frames the debates on macroeconomic theory and policy.

Activity 1
Which Side Are You On?

Aggregate Supply	Aggregate Demand
A factory producing computers	A company builds a new factory
A printing press	A U.S. company sells a jet to a foreign company
A tractor	A U.S. company buys coffee beans from South America
Trees	A woman buys a hamburger for her little boy
A corn field	Students purchase tickets for a rock concert
A coal mine	A woman buys a new car
A dentist	The government purchases a new submarine
An inventor	A farmer buys some fertilizer
A shoe salesperson	The government sends a woman to the moon
A rock star	Two newlyweds buy a house

Activity 2
Shifting Shapes and Curves

Increases Aggregate Demand:

1. People begin buying more food, clothing and cars.
2. The money supply increases.
3. Sales taxes in most states are cut 20%.
4 Other countries begin buying more goods and services from the U.S.

Increases Aggregate Supply:

1. A new invention makes solar energy the least expensive way to heat homes and fuel cars.
2. The percentage of people aged 62-72 who are employed or looking for jobs increases sharply.
3. A vast new oil field is discovered under the Great Salt Lake.
4. Education and training levels achieved by most new workers increase sharply.

Decreases Aggregate Demand:

1. The Federal Reserve increases the discount rate to increase other interest rates.
2. The federal government reduces military spending by 20%.
3. Private savings increase 8%.
4. This year the fashion industry features suits and dresses made with silk from China and Japan.

Decreases Aggregate Supply:

1. The OPEC nations reduce their production of crude oil by 30%.
2. More people begin taking early retirements.
3. Floods destroy 10% of the nation's corn and soybean crops.
4. Taxes on wages and salaries are increased 10%.

No Shift In Aggregate Supply or Aggregate Demand:

1. The price level for national output increases 10%.
2. The price level for national output decreases 2%.

From *Focus: High School Economics*, © National Council on Economic Education, New York, NY

Visual 1
A Century of U.S. Macroeconomic Performance

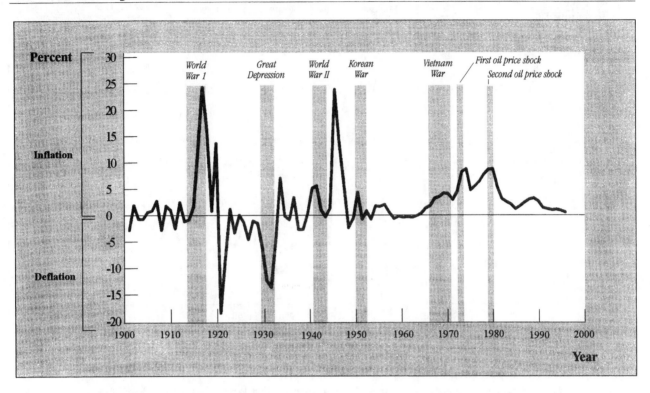

The Inflation Rate in the U.S. Economy

The inflation rate measures the percentage change in the average level of prices from the year before. A negative inflation rate indicates that prices are falling.

Adapted from: <u>Macroeconomics</u> by N. Gregory Mankiw © 1994, 2000 by Worth Publishers. Used with permission.

Visual 1 (continued)

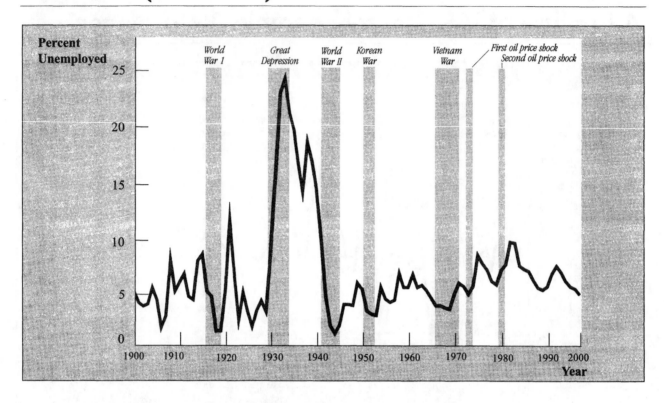

The Unemployment Rate in the U.S. Economy
The unemployment rate measures the fraction of the labor force that does
not have a job.

Adapted from: <u>Macroeconomics</u> by N. Gregory Mankiw © 1994, 2000 by Worth Publishers. Used with permission.

Visual 1 (continued)

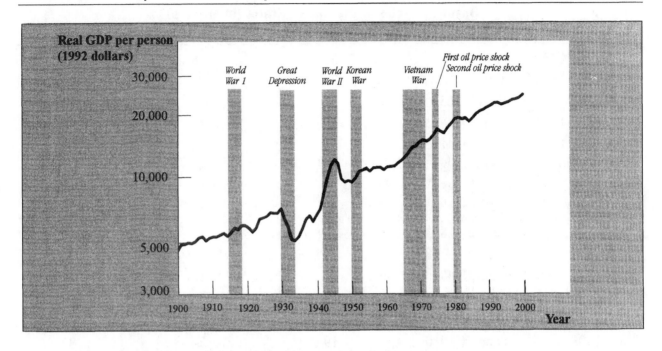

Real GDP per Person in the U.S. Economy

Real GDP measures the total income of everyone in the economy. Real GDP per person measures the income of the typical person in the economy.

Note: Real GDP per person is plotted here on a logarithmic scale. On such a scale, equal distances on the vertical axis represent equal *percentage* changes. Thus, the distance between $5,000 and $10,000 is the same as the distance between $10,000 and $20,000.

Adapted from: <u>Macroeconomics</u> by N. Gregory Mankiw © 1994, 2000 by Worth Publishers. Used with permission.

Visual 1 (continued)

Business Cycles in the United States (in months)

Trough	Peak	Length of upturn	Length of downturn	Length of cycle*
December 1854	June 1857	30	18	
December 1858	October 1860	22	8	40
June 1861	April 1865	46	32	54
December 1867	June 1869	18	18	50
December 1870	October 1873	34	65	52
March 1879	March 1882	36	38	101
May 1885	March 1887	22	13	60
April 1888	July 1890	27	10	40
May 1891	January 1893	20	17	30
June 1894	December 1895	18	18	35
June 1897	June 1899	24	18	42
December 1900	September 1902	21	23	39
August 1904	May 1907	33	13	56
June 1908	January 1910	19	24	32
January 1912	January 1913	12	23	36
December 1914	August 1918	44	7	67
March 1919	January 1920	10	18	17
July 1921	May 1923	22	14	40
July 1924	October 1926	27	13	41
November 1927	August 1929	21	43	34
March 1933	May 1937	50	13	93
June 1938	February 1945	80	8	93
October 1945	November 1948	37	11	45
October 1949	July 1953	45	10	56
May 1954	August 1957	39	8	49
April 1958	April 1960	24	10	32
February 1961	December 1969	106	11	116
November 1970	November 1973	36	16	47
March 1975	January 1980	58	6	74
July 1980	July 1981	12	16	18
November 1982	July 1990	92	19	108
May 1991				

* Peak to peak

SOURCES: U.S. Department of Commerce, *Handbook of Cyclical Indicators,* supplement to *Business Conditions Digest,* 1984, p. 178.; *Survey of Current Business,* p. C-25, annual editions.

From *Focus: High School Economics,* © National Council on Economic Education, New York, NY

LESSON TWENTY-ONE
ECONOMIC GROWTH AND DEVELOPMENT

INTRODUCTION

Economic growth is measured by a rise in real (inflation-adjusted) gross domestic product (GDP) over time. When a nation's production of goods and services rises faster than its population, real GDP per capita increases. That signals a rise in average income and the material standard of living. In other words, more production per person translates into more income and more consumption per person.

There are many different causes of, and obstacles to, economic growth. Over decades and even centuries, small differences in average annual growth rates in different nations are compounded, resulting in very large differences in average levels of income for the people who live in different countries. Institutions and policies that promote a stable political and economic climate, and help to encourage economic growth, are therefore extremely important.

CONCEPTS

Economic growth
Real GDP per capita
Investment
Production
Inputs
Human capital
Technology

CONTENT STANDARDS

Investment in factories, machinery, new technology, and the health, education, and training of people can raise future standards of living.

A nation's overall levels of income, employment, and prices are determined by the interaction of spending and production decisions made by all households, firms, government agencies, and others in the economy.

BENCHMARKS

Economic growth is a sustained rise in a nation's production of goods and services. It results from investments in human and physical capital, research and development, technological change, and improved institutional arrangements and incentives.

Historically, economic growth has been the primary vehicle for alleviating poverty and raising standards of living.

Gross domestic product (GDP) is a basic measure of a nation's economic output and income. It is the total market value, measured in dollars, of all final goods and services produced in the economy in one year.

Per capita GDP is GDP divided by the number of people living in a country.

GDP adjusted for price changes is called real GDP. Real GDP per capita is a measure that permits comparisons of material living standards over time and among people in different nations.

The potential level of real GDP for a nation is determined by the quantity and quality of its natural resources, the size and skills of its labor force, and the size and quality of its stock of capital resources.

Technological change is an advance in knowledge leading to new and improved goods and services and better ways of producing them.

The rate of productivity increase in an economy is strongly affected by the incentives that reward successful innovation and investments (in research and development, and in physical and human capital).

OBJECTIVES

♦ Students recognize the direct long-run link between economic growth and material standards of living.

♦ Students identify the major factors that promote economic growth, and some of the major factors that hinder economic growth.

LESSON DESCRIPTION

Students investigate the causes of, and obstacles to, economic growth by comparing data for high, middle, and low-income nations. Then they participate in an activity to see how changes in the quantity or quality of inputs can have different effects in different nations, depending on the nation's current mix of resources, technology, and educational achievements.

TIME REQUIRED

Two class periods. Day 1 – procedures 1-12. Day 2 – procedures 13-23 and Assessment.

MATERIALS

- Activity 1: Selected Countries and Centuries, one copy, cut up
- Activity 2: What Makes an Economy Grow, and Why Do We Care?, one per student
- Activity 3: Different Resources, Different Output and Growth, one per student
- Activity 4: Is It All in the Cards?, approximately one copy for each three students in the class – see Procedure 4 – cut up
- Visual 1: Sources of Growth in the U.S. Economy, 1929-1982
- Visual 2: Trends in National Income (real per capita GDP), 1870-2000
- Visual 3: The Growing Divergence of Income in High-Income and Low-Income Nations
- Visual 4: Factors Related to Economic Growth
- Visual 5: N. Gregory Mankiw's Four Secrets for Achieving High Rates of Economic Growth

PROCEDURES

1. Do this procedure quickly and informally, in about 10 minutes. Put the country slips from Activity 1 in one container, and the century slips in a second container. Have each student draw one country slip and one century slip, and write a paragraph describing the average standard of living for someone living at that time and in that country. What kind of jobs would most people have had? What kind of food would they likely have eaten? How long would they probably have lived?

2. Have some students read their paragraphs and poll the class to see how many students drew country and century slips that indicated a very low standard of living. (The late Kenneth Boulding used this assignment in his economics classes for over 40 years, and only once or twice did a student draw a country and century combination in which people were living in a wealthy, industrialized economy. Therefore, the key point of this activity is to show that throughout most human history, people lived in poor, usually agricultural societies. The average standard of living was not much higher than bare subsistence; food was plain, monotonous, and usually could not be refrigerated or stored for long periods; life expectancies were short, reflecting high rates of infant mortality, limited medical knowledge and services, and low and uncertain levels of agricultural production.)

3. To develop an overview of the current range of standards of living across the nations of the world, distribute a copy of Activity 2 to each student. Working individually or in small groups, have students answer the questions at the end of the activity:

A. List the five countries that have the highest and lowest values reported for each of the data series shown in the different columns of this table (e.g., average income, population, population growth, land area, etc.).

From *Focus: High School Economics*, © National Council on Economic Education, New York, NY

(*GNP* per capita* – High: USA, Norway, Denmark, Japan, Canada; Low: Nigeria, Kenya, Vietnam, India, Honduras).
* Some international data series still use Gross national product (GNP) rather than GDP. The technical differences between GNP and GDP are not important in this lesson – both are measures of a nation's annual income/output.

(Growth in GNP per capita – High: China, Taiwan, Hungary, Egypt, Australia and Poland (tie); Low: South Korea, Russia, Japan, Ukraine, Nigeria).

(Population – High: China, India, USA, Brazil, Russia; Low: Latvia, Norway, Denmark, Honduras, Hungary).

(Population growth: High: Saudi Arabia, Kenya, Honduras, Nigeria, Zimbabwe; Low: Russia, Hungary, Latvia, Ukraine, Italy).

(Land area – High: Russia, Canada, China, USA, Brazil; Low: Taiwan, Denmark, Latvia, Hungary, South Korea).

(Investment as % of GDP – High: China, Hungary, Honduras, Vietnam, Japan; Low: Kenya, Iran, Russia, South Africa, UK).

(Life expectancy – High: Japan, Canada, Australia, (four-way tie at 78 years); Low: Kenya, Zimbabwe, Nigeria, India, South Africa

(Index of Economic Freedom (note that a low numerical score indicates higher levels of freedom) – High: USA, Australia, UK, Canada, Taiwan; Low: Iran, Vietnam, Zimbabwe, India, Russia).

(Inflation – High: Ukraine, Brazil, Russia, Latvia, Nigeria; Low: Japan, Canada, Saudi Arabia, Denmark, Australia and France [tie]).

(Unemployment – High: Spain, Argentina, Latvia, Italy, France; Low: South Korea, China, Honduras, Japan, Mexico).

B. Based on these lists, which of the other variables seem to be closely related to a country's level of annual income and growth rate in real GNP, and which do not seem to be closely related to these income and growth levels? Point out that looking at these lists and the high and low subgroups can only suggest – not prove – the nature of the relationships between these measures. Still, some patterns seem fairly clear. (*High growth rates in population are more likely to occur in economies with low economic growth, but the overall size of a population can be high or low in both rich and poor economies. Geographic size (land area) does not guarantee high levels of income or economic growth. There are several cases where high rates of investment match up with high rates of growth, and vice versa. But there are exceptions, too – such as Japan, which has high rates of investment but was facing a severe recession in the years reflected in this table. High inflation is more likely to occur in countries with low income and growth, and low inflation in countries with higher income and growth.*) The Index of Economic Freedom is published annually by the Heritage Foundation and the *Wall Street Journal*. It is based on such features as trade policy (free trade or protectionist), tax rates, government's share of GDP, stable monetary policy and inflation, capital flows (or barriers to foreign investment), a free and stable banking system, flexibility or controls of wages and prices, property rights, the level of government regulation, and the extent of underground or "black market" activities. More freedom in these areas is correlated with higher levels of income and growth.

C. Which of the variables listed in the columns do you believe are most likely to be causes or determinants of a nation's levels of average income and **economic growth** – a sustained increase in real GNP or real GDP – and which of the variables listed in the columns do you believe are most likely to be results or effects of a nation's levels of income and growth? (*Students answers and beliefs will vary.*) Life expectancy is perhaps the clearest case of a variable that is partly determined by a nation's level of income and growth. Investment, public policies reflected in the economic freedom index, and low inflation rates are generally regarded by economists as factors that help to promote current and future economic growth.

4. By this point, the class should have a reasonably well informed idea about why economic growth and development is so important, and some understanding of factors that can promote or discourage growth. The obvious question that raises is: What has allowed some nations to experience high and sustained rates of economic growth for decades or even centuries, while other economies have not been able to do that? Discuss this question with the class for a few minutes, then announce that you will conduct a simulation to explore the question more systematically. Divide the class into either three, six, or nine groups, so that there are about three students in each group. Designate one third of the groups as "triangle groups," one-third as "rhombus groups," and one-third as "circle groups." If there are more than one group of each type, let the groups of

the same types sit fairly close together, but keep all of the groups slightly separated. Each type of group will work with a different deck of event cards in this activity.

5. Distribute one copy of Activity 3 to each student. Give one deck of 10 cards from Activity 4 to each group. Make sure each triangle group receives only one copy of each of the 10 triangle cards, each rhombus group receives one copy of each of the 10 rhombus cards, etc. To help keep these cards separated, you may want to draw or paste triangle, rhombus, and circle symbols on the back of the cards, or print the different decks on different colors of paper, or both. Have one student in each group shuffle the cards, but do not let students look at the cards at this time.

6. Explain that the table in Part I of Activity 3 is a numerical representation of what economists call a **production** function. In this activity, we will assume that each economy produces only one product – Quixotes. In sufficient quantity, Quixotes keep people alive and happy; but with too few Quixotes, people are miserable and may even die. Quixotes are produced using capital (K) and labor (L), as shown on the chart. But the three different groups (triangle, rhombus, and circle) will begin the activity in very different circumstances, represented by different locations on the table.

7. Announce that the triangle groups will begin the activity at the output level (or income level – for the overall economy, output and income are the same thing) of 1790 Quixotes, produced using 15 units of labor (L) and 19 units of capital (K). This output level is marked with a triangle on Activity 3. The rhombus groups start at the output level of 1000 Quixotes, produced using 10 units of labor (L) and 10 units of capital (K). This output level is marked with the rhombus on Activity 3 . The circle groups start at the output level of 196 Quixotes, produced using 15 units of labor (L) and 1 unit of capital (K). This output level is marked with the circle on Activity 3. The

locations of the different starting points for the three groups mean that the triangle groups represent high-income, industrialized economies, with relatively large quantities of both capital and labor. The rhombus groups represent middle-income economies, with somewhat less capital and labor than the triangle groups. The circle groups are low-income economies, with very little capital but relatively high amounts of labor.

8. Explain that after conducting the first part of the activity, the class will discuss the effects of differences in the quality as well as quantity of capital and labor in different kinds of economies. But for now ignore any quality differences, and concentrate on the number of capital (K) and labor (L) inputs, changes in those input levels, and the resulting changes in the level of output/income.

9. Have one person on each team draw the top card from their deck. In Part II of Activity 3, everyone on the team should write down the change in capital (K) and/or labor (L) shown on the card, the new level of output/income, and calculate the change in output/income.

10. Starting from the level of output/income produced *after* drawing the previous card, repeat procedure 9 four more times, until a total of five cards have been drawn from each team's deck. Do not draw more than five cards. This means that two teams from the same group (triangle, rhombus, or circle) may end up in different situations, even though they started from the same point.

11. Have each group report the total increase or decrease in their output/income level, compared to their initial starting point. Note whether the high, middle, or low-income groups experienced greater average gains. Explain that some of these differences reflect the luck of the draw, because each deck contained cards that increased and decreased capital (K) and labor (L) inputs, and some teams may have been

fortunate or unfortunate in drawing more of the increase or decrease cards. But there were other factors at work, too.

12. Debrief this part of the activity, first by pointing out that a one-unit change in capital or labor had a different effect on output depending on where a group was in the production schedule. Generally, one more unit of capital adds more to output for an economy that has very little capital (the circle groups) than it does for an economy that already has a lot of capital (the triangle groups). Similarly, one more unit of labor adds more to output in economies where workers have more capital to work with and labor is less abundant (the triangle groups) than it will in a country that already has a lot of labor and not much capital (the circle groups). (If you have covered the concept of diminishing marginal returns – see Lesson 15 – you may want to point out that, holding either the amount of capital or labor fixed while adding successive units of the other input, output will rise at a diminishing rate.) Note also that groups that drew cards that increased both their capital and labor inputs probably experienced greater gains in output/income than groups that only experienced an overall increase in one input. Also, groups that experienced net decreases in capital or labor inputs, or both, were naturally likely to do worse than groups that experienced increases in both inputs.

[In many class schedules, this will be an appropriate place to end Day 1 activities, with the remaining procedures covered on Day 2. Be sure students have Activity 3 to work with on both days.]

13. Note that several of the cards appeared in the decks for all three kinds of groups, namely the cards dealing with more women entering the labor force, older workers postponing their retirement, increased or decreased investments by individuals and companies from other nations, and the outbreak of World War III. All these cards had the same effect in terms of increasing or decreasing

capital (K) or labor (L) inputs, but the same change in K or L could lead to different changes in output/income in the different groups. You may want to take a minute to note that, despite some people claiming that wars, hurricanes, and other destructive natural or human events are good for the economy, in fact they destroy resources and make the fundamental economic problem of scarcity worse, not better. You might also want to discuss whether rich or poor nations are more likely to experience wars or natural disasters, but keep such discussions brief.

14. Explain that some of the cards were different in the three groups' decks, reflecting the different circumstances of high, middle, and low-income nations. Specifically:

A. The cards indicating an increase in population reflected different patterns, with immigration playing a larger role in the high-income nations, and high birth rates playing a large role in the low-income nations.

B. The cards indicating a decrease in the size of the labor force were based on a rising share of the population being elderly in high and middle-income nations, but resulted from deaths following droughts and crop failures in the low-income nations.

C. Changes in investment activity result from changes in private saving and interest rates in the high and middle-income nations, but changes in loans and grants from foreign governments and international agencies in the low income nations.

D. Political and economic stability are presented as a positive influence on international investments in the high-income nations, and instability is included as a negative influence in the deck for low-income nations.

Note that there are exceptions to these patterns of differences between high, middle, and low-income nations. Then ask students if they can give any examples of these kinds of patterns, or of exceptions to these patterns. *(Students may be familiar with low-income nations where birth rates and population growth are high, and famous cases of floods and famines. Political and economic instability continue to be key issues facing many of the transition economies that were part of the former Soviet Union, and most of the most successful transition economies were able to address this problem better than the transition economies that are reforming and growing more slowly. Japan is now the classic example of a nation facing huge demographic and economic changes as a rapidly growing share of its population becomes elderly.)*

15. Ask students to explain why, given the clear importance of the amount of investment in capital goods to the process of economic growth, low-income nations simply don't save and invest more? *(To invest in capital goods, current levels of consumption must be reduced somewhere, because you can't invest what you consume. Reducing consumption when income levels are low is, obviously, difficult to do. This creates what economists call "the vicious circle of poverty." Low income leads to low saving, low saving leads to low investment, and low investment leads to low economic growth and low future income. That is one reason why foreign investment is so important in low-income nations – as it was in colonial America and in the United States from 1492 through the 19th century. Actually, foreign investment is still very important in the United States today, largely because it is still such an attractive place to invest, given its high income, large population, and a high degree of political and economic stability.)*

16. Now lead a discussion to introduce the effects of differences in the quality of capital and labor inputs across different economies. For example, some capital goods use old

technologies, and some use new technologies. Usually, newer capital goods embody newer production technologies. Historically, countries that have led the way in developing and adopting new technologies have achieved higher levels of output/income. But investments in **human capital** – the education, training, and health of a nation's labor force – are also key to the process of economic growth. Labor productivity varies greatly across individual workers and across labor forces in different nations. Education and training account for a large part of those differences, in addition to differences in the quantity and quality of capital goods that workers have available to use in their jobs, and differences in institutions and public policies that affect workers' incentives to produce more. Some key incentives include wage differentials that are closely tied to productivity, and tax rates on wages, salaries, and profits.

17. Explain that differences in **technology** and other factors that affect the quality of labor and capital inputs are often treated as a variable that multiplies the outputs shown in production schedules like the one used in Part I of Activity 3. For example, suppose that we now assume that new capital investments are linked to the introduction of new technologies. That means that new investments of capital will increase output even more than the production schedule in Activity 3 indicated, because the increases shown in the table only reflect the increase in the quantity of capital, not changes in the quality of capital. To begin correcting that, have teams that experienced a net increase in capital (K) inputs multiply any net increases in output/income they experienced by the following amounts:

- if K increased by 1, multiply by 1.3;

- if K increased by 2, multiply by 1.5,

- if K increased by 3, multiply by 1.6.

- if K and output/income showed net decreases, or if K and output/income moved in opposite directions (because of offsetting changes in L), do not multiply the change in output.

If a team did multiply the change in output/income, have them write the new level of final income at the bottom of Part II in Activity 3. Note that the same kind of effect can be associated with increases in human capital, but do not make such calculations at this time.

18. Display Visual 1, and review the estimates of the factors responsible for economic growth in the U.S. economy through most of the 20th century. Note that some growth occurred simply because more labor and capital inputs were used, but new technologies and improvements in the quality of labor were also extremely important. The negative effects of laws and regulations reflect the costs of programs that deal with environmental issues, anti-discrimination programs, workplace safety rules, etc. The negative impact of these programs on economic growth does not, in and of itself, mean that these programs are not worthwhile. These programs have benefits as well as costs, and this data considers only costs of these programs.

19. Ask students to discuss which type of group (triangle, rhombus, or circle) had the best chance to experience economic growth in the activity. Then ask them whether they believe it is easier for high, middle, or low-income nations to sustain long periods of economic growth. *(The problems facing low-income nations are widely known and appreciated. It is likely that many students will suggest that high-income nations and the triangle groups have the best chance of sustaining economic growth.)* When this discussion is completed, say that you have one more factor for the class to consider.

20. Display Visual 2, and explain that this graph shows the rates of growth in real GDP per capita for the seven nations shown, from 1870

to 2000, with each nation starting from the level of national income it had achieved in 1870. The United Kingdom began this period with the highest level of income, but was surpassed by the United States around 1900. Since then, the United States has had the highest level of income, but the other nations have been catching up, or converging, to the U.S. level of income. Ask students to discuss or speculate why this convergence occurs. Then explain that economists have identified several factors, including:

A. Technology transfer – nations with lower incomes import and copy technology and business practices from the wealthiest nation.

B. Diminishing returns to capital – the wealthiest nation is likely to have the most capital, so additional capital is likely to be more productive in other nations, as shown in Activity 3.

C. International capital flows – businesses and individuals in the wealthiest nation are likely to finance some investments in other nations.

D. Research and development can increase output and income in all nations, so when technological progress is gradual and widespread, combined with the factors listed earlier, this helps other nations catch up with the richest nations.

E. Education and training in other nations also speeds the flow of capital goods from the richest nations.

21. Suggest that the pattern of convergence shown in Visual 2 means that countries in the rhombus and circle groups may well be improving the quality of their capital and labor inputs, not just the quantity. Therefore, have any groups in the rhombus groups that experienced a net increase in capital (K) and labor (L) inputs, combined, multiply their

increases in output by 1.1. Have them write the new level of income at the bottom of Part II in Activity 3.

22. Calculate the average level of final output/income for all of the triangle, rhombus, and circle groups, reflecting the adjustments made in procedures 17 and 21. Write the three average income figures on the board or an overhead transparency.

23. Ask students whether they believe low-income nations have been converging to the level of income enjoyed by high-income nations over the past century – because of the factors discussed in procedure 20 – or falling further behind – due to the "vicious circle of poverty," bad policies, a lack of investment in these nations by the wealthier nations of the world, or some combination of these and other effects. Accept any answers without comment, then display Visual 3. This shows clearly that income levels in the wealthiest and poorest nations in the world have diverged, rather than converged, over the past century. Explain that low levels of investment in physical and human capital, high population growth, poor public policies, and other factors discussed in this lesson are some of the main factors that explain this divergence.

CLOSURE

Display Visual 4, and use it to review with the class the factors that promote and impede economic growth, making reference to the activities presented in this lesson. In the discussion, note that the study that reported these results is based on data from 24 nations from 1960-1989. The nations are all members of the Organization of Economic Cooperation and Development (OECD) – predominantly industrialized, market economies. Adding low-income nations would add a much wider range of issues to consider, including nations with high rates of inflation (or even hyperinflation), more political instability, higher population growth, less spending for education, and higher trade barriers.

ASSESSMENT

Display Visual 5, or distribute a copy of this visual to the students. Ask them to write a short essay explaining how Harvard economist N. Gregory Mankiw's four secrets were illustrated in the activities covered in this lesson.

Activity 1
Selected Countries and Centuries

Albania	Iran	Singapore	21st century AD
Armenia	Iraq	Slovakia	20th century AD
Australia	Ireland	Slovenia	19th century AD
Austria	Israel	Somalia	18th century AD
Bangladesh	Italy	South Africa	17th century AD
Belarus	Jamaica	Spain	16th century AD
Belgium	Japan	Sri Lanka	15th century AD
Belize	Jordan	Sudan	14th century AD
Bolivia	Kazakhstan	Swaziland	13th century AD
Brazil	Kenya	Sweden	12th century AD
Bulgaria	Korea	Switzerland	11th century AD
Cambodia	Kuwait	Syria	10th century AD
Canada	Kyrgyzstan	Tajikistan	9th century AD
Chad	Laos	Tanzania	8th century AD
Chile	Latvia	Thailand	7th century AD
China	Lebanon	Tunisia	6th century AD
Columbia	Libya	Turkey	5th century AD
Congo	Lithuania	Uganda	4th century AD
Costa Rica	Madagascar	United Arab Emirates	3rd century AD
Cuba	Malaysia	United Kingdom	2nd century AD
Cyprus	Mexico	United States	1st century AD
Czech Republic	Mongolia	Uruguay	1st century BC
Denmark	Morocco	Uzbekistan	2nd century BC
Dominican Republic	Nepal	Venezuela	3rd century BC
Ecuador	The Netherlands	Vietnam	4th century BC
Egypt	New Zealand	Yemen	5th century BC
El Salvador	Nicaragua	Zambia	6th century BC
Estonia	Nigeria	Zimbabwe	7th century BC
Ethiopia	Norway		8th century BC
Fiji	Pakistan		9th century BC
Finland	Panama		10th century BC
France	Paraguay		11th century BC
Georgia	Peru		12th century BC
Germany	The Philippines		13th century BC
Ghana	Poland		14th century BC
Greece	Portugal		15th century BC
Guatamala	Romania		16th century BC
Haiti	Russia		17th century BC
Honduras	Rwanda		18th century BC
Hungary	Samoa		19th century BC
Iceland	Saudi Arabia		20th century BC
India	Senegal		21st century BC
Indonesia	Sierra Leone		

From *Focus: High School Economics*, © National Council on Economic Education, New York, NY

Activity 2
What Makes an Economy Grow, and Why Do We Care?

There is a very basic answer to the second part of this question. As President Kennedy once said, economic growth is a "rising tide that lifts all boats" – meaning that historically in the United States economic growth improved material standards of living for high, middle, and low-income families. Globally, nations that have experienced sustained economic growth – for decades or even centuries – have enjoyed much higher levels of production, income, and consumption than the economies that have achieved little or no growth.

What makes an economy grow is a more difficult question to answer. One place to start is by reviewing the basic categories of the factors of production: natural resources, capital resources, and human resources.

Certainly it helps to have large amounts of natural resources, as in the United States and Canada. But economies such as Japan and the Netherlands grew rapidly with comparatively little land and few other natural resources.

Investment in capital resources such as factories and machines can increase an economy's productive capacity and future levels of production and growth. But despite emphasizing capital investments in a series of five-year plans, the former Soviet Union faced falling levels of output and income in the 1980s, and eventually collapsed. That demonstrates that how and where resources are invested is important, as well as the overall level of investment.

Human resources are important to economic growth in several ways. First, labor is the single largest input used in most economies, including the United States. This is especially true in providing services to consumers and businesses, which is the fastest growing sector in most industrialized nations. (Services include professions such as health care, government, law, education, architecture, engineering, software development, and the arts – not just retail and fast food services.) Second, the education, training, and health of workers – which economists refer to as human capital – is directly related to workers' productivity, and therefore to levels of economic growth and income. Third, entrepreneurship and technological innovations developed through human innovation and creativity are key to the process of economic growth.

Despite all these positive effects that human resources can bring to the process of economic growth, it also seems clear that very rapid rates of population growth make it difficult, if not impossible, for economies to maintain high levels of economic growth and income. One of the most pervasive characteristics of low-income nations is a rapid rate of population growth.

Activity 2 (continued)

The system of incentives established by a nation's political and economic institutions can also have a crucial effect on economic growth. Are people allowed to own houses and cars as consumers, and are they allowed to own and operate businesses as producers? Are income levels set by the government or in the marketplace? How much of that income is then taxed away by the government? How much competition is there in the economy, and does the government try to increase or reduce the level of competition? How stable are a nation's political and economic institutions? Is there an orderly and predictable way for electing new administrations, or frequent and irregular turnovers? How high are inflation and unemployment?

It is sometimes said that recipes for economic growth are somewhat like recipes for making soups that have many ingredients. The most important ingredient is often the one that you don't have, or at least the one of which you have least. But sometimes there are ways to substitute more of other things to make up for what you don't have.

Look over the following table, which shows basic data related to these different kinds of inputs from countries that the World Bank has assigned to three different categories: High Income, Moderate Income, and Low Income. Notice how large some of the differences are between the wealthiest and poorest nations. Then answer the following questions at the end of the Activity.

Assignment and Discussion Questions:

A. List the five countries that have the highest and lowest values reported for each of the data series shown in the different columns of this table (e.g., average income, population, population growth, land area, etc.).

B. Based on these lists, which of the other variables seem to be closely related to a country's level of annual income and growth rate in GNP, and which do not seem to be closely related to these income and growth levels?

C. Which of the variables listed in the columns do you believe are most likely to be causes or determinants of a nation's levels of average income and economic growth, and which of the variables listed in the columns do you believe are most likely to be results or effects of a nation's levels of income and growth?

Activity 2 (continued)

Country	Average income (PPP[a] GNP per capita)		Population (million)	Average annual population growth rate (%,1980-98)	Land area (sq. km.)	Investment as a % of GDP	Life expectancy (years)	Index of economic freedom[b]	Average annual inflation rate (%,1990-98)	Annual unemployment rate (%, 1994-97)
	($ million)	growth (%, 97-98)								
USA	29,240	1.5	270	1	9364	19	77	1.80	1.9	4.9
Norway	26,196	1.7	4	0.4	324	25	78	2.30	1.8	4.1
Denmark	23,855	2.4	5	0.2	43	21	76	2.25	1.6	5.4
Japan	23,592	-2.9	126	0.4	378	29	81	2.15	0.2	3.4
Canada	22,814	2	30	1.2	9971	20	79	2.00	1.4	9.2
Germany	22,026	2.8	82	0.3	357	21	77	2.20	2.2	9.8
Australia	21,795	4.4	19	1.4	7741	22	79	1.90	1.7	8.4
France	21,214	2.8	59	0.5	552	17	78	2.50	1.7	12.3
Italy	20,365	1.3	58	0.1	301	18	78	2.30	4.4	12.5
UK	20,314	2	59	0.3	245	16	77	1.90	3	7.1
Spain	15,960	3.6	39	0.3	506	21	78	2.40	4.2	20.6
South Korea	13,286	-7.5	46	1.5	99	21	73	2.40	6.4	2.6
Taiwan	11,989	4.8	22	c	34	c	c	2.00	c	c
Argentina	11,728	2.6	36	1.4	2780	20	73	2.10	7.8	16.3
Saudi Arabia	10,498	-1	21	4.4	2150	21	72	2.95	1.4	c
Hungary	9,832	4.6	10	-0.3	93	31	71	2.55	22	8.7
South Africa	8,296	-1.3	41	2.3	1221	16	63	2.90	10.6	5.1
Poland	7,543	4.4	39	0.5	323	26	73	2.80	26.9	11.2
Mexico	7,450	3	96	1.9	1958	24	72	3.00	19.5	3.5
Brazil	6,460	-1.4	166	1.7	8547	21	67	3.50	347.4	6.9
Russia	6,180	-6.4	147	-0.4	17075	16	67	3.70	230.9	11.3
Latvia	5,777	4.3	2	-0.2	65	23	70	2.65	71.1	14.4
Iran	5,121	-0.2	62	2.6	1633	16	71	4.55	28.3	c
Egypt	3,146	4.5	61	2.3	1001	22	67	3.50	9.7	11.3
Ukraine	3,130	-1.6	50	0	604	21	67	3.60	440	8.9
China	3,051	6.4	1239	1.3	9597	38	70	3.40	9.7	3
Zimbabwe	2,489	-1.4	12	2.8	391	17	51	3.90	21.9	c
Honduras	2,338	1.1	6	3	112	30	69	3.35	20.6	3.2
India	2,060	4.3	980	2	3288	24	63	3.80	8.9	c
Vietnam	1,689	4.3	77	2	332	29	68	4.30	18.5	c
Kenya	964	0.3	29	3.1	580	14	51	3.05	15.8	c
Nigeria	740	-1.5	121	2.9	924	20	53	3.30	38.7	c

a. PPP = purchasing power parity, a method for comparing incomes looking at all goods and services produced and consumed in a nation, not just the goods and services traded with other countries that determine exchange rates for national currencies.

b. 1-5 scale, 1 = more freedom, 5 = less freedom.

c. information not reported

Source: World Bank, *World Development Report, 2000*

Activity 2 (continued)

Country	Major Industries
USA	petroleum, steel, motor vehicles, aerospace, telecommunications, chemicals, electronics, food processing, consumer goods, lumber, mining
Norway	petroleum and gas, food processing, shipbuilding, paper products, metals, chemicals, timber, mining, textiles, fishing
Denmark	food processing, textiles and clothing, machinery and equipment, chemical products, electronics, construction, furniture and other wood products, shipbuilding
Japan	steel and nonferrous metallurgy, heavy electrical equipment, construction and mining equipment, motor vehicles and parts, electronic and telecommunication equipment, machine tools, automated production systems, shops, locomotives, textiles, processed foods
Canada	processed and unprocessed minerals, food products, wood and paper products, transportation equipment, chemicals, fish products, petroleum, natural gas
Germany	iron, steel, coal, machinery, cement, chemicals, vehicles, machine tools, electronics, food and beverages, shipbuilding, petroleum refining
Australia	mining, industrial and transportation equipment, food processing, chemicals, steel
France	steel, machinery, chemicals, automobiles, metallurgy, aircraft, electronics, mining, textiles, food processing, tourism
Italy	tourism, machinery, iron and steel, chemicals, food processing, textiles, motor vehicles, clothing, footwear, ceramics
UK	production machinery, electric power equipment, automation equipment, railroad equipment, aircraft, shipbuilding, motor vehicles, electronics, metals, chemicals, paper products, food processing, textiles
Spain	textiles and apparel, food and beverages, metals and metal manufacturing, chemicals, shipbuilding, automobiles, machine tools, tourism
South Korea	electronics, textiles, chemicals, automobile production, food processing, clothing, footwear, shipbuilding, steel
Taiwan	electronics, textiles, chemicals, clothing, food processing, plywood, sugar milling, cement, shipbuilding, petroleum refining,
Argentina	food processing, motor vehicles, consumer durables, textiles, chemicals and petrochemicals, printing, metallurgy, steel
Saudi Arabia	crude oil, petroleum refining, basic petrochemicals, cement, construction, fertilizer, plastics
Hungary	mining, metallurgy, construction materials, processed foods, textiles, chemicals, motor vehicles
South Africa	mining (gold, platinum, chromium), automobile assembly, metalworking, machinery textiles, iron and steel, chemicals, fertilizers
Poland	machine building, iron and steel, coal mining, chemicals, shipbuilding, food processing, glass, beverages, textiles
Mexico	food and beverages, tobacco, chemicals, iron and steel, petroleum, mining, textiles, clothing, motor vehicles, tourism
Brazil	textiles, shoes, chemicals, cement, lumber, iron, ore, tin, steel, aircraft, motor vehicles and parts
Russia	coal, oil, gas, chemicals, metals, machine building, aircraft and space vehicles, shipbuilding, transportation equipment, medical and scientific equipment, construction equipment, textiles, handicraft
Latvia	buses, vans, street and railroad cars, synthetic fibers, agricultural machinery, fertilizers, washing machines, radios, electronics, pharmaceuticals, processed foods, textiles
Iran	petroleum, petrochemicals, textiles, cement and other construction materials, food processing, metal fabricating, armaments
Egypt	textiles, food processing, tourism, chemicals, petroleum, construction, cement, metals
Ukraine	coal, electric power, ferrous and nonferrous metals, machinery and transport equipment, chemicals, food processing
China	iron and steel, coal, machine building, armaments, textiles and apparel, petroleum, cement, chemical fertilizers, consumer durables, food processing, autos, consumer electronics, telecommunications
Zimbabwe	coal, clay, ores, copper, steel, nickel, tin, wood products, cement, chemicals, fertilizers, clothing and footwear, foodstuffs, beverages
Honduras	sugar, coffee, textiles, clothing, wood products
India	textiles, chemicals, food processing, steel, transportation equipment, cement, mining, petroleum, machinery
Vietnam	food processing, garments, shoes, machine building, mining, cement, fertilizers, glass, tires, oil
Kenya	small-scale consumer goods, agricultural product processing, oil refining, cement, tourism
Nigeria	crude oil, coal, tin, columbite, palm oil, peanuts, cotton, rubber, wood, textiles, cement

Activity 3
Different Resources, Different Output and Growth

Part I.

In this activity you will be working in small groups representing one of three different countries, named triangle, rhombus, and circle. In all three countries, only one good is produced and consumed, called Quixotes. In sufficient quantities, this good provides food, clothing, shelter, recreation, and all other material goods and services – in short, economic happiness. With too little Quixote, life cannot be sustained.

Quixotes are produced using labor (L) and capital (K). The table below shows how many units of Quixotes can be produced using different combinations of L and K. A starting point is shown for the triangle, rhombus, and circle economies: the triangle groups are initially producing 1790 Quixotes, using 15 units of labor (L) and 19 units of capital (K). This output level is marked with a triangle in the table below. The rhombus groups start at 1000 Quixotes, produced using 10 units of labor (L) and 10 units of capital (K). This output level is marked with the rhombus. The circle groups start at 196 Quixotes, produced using 15 units of labor (L) and 1 unit of capital (K). This output level is marked with the circle. Write down your starting level at the end of question 1 in Part II of this activity.

After your teacher gives each group a small deck of event cards, shuffle the deck but do not deal out or look at the cards. When the teacher tells you to begin, have someone in the group draw the first card and then have everyone in the group complete question 2 in Part II of this activity. Taking turns, draw four more cards and complete questions 3-6 in Part II. Your teacher will then give you some information to use in making some additional calculations, and lead a discussion of the results your team and other teams experienced.

Activity 3 (continued)

Units of labor inputs (L)

Units of capital inputs (K)

K \ L	1	2	3	4	5	6	7	8	9	10	11	12	13	14	15	16	17	18	19	20
1	100	118	131	141	149	156	162	168	173	177	182	186	189	193	(196)	200	203	205	208	211
2	168	200	221	237	251	263	273	282	291	299	306	313	319	325	330	336	341	346	351	355
3	227	271	300	322	340	356	370	383	394	405	415	424	432	440	448	455	462	469	475	482
4	282	336	372	400	422	442	460	475	489	502	515	526	537	547	556	565	574	582	590	598
5	334	397	440	472	500	523	543	562	579	594	608	622	634	646	658	668	678	688	698	707
6	383	455	504	542	573	600	623	644	664	681	698	713	727	741	754	766	778	789	800	810
7	430	511	566	608	643	673	700	723	745	765	783	800	817	832	846	860	873	886	898	910
8	475	565	626	672	711	744	773	800	823	845	866	885	903	920	936	951	965	979	993	1005
9	519	617	683	734	777	813	845	873	900	924	946	967	986	1005	1022	1039	1055	1070	1084	1098
10	562	668	740	795	840	880	914	945	974	/1000/	1024	1046	1067	1087	1106	1124	1141	1158	1174	1189
11	604	718	794	854	903	945	982	1015	1046	1074	1100	1124	1146	1168	1188	1208	1226	1244	1261	1277
12	644	766	848	911	964	1009	1048	1084	1116	1146	1174	1200	1224	1247	1268	1289	1309	1328	1346	1363
13	684	814	901	968	1023	1071	1113	1151	1185	1217	1246	1274	1300	1324	1347	1369	1390	1410	1429	1447
14	723	860	952	1023	1082	1132	1177	1217	1253	1287	1318	1347	1374	1400	1424	1447	1469	1490	1511	1530
15	762	906	1003	1077	1139	1192	1239	1281	1320	1355	1388	1418	1447	1474	1500	1524	1547	1569	1591	1611
16	800	951	1052	1131	1196	1252	1301	1345	1385	1422	1456	1488	1519	1547	1574	1600	1624	1647	1670	1691
17	837	995	1101	1183	1251	1310	1361	1408	1450	1488	1524	1558	1589	1619	1647	1674	1700	1724	1747	1770
18	873	1039	1150	1235	1306	1367	1421	1469	1513	1554	1591	1626	1659	1690	1719	1747	1774	1800	1824	1848
19	910	1082	1197	1287	1360	1424	1480	1530	1576	1618	1657	1693	1728	1760	△1790	1820	1847	1874	1900	1924
20	945	1124	1244	1337	1414	1480	1538	1590	1638	1681	1722	1760	1795	1829	1861	1891	1920	1948	1974	2000
21	980	1166	1291	1387	1466	1535	1595	1649	1699	1744	1786	1825	1862	1897	1930	1961	1991	2020	2048	2074
22	1015	1208	1336	1436	1519	1589	1652	1708	1759	1806	1849	1890	1928	1964	1999	2031	2062	2092	2120	2148
23	1050	1248	1382	1485	1570	1643	1708	1766	1819	1867	1912	1954	1994	2031	2066	2100	2132	2163	2192	2221
24	1084	1289	1427	1533	1621	1697	1763	1823	1878	1928	1974	2018	2058	2097	2133	2168	2201	2233	2263	2293

Activity 3 (continued)

Part II.

1. What is your starting level of output/income? (Write the number from the table indicated by your symbol (triangle, rhombus, or circle). _____

2. (Card 1) How much did capital (K) and/or labor (L) inputs change after drawing the card? (Write +1, -1, +2, -2, etc.)   K ___ L ___

How much did the change in capital and/or labor inputs change your economy's level of output/income? (Show a + before an increase and a – before a decrease.) _____

3. (Card 2) How much did capital (K) and/or labor (L) inputs change after drawing the card? (Write +1, -1, +2, -2, etc.)   K ___ L ___

Starting from the level of output in question 2, how much did this change in capital and/or labor inputs change your economy's level of output/income? (Show a + before an increase and a – before a decrease.) _____

4. (Card 3) How much did capital (K) and/or labor (L) inputs change after drawing the card? (Write +1, -1, +2, -2, etc.)   K ___ L ___

Starting from the level of output in question 3, how much did this change in capital and/or labor inputs change your economy's level of output/income? (Show a + before an increase and a – before a decrease.) _____

5. (Card 4) How much did capital (K) and/or labor (L) inputs change after drawing the card? (Write +1, -1, +2, -2, etc.)   K ___ L ___

Starting from the level of output in question 4, how much did this change in capital and/or labor inputs change your economy's level of output/income? (Show a + before an increase and a – before a decrease.) _____

6. (Card 5) How much did capital (K) and/or labor (L) inputs change after drawing the card? (Write +1, -1, +2, -2, etc.)   K ___ L ___

Starting from the level of output in question 5, how much did this change in capital and/or labor inputs change your economy's level of output/income? (Show a + before an increase and a – before a decrease.) _____

7. What was your final level of output/income? _____

8. How much did your level of output/income change, comparing your starting level (question 1) to your final level (question 7)? (Show a + before an increase and a – before a decrease.) _____

Activity 4
Is It All in the Cards?

Deck 1 Cards: Triangle Group(s) △	Deck 2 Cards: Rhombus Group(s) ▱	Deck 3 Cards: Circle Group(s) ○
After years of little or no population growth, immigration and a higher birth rate increase the labor supply. L +1 △	Population increases moderately. L +1 ▱	Population growth is extremely high due to high birth rates and falling mortality rates. L +2 ○
More women enter the nation's labor force. L +1 △	More women enter the nation's labor force. L +1 ▱	More women enter the nation's labor force. L +1 ○
Older workers postpone their retirement. L +1 △	Older workers postpone their retirement. L +1 ▱	Older workers postpone their retirement. L +1 ○
A growing portion of the population is elderly and retiring. L −1 △	A growing portion of the population is elderly and retiring. L −1 ▱	Droughts and crop failures reduce the population and labor force. L −1 ○
Private savings increase, interest rates fall, and businesses borrow more for new factories and equipment. K +1 △	Private savings increase, interest rates fall, and businesses borrow more for new factories and equipment. K +1 ▱	A sharp increase in loans and grants from foreign governments and international agencies is used to fund new public and private investments. K +1 ○
Private savings decrease, interest rates increase, and businesses borrow less for new factories and equipment. K −1 △	Private savings decrease, interest rates increase, and businesses borrow less for new factories and equipment. K −1 ▱	A sharp decrease in loans and grants from foreign governments and international agencies reduces public and private investments. K −1 ○
Individuals and businesses from other nations decide to invest more in your country. K +1 △	Individuals and businesses from other nations decide to invest more in your country. K +1 ▱	Individuals and businesses from other nations decide to invest more in your country. K +1 ○
Individuals and businesses from other nations decide to invest less in your country. K −1 △	Individuals and businesses from other nations decide to invest less in your country. K −1 ▱	Individuals and businesses from other nations decide to invest less in your country. K −1 ○
Political and economic stability in other nations leads to more investment in your country. K +1 △	Political and ineconomic stability in other nations lead some people and firms in other countries to invest more in your country, but others fear that the instability will develop in your country, too, and so invest less. No net change in K. ▱	Political and economic stability in your nation lead to less investment in factories and equipment. K −1 ○
World War III breaks out. Many young adults are killed, and many cities and factories are destroyed. L −2 K −3 △	World War III breaks out. Many young adults are killed, and many cities and factories are destroyed. L −2 K −3 ▱	World War III breaks out. Many young adults are killed, and many cities and factories are destroyed. L −2 K −3 ○

From *Focus: High School Economics,* © National Council on Economic Education, New York, NY

Visual 1
Sources of Growth in the U.S. Economy, 1929 - 1982

Sources of growth		Percent of total growth
(1) Increase in quantity of labor		32
(2) Increase in labor productivity		68
(3) Technological advance	28	
(4) Quantity of capital	19	
(5) Education and training	14	
(6) Economies of scale	9	
(7) Improved resource allocation	8	
(8) Legal, human, environment and other	-9	
		100

Note: Because of rounding, lines 3 through 8 do not sum to 68 percent.

Source: Edward F. Denison. *Trends in American Economic Growth, 1929-1982,* Washington: The Brookings Institution, 1985, p. 30.

Visual 2
Trends in National Income (real per capita GDP), 1870 - 2000

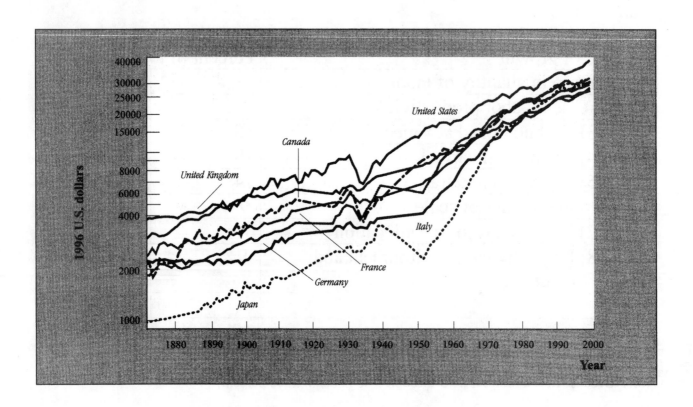

Note: National income in U.S. dollars is plotted on a logarithmic scale. On such a scale, equal distances represent equal *percentage* changes. Thus, the distance between $1,000 and $2,000 is the same as the distance between $2,000 and $4,000.

Source: R.J. Gordon, *Macroeconomics*, Eighth Edition. (page 288) ©2000 Addison Wesley Longman, Inc. Reprinted by permission of Pearson Education, Inc.

Visual 3
The Growing Divergence of Income in High-Income and Low-Income Nations

	1870	1960	1990
Per capita income in USA	$2063	$9895	$18054
Per capita income in world's poorest nation	$250	$257	$399
Ratio of GDP per capita of richest to poorest nation	8.3	38.5	45.2

Estimates of divergence of per capita incomes (in dollars) since 1870 using 1985 purchasing power parity dollars. Purchasing power parity is a method for comparing incomes looking at all goods and services produced and consumed in a nation, not just the goods and services traded with other countries that determine exchange rates for national currencies.

Some Reasons for Divergence:

1)   Lower saving and investment rates in poorer nations

2)   Faster population growth in poorer nations

3)   Political and economic instability in poorer nations

4)   Restrictions on business and international trade in some poorer nations

Source: Lant Pritchett, "Divergence, Big Time," *Journal of Economic Perspectives*, Summer 1997, p. 11.

Visual 4
Factors Related to Economic Growth*

Strong positive relationship:
   Investment in capital goods as a percent of GDP

Weak positive relationship:
   Enrollment rates in elementary schools
   Moderate price inflation

Weak negative relationship:
   Enrollment rates in secondary schools
   Population growth
   Imports and exports as a percent of GDP

Strong negative relationship:
   Government spending on services/consumption
   Income and profit taxes as a percent of GDP

*Based on results reported by Charles I. Plosser, "The Search for Economic Growth," *Symposium on Economic Growth*, Federal Reserve Bank of Kansas City, 1992, pp. 57 – 86.

From *Focus: High School Economics*, © National Council on Economic Education, New York, NY